Forcing Our Hand

Other Books by the Author

Managing Foreign Investments in Southern Italy
Foreign State Enterprises: A Threat to American Business

Forcing Our Hand

America's Trade Wars in the 1980s

Douglas F. Lamont

Lexington Books

D.C. Heath and Company/Lexington, Massachusetts/Toronto

Library of Congress Cataloging-in-Publication Data

Lamont, Douglas F.
Forcing our hand : America's trade wars in the 1980s.

Includes index.
1. United States—Commercial policy. 2. Competition, International. I. Title.
HF1455.L36 1986 382'.3'0973 85-46018
ISBN 0-669-12668-3 (alk. paper)

Published simultaneously in Canada
Printed in the United States of America
International Standard Book Number: 0-669-12668-3
Library of Congress Catalog Card Number: 85-46018

The paper used in this publication meets the minimum requirements of American National Standard for Information Sciences—Permanance of Paper for Printed Library Materials, ANSI Z39.48-1984.

ISBN 0-669-12668-3

The last numbers on the right below indicate the number and date of printing.

10 9 8 7 6 5 4 3 2 1

95 94 93 92 91 90 89 88 87 86

To Kate and Kris

Contents

Prologue ix

Introduction: Obsolete Views xi

Part One: Illusions and Insults 1

1. Free Trade 3
2. Fear: Parent of Protectionism 17
3. The Fix Is In 29
4. MITI 43

Part Two: Contagion and Cures 55

5. Comparative Advantage 57
6. Foreign Investments 69
7. National Energy Policy 87
8. Sectoral Free Trade 93

Part Three: Realities and Results 105

9. Managed Trade 107

10. GATT 121

11. The European Community 135

12. Preferential Trade Agreements 157

Part Four: Prospects and Problems 161

13. Lomé 163

14. Graduation 177

15. Debt 191

16. A New Order 205

Conclusion: U.S. Policies 219

Paraphernalia 227

Endnotes 233

Index 243

About the Author 259

Prologue

Within a matter of days after writing my February 20, 1984, international business column "Winds of trade policy have shifted . . . and in blows brutal 'managed trade' from European Community"[1] I got a call from the National Machine Tool Builders Association offering a Spring speaking engagement. I said in my column and in my speech, "The EC is a protectionist animal. It now dominates the GATT system. The EC has an overdeveloped appetite for causing economic injury upon the United States." I wrote and said that dry rot had set in at the General Agreement on Tariffs and Trade (GATT) and this decomposition was affecting the foreign trade policy of the United States. I called for action now before it was too late.

I mention the column and speech as evidence of a budding constituency that takes the trouble to read, listen, and act. This book I construe as a joint labor engaging both writer and reader. Without the writer, the reader has no framework, no analysis, no interpretation. Without the reader, the writer has no audience, no fans, no converts. *Forcing Our Hand* gives us a common language in which the numerous foreign trade publics can address one another and develop a common interest in public policy.

The book focuses on America's trade wars in the 1980s. The heart of my analysis is devoted to what the Japanese, Canadians, Europeans, Africans, Asians, Latin Americans, and others are doing to combat the preeminence of the United States in the world's economy. Following the central sections, the Conclusion deals with what American trade policy should be for the last few years of this century.

That America knows not what it is doing is both comic and tragic. That America must quickly do something is now self-evident. Whence this effort.

How then to arrange the bewildering fragments of foreign government practice, thought, and experience into an understandable design for Americans? Exporters, importers, freight forwarders, manufacturers, bankers routinely mention the "world's trading system" and the "international economy," but what do these phrases mean? How can we make plausible generalizations in a universe of specialized nationalisms? Much of the shrill argument over trade reflects the longing for meaningful integration, for norms of behavior, for ideals to live by before some new oil shock brings us down again.

What is common to many of these economic nationalisms is an aura of thoughtful bankruptcy. Having accepted the premises of interventionists revealed in the past two decades, the U.S. International Trade Commission continues to insist on the myth of the duped company fighting a losing battle against goods dumped by foreign conspirators. The myth has little to do with anything other than exorbitant legal fees, but it encourages the belief that no individual company, especially a firm given to paying high wages for slovenly work, can hope to resolve the problem of foreign competition.

For an author, the prevalence of this attitude presents problems, both of what to say and how to say it. *Forcing Our Hand* is a product of the new journalism, and it is written for opinion leaders—those who are willing to change their minds, those who are willing to change the minds of others.

Introduction: Obsolete Views

America has a narrow, humdrum vision of reality with which it is satisfied, in its foreign trade. Its export policies are stale and indifferent to changes in labor costs, and they suggest to foreigners an exhaustion of the spirit—a fatal perception, if it is accurate, because jobs and markets will be lost to new "Yankee" traders. A sense of nostalgia has settled over the country. We Americans are caught in the vise of traditional ideas: we are immune both to new experience and to new thoughts on how to manage our international trade policy. Our mistakes today are the same ones we made yesterday and the day before. For example, the American automobile companies insist on paying, and the United Auto Workers insist on receiving, total compensation (that is, wages plus fringe benefits)*double* that provided to Japanese automobile workers. So the Japanese maintain a $1500-per-car production cost advantage over us. We insisted that they limit their exports to us—the so-called voluntary marketing agreement negotiated by the federal government on behalf of the industry—to one out of every five cars sold in the United States. But do our automobile companies and the UAW understand the enormity of the cost differential and the seriousness of their financial predicament? No. Will they cut costs drastically so our automobile industry can thrive without government protection from Japanese rivals? No. They prefer to compensate automobile workers at roughly twice the amount earned by the average U.S. industrial worker. Those of us who earn $10 to $15 per hour—those of us who buy cars—guarantee the jobs of the automobile workers who are earning $26 to $28 per hour. This is after the federal and state governments bailed out Chrysler and after that company turned itself around to become competitive again with

General Motors and Ford—but not, of course, with Toyota and Nissan. The American automobile industry is analogous to a psychiatric patient who tries inappropriately in his present life to reenact a traumatic event of the past: another Chrysler-type government bailout, this time for the Big Three all together. Such are the wages of protectionism. We suffer from a compulsion to repeat our disasters (in automobiles, steel, textiles, motorcycles) in the hope that they will come out differently. Ours is a self-destructive behavior, a mental disorder that causes us to invent superfluous tragedies and replay them again and again. I call this our constipated outlook toward international trade.

We have condensed our views on exports into a sacred phrase, *free trade,* and crammed them together as relics to be honored because they are hallowed through association with our post–World War II hegemony over the world. These views have caused us to suspend our senses vis-a-vis the political and economic changes occurring around the world; to confine the expression of our spirit to the outmoded impracticalities of adversarial relationships among government, business, and labor; and to burden ourselves with an obsolete international trade policy.

Our foreign trade policy is obsolete because we have fenced it in by one of those "terrible simplifiers," the concept of fair trade. We look for the easy solution, since it's comfortable, and avoid the complex solution, which is uncomfortable. The complexity of the solution requires the creation of superior technology, better management, and improved craftsmanship by workers: solutions to design, engineering, production, investment, and marketing problems are so intricate that the best brains must stretch themselves to understand all the interlocking parts: the alternative is failure. It requires a government response to the felt needs of workers, shippers, freight forwarders, bankers, exporters, investors, importers, and consumers—in fact, the solution requires a government-sponsored consensus on the dollar-exchange rate, the level of interest rates and the cost of money, quotas for protected goods, nontariff barriers for other products and services, liability for sovereign country debt, and administrative procedures for resolving dumping questions and a host of important policy issues. An organizational structure in Washington is needed whereby all who are a party to the problem become a party to the solution. These discussions, consensus-building strategies, and political activities to build networks in support of export and import initiatives are all carried out by government in a mixed society. Government could prod American business and labor to do their best without at the same time forcing consumers to subsidize certain workers whose wages are above the national average and who will strike at the first sign that their days on Easy Street are over. These activities are worth pursuing because in the real world (though not in our fantasy world) they are being pursued successfully by others—most notably the Japanese—and these foreigners are simply doing a better job in selling their goods to us than we are in selling our goods to them. Exports are the key to prosperity in this interrelated world. One in every five American jobs produces goods for sale overseas, and every $1 billion in additional exports means 26,200 new jobs. It's a mistake to think that the private sector, doing business as usual, will rush in with alternatives without a clear, definitive government policy set before it. The desire to keep things as they are is based on a critical deception—namely, the idea that the Japanese will indeed change their ways and open their domestic markets to free and fair competition. When will this happen? Never! We fail to see the true character of the competition with our machine tool industry. For example, in the Houdaille case, even with a cabinet recommendation to condemn the Japanese for their anticompetitive behavior, President Reagan agreed with his good friend the prime minister of Japan and did nothing to protect and save the numerical control machines produced in the United States. Is this a case of an abnormal illusion? Do we have pathological illusions about foreign competition that cast a veil over our eyes and mind? Government must set some boundaries for acceptable foreign participation in our domestic markets. Right now we fail because, except in the case of federal lands in the West, where the Mineral Leasing Act of 1920 protects us, we post no signs saying Keep Off, Stay Out, Hunting Prohibited. Foreign governments do take such protective measures. They have an enclosing barrier to keep unacceptable intruders out. We have a debating society in which lawyers practice skillful repartee before the U.S. International Trade Commission (ITC), the U.S. Special Trade representative, and the International Trade Administration

(ITA) of the Department of Commerce. Our federal agencies do not protect the public's interest in jobs and cheap goods. Our simple belief in free and fair trade has permitted others to fence their goods to us, to offer us products below cost—products which are paid for by workers who earn, in some cases, subsistence wages. These workers' labor is stolen from them, and America has become the place where the goods they sweat to produce are received, sold, and distributed to eager, worldly buyers.

Such is foreign governments' comparative advantage. Theirs is a world of wages below the average American wage, of better management (particularly in terms of inventory and quality control), of government subsidies that undercut American firms, of government-owned firms (state enterprises) that freely engage in monopoly at home and competition abroad. Foreign governments do everything in their power to create jobs domestically for the purpose of exporting products overseas. But they don't prop up inefficient firms. They insist that firms invest in modernizing their plants; if a firm fails to do so, its tariff protection ceases. Foreign governments prefer to pay workers to work rather than give them welfare checks or adjustment assistance because their jobs are discontinued, owing to imports; when necessary, at government expense, they retrain workers so they can work for new investors.

Americans must come to grips with this approach toward international trade. Here's what we must do:

Recognize that the developed countries are forced by their internal politics to protect their traditional markets, industries, products, and customers.

Perceive that the less developed countries (LDCs) are driven by poverty, debt, and incipient revolution to assume high risks in protecting their home markets and breaking into world markets.

Acknowledge that no force of concept, authority, or perceived interest exists within the international trading system to halt the drive toward protectionism overseas and the foreigners' quest for open markets in the United States.

These trade wars of foreign governments are a real war for us.

Trade Wars

Let's be more specific about the results.

Our basic industries are faltering. Steel's fears about free trade drive it to demand protection: voluntary and mandatory quotas, trigger prices, and guaranteed market share. Chrysler gets a "fix" from the federal government and supervision from Washington. Also textiles, motorcycles, and others: the list grows longer every day. We haven't learned Japan's habit of ending the production of low-value-added goods and simultaneously starting up the production of higher-value-added goods. Unlike Japan's MITI (Ministry of International Trade and Industry), we haven't adopted the practice of deciding which industries to save and which to let go. We need to determine how we are going to do this before it's too late.

Although we continue to make advances in high technology, we have contracted a British disease: basic research is done at home, but foreigners capitalize on improvements in semiconductors, artificial blood, and random access memories. They make a quantum leap forward through a combination of government support for applied research, the purchase of American subsidiaries and seduction of American executives, and the use of elaborate public-relations programs to capture an unassailable market share even before American firms can join the battle. While MITI creates a comparative advantage for Japan, we flounder—captured by illusions, humiliated by our weakness and their strength.

Moreover, our corporations invest where foreign governments give them the best deal. This creates comparative advantage, too. High tariffs that protect the domestic markets of foreign governments, together with lower corporate taxes relative to those in the United States, force-feed the construction of branch plants in Canada, Europe, Asia, and even Third World countries. Each inducement to capture American direct investment breeds the inevitable nationalistic reaction by host governments. For example, Canada created the Foreign Investment Review Agency (FIRA), which demanded that American investors create Canadian exports, and also used its National Energy Policy (NEP) to squeeze, silence, and take over the American-owned oil companies. Both Canadian policies showed the world what a determined government could do, as well as how, when Canada realized it had gone too far, a modest free-trade proposal, followed by a change in government, could end

Canada's bickering with its largest trading partner, the United States. A contagion of foreign government self-interest has spread across our foreign trade. Attempted cures like free trade for a limited number of goods may have a salutary effect, but they won't bring the world's multilateral trading system back to full health.

Also, our government pays no attention to how the European Community manages trade among its ten member states, with the Mediterranean, African, Caribbean, and Pacific nations, and through the General Agreement on Tariffs and Trade (GATT). The Tokyo Round of Trade Negotiations in the 1970s saw the European Community unsettle the United States and dominate the free world's trading system. As a result, GATT does the Community's bidding in terms of export subsidies, safeguards, border tax adjustments, and regional common market arrangements.

The specifics of how the European Community uses its preferential trade agreements with Third World countries to create comparative advantage in its own favor are unknown to us. But the results stare us in the face—comparative advantage created for everyone's good except our own.

The multilateral trading system exists within an interdependent world, with Third World demands for market access and differential treatment, and with scary national debt structures and a new international economic order. One refusal by a Brazil or a Mexico to repay its debt—a moratorium on interest and principal repayments—means that private international banks would lose their proper asset base and the Federal Reserve (along with other central banks) would have to step in and prop up the whole house of cards.

One of the things we don't understand very well is how Third World countries use the crisis of the world economy to bring about a trade and investment climate more to their liking, again creating comparative advantage in their own favor. For example, Brazil created such an overseas market position by informing the United States that if the number of Brazilian shoes exported to our shores were reduced, Brazil would be unable to make payments on its $100 billion sovereign country debt. There may be trade opportunities in the Third World. However, given the risks that less developed countries are willing to run in order to gain and keep market share in the United States, these opportunities are hard to find. Against determined foreign governments, they are even harder to keep open for U.S. firms.

So, too many foreign products are coming into the United States. This influx far exceeds the ability of the American worker-consumer to absorb these goods without a permanent loss of traditional manufacturing jobs. At last count, some 10 to 12 million Americans are condemned to the human scrap pile either because they are low-skilled workers in declining industries or because they are semiskilled workers in high-technology industries. Their jobs will be automated out of existence. Those who have jobs will use government to protect these jobs and to preserve their wage levels. Those who manage business will use government to prevent newcomers from entering the market. Idle workers and idle plants will march hand in hand asking for special government help to provide them with a risk-free business environment, profits will belong to the companies, but the risks will be borne by government, the taxpayers, and those on welfare. Do we want such make-believe socialism here in the United States?

The European Community demonstrates what lies before us. For agriculture, it sets support prices, buys excess output, destroys or dumps goods. For manufactured goods, it imposes mandatory price controls, sets production quotas, pays out subsidies, and negotiates export restraints. The list of protected goods includes textiles and clothing, quartz watches, hi-fi equipment, color TVs, motorcycles, forklift trucks, light vans and passenger cars. The national governments spend Community funds retraining workers and subsidizing exports. Such is the face of protectionism in Western Europe.

Protectionism

However, no matter what the European community does—in fact, no matter what we do in the United States—protectionism no longer protects but instead is counterproductive. Through raising tariffs, imposing quotas, introducing nontariff barriers, and legislating domestic content requirements, protectionism aggravates industrial decline, creates more unemployment, and forces consumers to spend more and save less. It puts the day of reckoning off, but just for one more day. Protectionism is hailed as the means to give noncompetitive industries time to rebuild themselves so they can compete once again; instead, the textile industry, which is protected by the Multifibre Agreement (MFA), finds competing goods coming in from new overseas locations instead of from older ones that were given quotas under the agreement. Here's America's scorecard from the MFA: a 10 percent increase in the cost of textiles to American consumers and a noncompetitive domestic textile industry in the American South. Another example: the steel industry, for whom the federal government imposed the trigger-price system and negotiated quotas with the European Community and Japan, subsequently demands protection from Brazilian and Mexican steel imports. The source of our imports is changing without anything being done about the real problem. Sure, these Third World producers have a comparative advantage over us. Sure, West Germany and Japan do, too. Their labor costs are $10 an hour less than ours, and no matter how much American management strives to increase productivity, it cannot overcome this labor-cost disadvantage. So long as we protect the steel industry, it can pass on its labor costs to American consumers, and each "union victory," each "gain for the working man," means management gave in for the sake of labor peace (management did not want a strike) and to maintain its protected market share. In terms of automobiles, machine tools, and construction machinery, American production technology and equipment are as advanced as our competitors' and, in some cases superior to theirs. We have poured money into robots and factory automation. But we have done nothing to pay workers and executives based upon their performance, with cash wages being a great deal more in good-performance years and much lower in bad-performance years; labor leaders and supervisors prefer a fixed wage with a bonus *on top of* those given for productivity increases and gains in profitability. A flexible wage structure is needed to get our smokestack industries through the structural crisis that will not go away. The prevailing wage structure for these industries, which is one-third higher than the average American industrial wage, must be brought down by one-third until American steel and automobiles can compete on a price basis with Japanese and German models. Management must be willing to take a strike to hold down labor costs. Management must do a better job of keeping inventories at a minimum and insisting quality be maintained at the highest possible level.

American management, both in the corporations and the unions, is the problem. It must give up its obsolete views about what it can and cannot do, and accomplish the hard work of insisting on change. The old ways are done for because capital is so mobile today. No industry, and no company, is bound to its original home base. They can flee from the Midwest's foundry to the Sun Belt, from there to border factories on the Mexican side of the Rio Grande River, or to anywhere in the world where labor costs are lower, where there is less taxation, and when management feels comfortable with government. There is no law of nature that requires American consumers to bankrupt themselves for high-priced steel and automobile executives and workers; no law of economics that says noncompetitive American industries must survive the onslaught of foreign exports; and no law of business management that gives executives and unionized workers a lifetime right to jobs.

What our steel management wants is a dower in the American economy. They let so much of their own industrial plant decay and die that they want the federal and state governments to give them the right to claim a portion of the consumer's income in perpetuity. This right of dower, a vested legal interest in the future prosperity of the United States, is theirs, they claim, by right, because they are America's smokestack industry and are not subject to the basic laws of competiton and comparative advantage. The politicians who heed the words of steel executives are naive and even foolish, for the latter are as out of touch with reality as were the railroad executives before the collapse of the Pennsylvania and New York Central railroads. Theirs is a poor vision for the United States. They have suspended their senses, constipated their spirit, and constricted their mind. Each time we follow their lead and fence ourselves into a narrower territory, we face the eventual day of reckoning with an even larger bill to pay in terms of lost jobs and income, industrial poverty, and a ruined position in the world market.

U.S. Policy

Yet the truth about America's international trade position is usually not known by those who shout the loudest for protection. Here are the facts for all to see: The world market is the largest single customer for American factory labor. Our manufacturing industry exports twice as large a proportion of its output as Japan's does. The export share of U.S. industrial production exceeds that of any major industrial nation except West Germany. Exports of manufactured goods in 1984 accounted for one of every five jobs in U.S. factories. One fourth of our manufactured goods and two fifths of our farm goods are sold in world markets. This is an exceptionally good record.

But we could do better if we paid attention to how government decisions influence the competitive position of American industry. For example, the Reagan administration's strong-dollar policy since 1981 (one that was difficult to change without investors losing confidence and causing a run on the dollar) cost more American manufacturing jobs and created more unemployment than the crisis in the steel and automobile industries. We must build a concern for foreign trade into the policy-making process and, if we want to be as successful as the Japanese, who are the real pros at this, or as long-lasting as the French (since the seventeenth century), or as dedicated as the Canadians, who can't shake their geographic proximity to us, we must learn to subordinate other considerations to the needs of our international trade policy. The West Germans ask for an impact statement describing the foreign trade consequences of proposed government policies. That may be going too far for the United States. However, if we had done so, we would have known that a 10 percent lower dollar in the early 1980s would have raised the level of American exports a full quarter higher than they were in 1983. In 1981 and 1982, the dollar was thought to be overvalued by about 25 percent. In those years, this exchange-rate imbalance levied a heavy cost of the United States: a 25 percent tax on our exports and a 25 percent subsidy on the imports from Japan and Europe. Our trade deterioration in 1981 and 1982 was the largest single cause of our recession. Our gross national product was off by

$100 billion because of imports; 10 to 12 million workers became permanently unemployed because of our trade-induced recession and the refusal of investors to create new jobs here as long as the dollar remained strong; and the balance was tipped away from a liberal trade policy toward protectionism.

What's America to do? It must review carefully what it can do alone. An uncommon amount of discernment and foresight will be required to overcome its restricted outlook and outmoded views. America must suspend its desire for revenge and show by example that it means to take appropriate action to defend its domestic economy. This action may take the form of a national industrial policy toward trade whereby jobs here at home are given paramount importance and the exchange rate is seen as part of the solution rather than an end in itself. A strong dollar is a given today. Executives must learn how to cut costs and improve productivity so that they can reduce prices on products they export. Executives must not give up more market share or they face the prospect of breaking off their distribution and financial connections with overseas markets. Even if the dollar should come down significantly in terms of the Japanese yen or the West German mark, severed world connections take many years to be reestablished. These lost business contacts are one of the hidden costs of refusing to compete in spite of the strong dollar. One thing the federal government could do is impose a negative interest-equalization tax on foreign portfolio investments. Foreign investors would have to pay us for their investments here. The Swiss use this approach—you pay them for the security and secrecy of your investments there—to keep the Swiss franc from rising too high against the West German mark. We could do the same against the yen, mark, and other currencies when our trade imbalance gets too high with Japan or West Germany. Barriers to trade, such as quotas, high tariffs, and voluntary market orders, are not the answer. Their cost to the American consumer is too high. America must awaken itself from its long sleep and get on with building a constituency for international trade. American labor is carefully watching American management and government. All three are looking for the big breakthrough in ideas for the future. Regrettably, they fail to use the tools already in place (for example, export trading companies and foreign sales corporations) and those that could be put in place (such as a negative interest-equalization tax or a department of international trade and industry).

Here is America's trade agenda for the last fifteen years of the twentieth century.

First, unless the developed countries are willing to deal effectively with the trade-debilitating effects of national industrial policies, downplay the multilateral trading system of the General Agreement on Tariffs and Trade.

Second, upgrade our bilateral trading efforts with Canada and Mexico and with the Caribbean and Latin American countries. These countries must have special access to our home market, including free trade with Canada and the elimination of special-interest restrictions on goods coming in from Mexico and the Caribbean Basin Initiative countries. Other Latin American and Third World countries must have access to our home market based upon a price auction system that helps them service their sovereign country debt and guarantees them the share of our market now held by the Japanese and Europeans.

Third, insist that the developed countries of East Asia and Western Europe play by the GATT rules or risk equivalent negative actions on our part.

Finally, purge ourselves of the temptation to follow the Canadian, Japanese, and European interventionist models in seeking to protect American markets, industries, products, and customers. Instead, show the benefits from freer trade by widening its impact among the countries of North and Central America, and in the Caribbean Sea.

With these four elements in place, American business executives will be able to make trade and investment decisions that will benefit some 400 million people in the Western Hemisphere. This is America's real work for the last fifteen years of the twentieth century.

Part I
Illusions and Insults

1
Free Trade

Free trade holds to one idea and one way of performing in the world: among industrialized countries, eliminate tariffs and nontariff barriers; don't impose quotas, voluntary marketing arrangements, and other surveillance schemes; stop using embargoes. Between the developed and less developed countries, the same open-economy illusion holds (as far as the infant industry argument allows.) With the centrally planned countries, don't pretend the free trade phantom exists. Economists believe free trade moves the world economy in a thousand ways: for consumers it forces prices down; for producers it adds needed competition; for governments, it severs, like an axe, their spending appetites and brings them to account for their mismanagement of a nation's economy.

The exporters and importers of the United States, the European Community, and Japan believe differently, and their popularly held views are supported by the evidence. Andrzej Olechowski and Gary Sampson wrote in 1980 that "Tariff rates are . . . the least serious obstacle to international trade."[1] Instead, nontariff barriers, such as safety regulations and voluntary quotas, make up the vast number of discriminatory trading practices among the developed countries. And Japan uses unconventional means—for example, explicit guidance by its Ministry of International Trade and Industry—to restrict the flow of imports into its home markets and speed up the flow of exports overseas. So much for the illusion that free trade exists among the three leading industrial powers of the world.

The Olechowski and Sampson conclusions are drawn from studies on the weighted averages of tariff rates. Under the General Agreement on Tariffs and Trade, countries grant their neighbors, friends, and allies the status of "most favored nations"; if one country obtains a tariff reduction from another friendly country, all countries that agree to grant the most favored nations status to one another get the benefit of the same low tariff rate. Most favored nations is the fundamental trading principle of GATT. Special regional preference rates, such as those under the Canada–U.S. Automobile Pact or between the European Community and the Lomé Convention countries of Africa, the Caribbean, and the Pacific, also are acceptable under GATT.

During the 1970s, the United States gave more emphasis to trade protection than did the European Community—in terms of all manufactured goods imported from the developed countries and less developed countries.[2] Notwithstanding this conclusion, of the eight thousand four-digit items on the Brussels Tariff Nomenclature (BTN),* 22 percent, when imported into the European Community, were subject to nontariff barriers (such as controls over the quantity imported) that were discriminatorily applied against the exporting country.[3] Both the United States and the European Community imposed stringent restrictive barriers against footwear and textiles—57 percent of all BTN items for footwear were restricted by the United States; and 46 percent of all BTN items for textiles were restricted by discriminatory barriers of the European community.[4] Japan kept these products out through its use of the Ministry of International Trade and Industry as the doorman against foreign manufactured goods. The three major industrial powers had talked a good game about freeing up world trade, but these partial pieces of evidence shut them up. During the 1970s' Tokyo Round of Trade Negotiations, the United States, Europe, and Japan could not wipe out the stain of their protectionist past, and the less developed countries played upon this guilt feeling to win more concessions under GATT.

In the 1980s, the three big industrial powers stopped submerged, dead in the water. Where could they go? Not backward, for they had invested free trade with the wrong attributes. Not forward, for they had perceived protectionism as free trade. They had

---

*Brussels Tariff Nomenclature now is called the Nomenclature of the Customs Cooperation Council (CCCN).

lost their way and finding it again in circumstances where light was barely visible, where sounds pinged and then died away, where false thoughts led them to greater disasters, would be the most difficult task facing them. They had to avert an all-out trade war.

The United States' self-inflicted wounds included banning the export of Alaskan oil; prohibiting the sale of timber from federal lands west of the 100th meridian; excluding foreign shipping from intracoastal trade; imposing voluntary marketing quotas for automobiles; raising high tariffs against textiles (20 percent), fruit juices (27 percent) and ceramics (14 percent); and setting up a host of special deals, all to favor special interests. America mocked free trade by these actions.

Looking for relief by acting similar to the Japanese: easier said than done! Absenteeism in the United States is four times greater than in Japan; labor turnover in the United States is seven times greater than in Japan. Japan's productivity goes up while ours goes down. Their labor costs go down while ours go up. Their costs of materials (because of better inventory management) are lower, too. We must correct these problems, industry by industry, supplier by supplier, firm by firm, worker by worker, bearing in mind the consequences if we do not in terms of lost jobs and industrial competitiveness. Mercantilism (that pernicious actor) waits in the wings for the sick star to give up, dance off stage, pack her bags, and go home.

Japan wants us to be competitive so we will keep our domestic markets and the international trading system open for its goods, but not so open that Japan must be a free-trade economy, too. And that's no illusion. Those are the facts the United States faces today.

Japan's Challenge

Here are the research findings from the University of California about U.S.–Japanese competition in the semiconductor industry. Michael Borrus, James Millstein, and John Zysman wrote that Japan wanted to establish its international industrial superiority by possessing its own technology.[5] Moreover, through government actions and by collaboration of the firms and their banks, competition among firms in targeted industries was both directed and limited.[6]

Government bureaucrats manipulated the market to favor Japanese producers.[7] Finally, Borrus et al. concluded that these government actions on the part of MITI "represent political tactics of industrial development and should be made the subject of international trade negotiations."[8]

There we have it, worked out for us: the enormous cultural obstacles barring penetration of the Japanese market are reenforced by direct government intervention; let's not equate this to free trade. We now know that the Japanese Ministry of International Trade and Industry was an "official doorman between domestic Japanese society and the international arena determining what, and under what conditions, capital, technology and manufactured goods enter and leave Japan."[9]

We believed, falsely, as it turns out, in two myths about the Japanese. We saw "Japan, Inc." as the external symbol of government-business collabortion on every decision to do with American and European international trade interests. No such entity, with the attributes of power and decisionmaking we gave it was ever present in Japan. We also saw Japan as the Land of Cutthroat Competition where local businessmen do each other in. This too was a myth that did not exist. Our perceptions were wrong. Our western eyes saw things not as they were, but as we wished them to be.

At long last, we are seeing reality: market shares are tolerated but fierce competition is used over expanding shares of growing markets. Japanese firms collaborate when foreigners seek to penetrate domestic Japanese markets, and the state acts in concert against foreigners.[10] This arrangement provides a stable availability of capital. Debt financing (bonds rather than stocks) permits the corporation to diffuse its risk to the banks, to other firms in the industry, and to the government itself, and encourages executives to think about the long term, about research and development, about capturing technological leadership, about the controlled diffusion of products in world markets.

Monopsonist. This is MITI. It controls access to Japanese markets. And MITI dictates how much Japanese firms pay in royalties for licenses of foreign technology. If they want foreign technology, they must learn to export. They must sell this foreign technology to other Japanese firms.[11] Only a small amount of market access by foreign firms is permitted. There will be no repeat of IBM's success story. Texas Instruments, in return for a 50 percent joint venture with Sony, had to license its integrated circuit patents to these Japanese firms: NEC, Hitachi, Mitsubishi, and Toshiba.

Free trade does not exist between the United States and Japan. The latter restricts access to its domestic markets. So does the former. But we place restrictions on access to our markets after the fact—after the Japanese have captured so large a market share that they cannot be dislodged. They are smarter; they don't let foreign firms capture a large share of their domestic markets. Instead, Japanese firms, together with the banks and MITI, collaborate to keep foreigners out. Theirs is an industrial policy worthy of serious international trade negotiations. This is the unfinished agenda of GATT.

Let us also be realistic about GATT. Japan's industrial policy is not going to be the subject of serious GATT negotiations during the Reagan round of trade talks in the 1980s. So the United States must find other ways to deal with Japan's real restrictions to their domestic markets. The one advantage we have is that we can control access to our own domestic markets. Let the Japanese bid to gain access to our home markets. Since other countries want to sell in the United States, too, let them or the Japanese pay a premium auction price for the privilege of selling their goods in the United States. Otherwise, we will have to negotiate a binding, ironclad reciprocal bilateral trade agreement with the Japanese to ensure that they do indeed open their domestic markets to our goods.

Protectionism Costs Money

Because protectionism is what we are about, and because there will be more attempts by special interests to keep foreigners out of domestic markets, we must understand what protectionism costs us and decide whether it is in our best interest. Protectionism is a bad idea. Capitalism may even be destroyed because protectionism is pure waste, a deadweight loss. Self-sufficiency in goods and services, a corollary idea, makes our problems worse, not better. The sad truth is that the United States cannot seal itself off from the world. If we follow this appealing but deleterious notion, we would all be poorer through higher prices, more inflation, heavier taxes, and the loss of our international competitiveness.

That mercantilism is an old and discredited doctrine is known. That protectionism gives us little and costs us much is *not* known. Let's inspect this statement.

In 1980, the direct cost of American protectionist policies to American consumers was $58.4 billion; that's an implicit tax cost of $255 per person.[12] Tariffs accounted for $45.8 billion, or 78 percent, of the direct costs.[13] Quotas, voluntary marketing agreements, Buy American legislation, and regulatory barriers accounted for the rest. There, from a separate piece of research, we extract evidence to confirm the conclusions of Olechowski and Sampson. Tariffs are the weapon the United States uses to shield its inefficient producers from international competition. In the absence of high tariff rates on textiles, fruit juices, and ceramics, consumers would buy their goods from foreigners at lower prices. What consumers actually must pay over what they could be paying is the deadweight loss. The difference does not become public revenues but goes into the pockets of the protected steel and textile companies. It's a hidden cost that is passed on to the consumer in the price of the goods, benefiting those firms that stay in business and the employees who keep their jobs in those firms. Sadly, these benefits are of a short-run nature, because foreign firms improve productivity, cut their costs, reduce their prices, pay the higher tariffs, and still undercut domestic firms. Since the high cost structure of American firms is protected, high tariff rates offer them no incentive to do better.

Nontariff barriers such as quotas don't even offer foreign firms the incentive to improve productivity, cut costs, reduce prices, and compete more efficiently. These restrictions guarantee foreigners a certain percentage of the market no matter what they do. If they are smart businessmen, and, like the Japanese, they usually are, they will supply our market with goods that have the highest profit margins. The mix of our imports shifts toward luxury goods; quotas are a regressive tax on those least able to pay for more expensive imports.

The opportunities for restrictions are endless. Some are difficult to quantify. Who knows what the Buy American legislation of the federal and state governments will cost? Who can tell how much we lost by banning foreign-flag ships (that is, ships registered in other countries where labor and safety costs are lower) from intracoastal trade? How can we calculate what the steel trigger-price mechanism costs us in terms of the reduced demand for high-priced steel in automobiles and other products? We have effectively removed any incentive for domestic producers to make these goods at reduced costs. Instead, protectionism subsidizes the least efficient firms, in these cases domestic businesses, and no one can force our businessmen to change their ways before it's too late.

American executives have a vision about protectionism. They prefer to keep foreign goods from reaching American consumers through tariffs and quotas rather than go on the federal dole until they can become competitive again. They don't like the Chrysler model of protectionism. They prefer to not be held accountable for their protectionist actions, and the hidden costs of their subsidies are passed on to the consumers. The businessmen (who produce steel, automobiles, cement, industrial fasteners, heavy-duty motorcycles, textiles, and so on) should be pleased with themselves; they have eaten well at the federal table. And have grown fat.

All is rot and decline. Once begun, protectionism takes on a thousand forms, holds to a thousand pernicious ideas, and costs the consumer in a thousand ways. The blatant attack on free trade spreads country by country, industry by industry, to all markets, firms, and goods.

No Restrictions

"Defeatism." That's what Colin Clark called it when the Cambridge School of economists said the only way to restore the British economy to full employment is through a drastic and permanent restriction on imports.[14]

Clark showed that neither keeping costs down nor depreciating the currency substantially increases the volume of exports, for without reserve production capacity, a large gain in exports is not possible. To get manufacturing going takes time. Making market surveys, choosing distributors, finding financing, purchasing shipping space, hiring export personnel, all takes time. Large export gains are achieved when a country has more capacity than it is utilizing and when the technology in the factories is modern enough to compete with foreign-owned technology.

High technology? Not necessarily.

Appropriate technology for the industry, availability of skilled labor, costs that are in line with the world's low-cost producer, just-in-time inventory practices, zero defects, management willing to make the necessary changes: these are the ingredients for success.

America's steel industry, a vertically integrated shadow of its former self, and automobile industry, the three big buyers of tires, parts, and other original equipment, have closed plants throughout the country. Without thinking of the nation's future needs, both industries tore down mills, disassembled production lines, and deposited skilled workers on the dole. Their vision is that of the short run. They didn't consider the need we would have for these factories when demand turned up. Rising internal demand fueled by a long-term economic recovery will force us to import more steel, more cars, more parts, not less. The best thing these industries can do is to stop thinking about themselves and think about the nation.

The Japanese will not let themselves be defeated. They insist that their mills and plants be kept open, that management introduce the best technology at the lowest possible cost, and that the firms get out and sell their products worldwide. MITI will collaborate with these firms and help them to succeed. Japan makes protectionism work for itself.

The Canadians hope they won't defeat themselves. By raising high tariff walls and lowering corporate income taxes, they create the best market for branch plants, owned mostly by Americans. They reverse course and impose excessive restrictions on foreign direct investment. Canada stalls the engine that powers growth, employment, and exports.

The Europeans will themselves to be one continental economy by imposing protectonism against all comers. They target losing rather than winning industries and follow the United States down the same road toward very expensive protectionism of home markets.

The Mexicans and other Latin Americans will themselves to be defeated. They bought the tenets of the Cambridge School of economics hook, line, and sinker. Between 1976 and 1982, under President José Lopez Portillo, they refused to join GATT, to subject their industry to a breadth of competition from world producers, and to receive the benefits of most favored nations. Instead, they imposed tight restrictions on imports, borrowed heavily from the world's private capital markets, used their scarce dollars for big purchases (such as new ports and pipelines), created triple-digit inflation, devalued the Mexican peso, and made themselves poorer. Mexico makes protectionism work against itself.

Or read in the following chapters about all the cases of how the European Community, together with the Lomé countries—its former colonies—overturned GATT's fundamental principle of multilateral free trade in favor of bilateral free trade between these two economic groups. This is protectionism run amok in the western world. No consensus for ultilateral free trade exists among the members of GATT. The United States has tried many times through GATT to ease its international trading problems; none of these attempts have been successful. Let's look at some explanations for why the United States tried and failed.

Devaluations Cost Money

One day in the 1970s, as soon as our 1971–1972 devaluations of the dollar had been completed, we woke up to find our foreign trade subject to the J curve, the eighteen-to-twenty-four-month lag in the changes in prices and quantities of imported and exported goods. After devaluation, prices on imports went up but volume didn't come down, because foreigners worked harder to keep their U.S. market share and American consumers had come to prefer their foreign goods. So we had more adverse problems with our balance of payments after devaluation than before. To reach the goal promised by the devaluations, we had to wait two years in the case of a few goods, sometimes longer in the case of others, before prices and quantities changed. Eventually, these time lags were overcome; the quantity of exports rose and the quantity of price-elastic imports came down. And we should have had favorable terms of trade in our merchandise account, the current account of the balance of payments.

But relative prices didn't remain the same over the time period, because energy costs exploded; wages changed because prices changed; give-backs were forced upon labor when labor costs got out of line; middle management was cashiered to get productivity up. These items are not shown in simple price-quantity comparisons.

Furthermore, government subsidies of protected industries created additional demand for the service industries. Someone had to monitor whether tariffs were being paid, whether quotas were being observed, and whether Buy American provisions were being honored by contractors. Government bureaucrats were paid to impose the new rules, and lawyers were hired to defend or oppose these rules and their application to specific industrial problems. None of these services can be imported, so the demand for them must be satisfied from domestic resources. In Britain and Canada, the government bureaucracy became so bloated in the quest to protect domestic markets that too few resources were left for manufacturers to call upon when they needed help in exporting, and their export links were severed completely, owing to protectionism. It will be many years before a profitable commercial relationship with overseas buyers can be restored.

Such government and private services represent an increasing share of the gross national product, both in terms of imports and exports. If the United States continued to follow in the footsteps of Britain, America also would have too few producers available with the right technology when things looked up, when the world recovered from its deep recession of the early 1980s and slow growth of the mid-1980s, and exporters learned to sell goods overseas in spite of a strong dollar or its eventual weakening.

What are America's prospects for the next few years?

With critical constraints, such as obsolete factories, inefficient logistics support systems, poorly trained labor, and moribund networks of overseas buyers, the United States will be unable to take advantage of any depreciation of the dollar for at least two years after it hits its new low. We will be unable to shed our trade deficit; it will remain high—over $150 billion—for a long time. We will be unable to rid ourselves of our enormous federal budget deficit, whereby public goods displace private goods, and which causes us to argue among ourselves over dumping cases, unfair labor practices, and restraints of trade as counsel for foreigners, adversaries to our people. Agricultural goods and services will earn export revenue, but not enough to reduce the trade deficit and end the quest for import protection.

Manufacturers won't make up their minds to produce more for exports until they are sure things have really changed. It will take at least two years to convince them.

Add that to your time lag. Four to five years before things really take hold and American businessmen are ready to export.

By jove, suddenly it's 1992.

It is wrong to assume that new factories and manufacturing technology will supply themselves. There will be capital costs. These will be in excess of the cost of providing the same quantity of goods today. These costs mean that resources must be diverted from the public sector. Government expenditures for defense, entitlement programs, roads, bridges, and so on cannot be permitted to crowd out industrial investment. This time, we won't have the portfolio investment we had from foreigners between 1981 and 1985; this time, we won't have the excessive international liquidity we had between 1960 and 1974.

Up until the sovereign loan crises of 1982 (for Mexico) and 1983 (for Brazil), America's export growth with the developing countries was stronger than with the developed countries. Notwithstanding the OPEC oil crisis in the 1970s, the gross national products of the LDCs slowed less than those of the developed countries. We had force-fed the developing countries with loans. Theirs was a "dash for growth." Money was pumped into these societies at rates faster than the local economies could absorb. Economists call this *lumpiness*.

For example, although a large amount of oil was found in southern Mexico, that country neither had the pipelines laid to move the oil nor the steel fabrication mills to manufacture the pipelines. Mexico didn't have enough deep-water ports or berths for the tankers or a large enough rail system or enough rolling stock to move the pylons, steel, and other materials to its southern oil fields. Everything was in short supply during the debt-ridden oil boom: no telephones, limited quantities of electricity, and too few managers and entrepreneurs. Lumpiness led to chaos for the lucky few and triple-digit inflation for almost everybody.

By the 1990s, all nations (including the United States) will be comrades on the same roller coaster. Our bottlenecks are in obsolete factories, broken-down interstate highways, few deep-water ports, high-cost labor, and ineffective management. There will be no special dispensation for the United States, no window of opportunity, no grace period—no time lags—for us to work out our international trade problems.

America is deluding itself if it thinks it can be committed to the free-trade ideal and continue to impose protectionist measures on its imports; if it thinks it can let others play the protectionist game while it stays free of mercantilism's golden handcuffs. Japan, Canada, and France are showing us how to compete against them—that is, if we want to become another protectionist animal. They are mocking us because our private sector can't compete against their government-business partnerships. They are tempting us with their belief in this false god called protectionism.

And we deceive ourselves with this phantom.

Summary

The argument: Free trade as Americans like to think of it never really existed in the world economy. The United States believed in and convinced others to accept multilateral free trade—with exceptions, loopholes, and escape clauses; these are the bounty derived from protectionism. It used nontariff barriers to protect declining industries, and these efforts cost each one of us a lot of money. Japan used MITI to create a relatively closed domestic market that could thrust goods of all kinds, qualities, and prices into the world's export markets. The concept of free trade as defined under the GATT formula, that is, multilateral trade and most favored nations, is obsolete as a theory upon which the United States can build a political strategy for competing in today's world economy.

Results: The United States has been unable to present a coherent, well articulated, fully integrated international trading strategy for the world as it actually exists. Instead, we have become the export market of choice for all countries because we impose fewer restrictions on imports than do other countries. We have let the other industrial countries dictate our trade policy, and we have made our trade policy conform to their internal drives to protect domestic markets, industries, and levels of employment. Also, we have allowed the less developed countries to dictate our trade policy, and we have made ours subject to their willingness to assume extreme risk by opening our markets to their competing goods.

Recommendations: The United States must deal with these prevailing political, economic, and social realities, because no authority is going to alter the world's drive toward protectionism and away from free trade. We must end our unique commitment to multilateral free trade and do what the European Community and the Lomé countries have done—that is, strive for bilateral free trade with countries that are willing to give us reciprocity in the exchange of goods and services. Then we must use access to the U.S. domestic market as the critical bargaining chip in the export of American products overseas.

2
Fear: Parent of Protectionism

Fear is the original parent of protectionism. Consider the case of steel. Fear—or a collection of fears—is American steel's prime mover. Steel's fear of foreign competition is, of course, dominant. Mercantilist barriers in place today were raised after three decades of management's refusal to innovate quickly and through management's inability to keep labor costs in line with world levels. Steel executives have made so many bad decisions, refused so adamantly to invest surplus funds in high-valued-added steel products, thrown so many people out of work during slowdowns, closed so many mills, and followed United States Steel so much like sheep that they are now unable to deal with reality. They think the federal government will protect them because there's nothing else to do.

Throughout the post–World War II period, particularly in the 1960s, the Japanese took the measure of American steel executives and decided they could be beaten. Ours is a group that buys oil companies and imports foreign steel but won't admit there is anything wrong with these decisions. Our steel executives see themselves as saviors and accuse others of making inaccurate charges. Ours is a group that with mammoth lobbying efforts in Washington and the state capitals will defend what is dearest to their special interest: keeping low-cost foreign steel out of the reach of domestic consumers. In the 1970s, steel executives had no doubt that the federal government owed them everything, even driving the national economy into autarky, isolationism, and stagnation, and they forced the trigger price on a hapless Carter administration in need of votes in the industrial north. By traditional standards of business competition, however, these executives surrendered themselves to the coils of politics and bureaucracy. They are mandarins with corporate titles. To be sure, they keep up pretenses with their private jets and high, six-figure salaries; but they continue to protest long after the world has shown them to be incompetent, ineffective, inefficient, time-serving caretakers, and their loud complaints, like all complaints, carry the danger of crying wolf too often. Their only usefulness was in alerting us to the danger from an unlimited dumping of foreign steel. Their evidence was never really clearcut for the assertion that significant amounts of steel from Japan, Europe, and the Third World had been dumped, or, if it had been, that such foreign steel harmed American steel interests. They wanted us to believe that we must protect existing capacity in this "smokestack" industry; but they never came to grips with whether there was too much capacity and how much of it was obsolete.

The fears of the steel executives were fortified by their incredible misconception of world reality, shaped mainly by what they wanted to believe. No one has measured the impact of the steel industry's complaints on the national industrial policy debate. Common sense suggests that the industry's demands forced the Democrats to incorporate them as an issue in the 1984 campaign, and that former steelworkers would have jumped on the bandwagon led by their former steel bosses on the subject of government management of the industry. Common sense also suggests that targeting a declining industry for special help means we fail to give attention to winning industries. But the steel executives, in refusing to cease their drumbeating for special consideration, called attention to a wider problem: steel's inclination to do nothing until it was too late, then blame everyone else for its own failures. Trapped in a mad race for protection, steel executives insist the public "Buy American." Enthralled with state requirements to purchase domestic steel at any price, they do nothing to lower their costs. These executives can't tell the difference between their own puffed-up complaints and the challenges from the outside world, between what they want for themselves and what they've come to believe the public wants from them. They are like psychiatric patients who fear every new day because others don't behave exactly in accordance with their preconceptions of imaginary foreign steel manufacturers, domestic customers, and government.

Half a decade ago, on May 15, 1980, Robert B. Peabody, president of the American Iron and Steel Institute (AISI) and a full-time Washington lobbyist, wrote in a two-page letter to the editor of the Chicago *Sun-Times* that the steel industry does not seek additional "protection, but only adequate administration of present trade laws."[1] He said the AISI simply wanted the federal government to fulfill its obligations under the antidumping laws. The letter was in response to my May 5, 1980, column, "Protectionism is Wrong Answer for Steelmakers."[2] As in Monopoly, that children's game for adults, where you buy property with the intention of keeping your opponents weak and yourself strong when you round Go, the AISI had cleared everyone from the field and made steel the only trade issue worth caring about. Notwithstanding, the federal government's long involvement (since 1967) in protecting the American steel industry, the industry wound up in the 1980s with only 20 percent of its capacity in continuous casting, versus 60 percent for the Japanese. Regrettably, the American steel industry, having developed the continuous casting technology, showed it to the Japanese in the 1950s, and the Japanese, not us, marketed it to the world—including ourselves. So steel's fear is twofold; servitude, whereby punishment, not fault, is dreaded; and filial offspring, by which fault is feared. The AISI believes that "investment in nonsteel activities has supported investment in steel."[3] Yet buying Marathon Oil didn't do one whit for the steel business of United States Steel except divert funds from the mills. The steel executives have been shaken by Japanese intimidation, and our managers cringe at being blamed by their own countrymen for America's decline. Perhaps this fear is the beginning of wisdom. Following are the answers for the AISI.

Disinvestment

One: ROI, or rate of return on investment. That's why United States Steel offered $6.3 billion for Marathon Oil Company. Big Steel could have built a new mill or modernized all its existing facilities. Why did it buy an oil company?

Let's look at the deal with a financial eye. Investment in steel is not as profitable as investments in downtown commercial real estate or high-technology industrial parks or in oil, when OPEC oil is $34 a barrel. (It turns out United States Steel paid top dollar for Marathon Oil just before the price of OPEC oil dropped to $29 a barrel; Big Steel's executives weren't smart oil executives after all.) Steel executives have an interest in making money and not in whether America needs a steel industry. So they have been reducing steel-making capacity and investing in other things. They want to keep domestic steel prices up so they can siphon off the additional revenue into nonsteel investments. Hence, their emotional demands for emergency import quotas, accelerated depreciation of investment in machinery and buildings, a three-year deferral for complying with the Clean Air Act, and the trigger-price system.

Steel's effort at modernization is like throwing paint at a wall and hoping to produce a painting. The AISI believes the steel industry did all it could be expected to do, given its cash flow and long-term debt to equity ratio. But in reality, it did nothing with its tax breaks and special deals from the federal government. No foregone taxes had to be reinvested in steel because the federal government wasn't smart enough to ask for a quid pro quo.

U.S. Steel disinvested in steel. The company put its money into Pennsylvania shopping centers and Texas chemical plants instead of into giving Youngstown, Ohio, a modern, Japanese-style manufacturing operation: a basic oxygen process shop, where a batch of steel can be made in forty-five minutes rather than in seven hours in an open-hearth furnace, and a continuous caster to semifinish the raw steel as it comes out of the furnace.

ROI considerations are important even if tax breaks and subsidies are included in the calculation, but we must never forget that the federal government has given steel firms a new lease on life. Once the firms have accepted government handouts, they can't be allowed to do as they please. It's no longer a free lunch for steel. Theirs is a vital national industry. If they don't wish to modernize their plants and equipment, then it's time for others to do the job for them. Steel leaves us with no choice.

Under the Trade and Tariff Act of 1984, modernization and reinvestment in the steel industry have become concerns of the federal government, and they are to be taken into consideration as the president enforces U.S. trade law against foreign imported steel. The

United States has moved another step closer toward a national industrial policy for steel. This shift in national attitude is not to the liking of the steel executives, and they have no one to blame but themselves.

Disinformation

Two: The AISI never tells us about steel's disinvestment program, but it's been going on for a decade. The AISI never tells us that because the Japanese steelmakers installed modern equipment that reduces the cost of making a ton of steel, they can undersell American steelmakers.

Disinformation consists of filing with the Department of Commerce sixty-seven cartons of documents (weighing a thousand pounds) to prove that foreign steel producers dumped steel on American consumers below cost. On March 21, 1980, Big Steel and its industry colleagues alleged that foreign steel products were being imported into the United States between 40 and 70 percent below the cost of production, and they wanted the price of imports to be pushed upward. Their allegations were not upheld. Yet the politicians feared steel's political clout and did the industry's bidding anyway. Steel's disinformation fantasy says prices are never too high to be harmful.

That harms the interest of American consumers.

As long as steel refuses to modernize its mills and make them competitive with the world's best, steelworkers will suffer decreased employment and steel firms will suffer decreased sales. Fearful of lowered revenues, steel executives become bankers for shopping centers, savings and loan associations, petrochemical plants, and oil refineries. Clearly, what's good for United States Steel is bad for America.

Trigger Prices

Three: Tom-toms beat out the harsh, monotonous Pittsburgh sound. Every year since steel began its disinvestment-disinformation program, the steel firms have mounted a legal assault on free trade in steel products. Steel forced trigger prices on the Carter administration in 1977. These were scrapped in January 1980 and reintroduced in October 1981. On the basis of Japanese steel-making costs, the trigger-price system establishes minimum prices for foreign steel sold in the United States. These prices cannot be undercut without preclearance from the federal government. If imports exceed 15.2 percent of the market when our mills are operating below 87 pecent of capacity, government must investigate this surge in imports. As we listen to the tom-toms of United States Steel, we must hear the discordant tones and lack of harmony in the American composition. Suits involving countervailing duties and antidumping cases are filed against nine countries, as if America's foreign relations with France, Belgium, Luxembourg, Italy, Britain, the Netherlands, West Germany, and others are of no concern to the company. It is impossible to get the message through to steel executives that they are doing irreparable harm to the foreign trade of this country. In 1983, after the Williamsburg economic summit, where President Reagan proclaimed his unflinching loyalty to free trade, he slapped quotas and tariffs on imports of specialty steel, a mere $373 million in 1982. So trivial an amount. But because it's a Section 201 action under the U.S. Trade Act, foreigners can sue for damages under Article XXIX of GATT. To protect steel, we must lower tariffs on other goods, such as butter and cheese. Steelworkers who picketed the 1981 shareholders' meeting of United States Steel said it best: "The threat is real from U.S. Steel."

The *AISI* message is that it's all the government's fault. Pollution control. Misallocation of capital. New steel mills overseas. Failure to stamp out foreign-government–owned steel firms. Failure to raise tariffs and nontariff barriers high enough to keep out foreign steel. Is the Pittsburgh message correct?

Labor's to Blame

No industry can overcome a labor-cost disadvantage of $10 an hour in a competitive market, no matter how much it increases productivity. One evening I was thumbing through a rather long article by Arthur Laffer on the failure of protectionism in the steel industry,[4] and glancing at a piece by Peter Drucker about the need for union flexibility, when that statistic caught my attention.[5] It jumped off the page as the key piece of information because it has to do with competitiveness, not with trade, so there is no need to worry about net subsidy *ad valorem* rates, dumping margins and countervailing duties, or the exchange rate for yen and D-marks; and because it involves workers, not bureaucrats. It says that workers who are protected by the United Steelworkers Union, once the most powerful union in the United States, make twice as much as Japanese steelworkers, and that is saying American steelworkers are overpaid for what they do. Unionized steelworkers resist this notion. They have invented alternative concepts, with the result that workers making $18 in cash wages and another $10 in fringes and benefits—for a total compensation of $56,000 a year for a full-time steelworker—insist that this be the prevailing wage, thus driving up the costs of all other labor in the region where steel is the predominant industry. Expensive: that's what this labor is when compared to other steelworkers elsewhere in the industrialized world. Labor's traditional defense against the charge that our steelworkers are paid too much is that somehow our foreign competitors will let American steel management pass on these costs to U.S. customers. But to believe our steel firms are oligopolists and have price control over our domestic market is to try to turn fiction into fact. Japanese steel comes into the United States because it is produced more cheaply. European steel comes into the United States because the European Community has been more successful in rationalizing European steel, that is, closing excess mills. Brazilian steel comes into the United States because it is subsidized by that government in order to provide its own people with employment.

The reason labor prefers not to be confronted with the thought that steelworkers are paid too much is that the idea forces a response from the union's leadership—that is, the leadership would have to admit it was wrong. The common first reaction is to blame management for the plight in which this smokestack industry finds itself. Did management fail to invest in new technology? Yes. The battle of words can be argued as long as newspapers and magazines stand ready to print different points of view. Anyway, the argument between management and labor is less important than the question of America's international competitiveness. We are unable to keep our share of the domestic market and we cannot increase our share of foreign markets. Faced with that truth, we can enforce protectionist measures and let the issue fester; things will get worse, costs will get further out of line, and more jobs will be lost. Or we can attack the problem head on and automate, shift workers to higher-value-added jobs, and do a better job in after-sales servicing of customers, which will no doubt help the situation. Maybe some increase in productivity will narrow the gap in the cost of labor to say $9. Maybe even to $8.

Productivity experts like Elizabeth E. Bailey say incrementalism won't work. In a *New York Times* article in 1983, Bailey stated that there must be a significant change in how labor is paid, perhaps a fixed wage, lower than what is paid now; a bonus on top of that for outstanding performance, with benefits geared to current family needs rather than universal demands (the so-called cafeteria approach); and flexibility in paying both labor and management based on productivity, profitability, and control over world market share.[6] We are faced with a steel industry in which there is an ease of entry and exit in selling the product, in which technology is cheap and resalable, and in which low-cost labor is abundant to produce whatever steel product is demanded. Others have contested for our markets and won. Organized labor opposes changes in its relationship with management, and the former helped the latter put quotas and trigger prices in place. All to no avail. Their protectionist policies did not, according to Laffer, "increase significantly domestic steelmakers' market share, profitability, employment or investment."[7] Rather, these ill-conceived policies "will increase foreign competition for domestic industries intensive in the use of steel including autos, appliances and oil and gas."[8] Productivity experts tell us to renounce protectionism—end Section 201 and Section 301 cases, eliminate dumping and voluntary quotas from our trade vocabulary, get the government out of trade regulation, stop the government from setting industrial policy through the U.S. International Trade Commission. This would mean no more trigger prices, high tariffs, and countervailing duties. Renouncing protectionism is a step that at first, for steel, will be painful, but it is necessary—because we want to hide from the idea that our prevailing wage is too high. Laffer shows us the dismal trade results from the imposition of protectionism on the steel industry. What goes into producing goods and how they are processed are the crucial ingredients of our international competitiveness, or lack thereof.

Management's to Blame

The problem of steel's lack of international competitiveness can also be attributed to poor management decisions, particularly in capital spending. Thomas F. O'Boyle says poor management decisions bear as much responsibility for the mills' current plight as do high wages and benefits.[9] Thirty years ago, the fearful steel executives failed to adopt the two breakthrough advances in steelmaking: the basic oxygen furnace and continuous casting. Since the 1960s, the future has been passing them by. Steel management has been united in its aversion to risk. In its relentless pursuit of the past, steel was hesitant to abandon its "proven" open-hearth furnaces. Whereas the Japanese closed their last open-hearth furnace in 1978, United States Steel still produced 28.5 percent of its steel by that obsolete method in 1983. The American steel industry is a past that doesn't work. Like its nightmares, steel's symbols haven't changed, either. The ingot being poured—a process tenaciously held to even when cheap energy vanished; it did not yield to continuous casting in the mills—is steel's logo as it presents itself to the world.

Government's to Blame

The problem of steel's vanishing presence in the world also can be attributed to the federal government's poor understanding of what was going on elsewhere in the world, at first in Japan, then in the European Community, and now in Third World countries such as Brazil and Mexico. During the 1950s, Japan restricted imports through high tariffs and controls over foreign exchange. Then, in the 1960s, Japan stopped Japanese steel makers from competing against each other when bidding on licenses for imported technology, and it did not permit foreign steel firms to export to Japan or to set up a subsidiary there. Throughout these twenty years, the Japanese government gave financial assistance to its steel industry with low-interest loans, special tax benefits (such as accelerated depreciation), and investment funds to improve exports. Japanese steel firms worked under MITI's administrative guidance and when they failed to follow MITI's instructions, MITI restricted their allocation of imported coking coal. By 1978, electric furnace steel makers, 19.1 percent of Japan's steel industry capacity, were designated a depressed industry and were given special protection and aids to help them through the crisis.

Since the 1950s, Japan has been the single largest source of America's steel imports, accounting for over 40 percent of total imports during the late 1970s, when import growth came to a halt as the result of the trigger-price system. This was true even though both Japan and Europe agreed to voluntary restraints starting in 1969 and extending through 1974. Quotas were imposed on the imports of specialty steel between 1976 and 1980, and again in 1983, for four years, until 1987. Also, trigger prices came into being in 1978, were suspended for a time in 1980, and were suspended again in 1982, when American steel companies filed antidumping and countervailing duty petitions before the U.S. International Trade Commission.

While American steel makers sold their steel products mainly in the U.S. market, Japanese and European steel makers built their facilities at coastal ports to sell steel in international markets, particularly in the United States. Now Latin American steel makers do the same. So today Brazil, Mexico, and others are subject to the same antidumping and countervailing duties that United States Steel and Bethlehem Steel obtained from the U.S. International Trade Commission against the Japanese and Europeans in the 1970s.

In 1983, Bethlehem filed a comprehensive 201 petition alleging that the domestic steel industry was seriously injured as a result of increased imports. According to Bethlehem, "Brazil is engaged in flagrant dumping in the U.S. market."[10] This made Brazil and the other Latin American countries angry. Brazil, Mexico, and Argentina want to sell their steel to us so they can pay off their sovereign country debts.

In its November 28, 1983, editorial, the *New York Times* said "Protect Steel, Damage All."[11] The editorial was making the point that it's hard to see how additional protection for American steel will benefit either the public or the long-term prospects of the domestic industry. More protection is bad public policy, plain and simple.

Republican Senator John H. Chafee of Rhode Island said that if we were to guarantee American steel makers 85 percent of our domestic market, we would be violating our international trade agreements and would force up prices for steel and steel-intensive products in the United States. "The only answer," he said, "is to put an end to this kind of protection now."[12] Donald F. Barnett and Louis Schorsch concluded that government must stop relying on politically easy options such as trade barriers, which only postpone the changes needed to make U.S. steel plants competitive.[13] Steel already has a de facto industrial policy comprised of a crazy quilt of trade barriers, special tax provisions, environmental regulations, and antitrust exemptions. No federal program, and no combination of federal programs, will work for the steel industry. All of them have been bad public policy, plain and simple.

Unfortunately, we Americans like quick fixes. And we are especially likely to go astray when we try to shift the blame for problems onto the multilateral trading system. At present, our chief remedies are as follows: Section 301 of the Trade Act requires proof of unfair trade practices such as dumping or government subsidies; and Section 201 requires simply that the facts show that swelling imports have wrought serious economic damage to the industry. To hear steel executives, Florida orange growers, and others tell it, all foreign firms are guilty of dumping: an unfair trade practice where the price of goods sold in the United States is cheaper than the same goods sold in the home country. They want the U.S. International Trade Commission to make a finding in their favor under Section 301. And they want the president, as a partisan in their worldwide struggle against their foreign competitors, to deal with their grievance. The main flaw in this remedy, however, lies not in the projected results, with which it is hard to quarrel, but in the fact that it is the quick fixers who champion it. They want foreigners to fear them. It is our inability to breed fear among foreigners that permits the Japanese to fight and win. In order to win, our firms must be freed from the lobbying efforts of the Japanese and European Community in Washington. We have to tell them to go home and stop interfering in our orderly process of compromise and consensus. Our failure to do this is the reason that the Japanese, much to our amazement, can lose every round and still convince the president not to impose quotas on their imported goods. We are unwilling to tell the Japanese government to cease and desist. And we are unwilling to work hard on the necessary long-term solutions. For some time now, our remedies have been like horror movies that might frighten only chidren, and we have only ourselves to fear.

Summary

The argument: Free trade doesn't exist in steel. American steel executives have seen to that by their cries for more and more protectionism. The government is to blame because we gave in to steel and let the industry have all the tariff and nontariff barriers possible. However, the government didn't demand a quid pro quo for this protectionism; it didn't demand that the monies earned from protectionism go into modernizing or building mills.

Results: We have protected an inefficient steel industry that has been unable to find a way to become competitive again. We have been unable to gain access to overseas markets. We have let the steel industry become an agent for protectionism within the United States. We have become the captive of our own phantoms, illusions, and fears.

Recommendations: The United States must apply the Trade and Tariff Act of 1984 with a new sense of purpose. The steel industry must be modernized with the monies earned from protectionism irrespective of the desire of American steel executives to buy oil companies and shopping centers. Moreover, the United States must negotiate several reciprocal bilateral trade agreements for steel with Canada, Mexico, and one or two other Latin American countries; the multilateral approach through which Japan and the European Community have primary access to our domestic market should be terminated.

3
The Fix Is In

The success of steel in directing America's protectionist sentiments is undeniable. To be sure, what nonsteel executives tried most eagerly to imitate was the wide range of lobbying efforts: political support from congressional delegations and state officials; friendly picketing by labor, suppliers, and dealers; encouragement from media personalities paid to spread the good word about why a Chrysler car or a Harley-Davidson 700 cc. heavy-duty motorcycle is as American as apple pie. Few industries have clout in all regions of the nation—clout that includes the most powerful union in the country and so many reporters who make their living by seeking inside information and writing about the comings and goings of steel. More difficult though not impossible to imitate was the romance of the industry's history: Northern iron and steel drove Old Dixie down, conquered Spain's colonies, threw the Kaiser out and made Germany, Japan, and many older nations part of the American empire; Pittsburgh, Youngstown, Gary, all mill towns, took eastern and central Europeans and made them affluent ethnic Americans. Some remember the religious fights among Poles over the Black Madonna when a small minority supported the fledgling Polish National Catholic Church, Catholicism without the pope but Jansenist in belief, and the majority who were staunch Polish Roman Catholics but unconvinced the Irish-American hierarchy knew much about Polish Catholicism. Even the Episcopal church, Protestant and low church along Philadelphia's Main Line, rushed into battle its high-church, Catholic colors with Mary statues, burning candles and saying rosaries in its Polish parish churches. Good old American religious pluralism! Or the fights between Orthodox

Christians (these look to the patriarch in Constantinople–Istanbul) and Uniate Christians (they're the pope's Eastern troops), between old calendar and new calendar Ukranians, some Orthodox, some Uniate. The luxury of their gold-domed churches, the richness of their altars and parish houses attest to the wealth these steelworkers found in the land of the free. Dreams came true in the mill towns of Pennsylvania, Ohio, Indiana, and Illinois. Some other industries talked about Rosie the Riveter, the heroine of our World War II effort. When the men who made Model A Fords and Chevies went to war, their wives, sweethearts, and women built the tanks that took Europe by storm. In the post World War II period, there was the annual model change for automobiles. Throughout the 1950s and 1960s people flocked to the annual car shows. Tail fins on Cadillacs were designed to commit us forever to conspicuous consumption. We sat in Pal's Cabin (my diner on top of Second Mountain in West Orange, New Jersey) deciding which back seat was best for picking up girls, petting, and, if we dared, a three-point landing, and which car (mine was a converted Oldsmobile police cruiser) could go from zero to sixty miles an hour in the fewest seconds possible. It is because of these dreams of good times past, of course, that Lee Iacocca succeeded in convincing us that Chrysler was worth saving.

Chrysler

What is protectionism? It is fear personified, an instance of emotion, apprehensive of a future evil, when old hopes grow dim. Auto executives know that their decisions will depend on an accurate estimate of the probable behavior of the federal government. A wrong guess may spell the end of models, makes, and manufacturers, a further shakeout of an industry which seemed concentrated on the Big Three plus American Motors and Volkswagen as late as the 1960s. There is, of course, no one answer that is good for all administrations; rather, there are many answers, most of them probably good, all of them possible under the right combination of political circumstances. The government itself cannot always be depended on for a reliable prediction of what it will do. One can rarely trust a politician for an objective opinion about a problem he does not have to do anything about right now. Of course, politicians who built military bases in the south and bailed out New York City expect their colleagues to rally 'round Michigan's banner when disaster strikes its most important industry. But a reliable definition of protectionism is something else. Political forces determine its destiny.

Back in 1979, you heard a lot of people saying "The fix is in for Chrysler." Senator William Proxmire coined these code words. What they told us is that President Jimmy Carter; his cabinet; congressmen; the mayor of Detroit; the governors of Michigan, Indiana, and Illinois; the clean and honest United Automobile Workers; the banks; 119,500 employees and their families in six states; suppliers who employ hundreds of thousands in many more states; the dealers across the nation; the Washington lobbyists; the Canadian and Mexican governments and their citizens who work for the firm; all were on one side—for Chrysler's survival. They said five hundred thousand jobs were at stake. The truth is that no other bankruptcy led to such a high proportion of job loss, because under any reorganization plan approved by the federal courts (so-called Chapter 11 bankruptcy), the intent is to keep plants open and maintain jobs while looking for new business. Their figure was a scare tactic. They said competition would end; but foreign competition is the crucial force operating against the Big Three. They blamed federal regulation that insists on fuel-efficient cars; but that's a public good whose expense is to be paid for by all firms and then passed onto the consumers. They blamed the economy, the business cycle, a recession, or whatever economic data they could massage. Free traders didn't accept these data as valid and were against the bailout. Others reasoned that if we must give a federal handout to corporations, it should be done for the only good reason possible: it's in the national interest because the company is a key defense supplier. If we can't say that—if we have to muster all these other arguments, and maybe we must to keep the fabric of the nation together, to pay back political debts, to get the nation working again, for instance, then begging at Uncle Sam's door should be done with our eyes open, which means that government must set the terms. What's good about a fix, anyway? In short, it's the last-resort option when government bureaucrats must step in and supervise management.

Even before Lee Iacocca went to Washington like a used-car salesman to haggle over the terms of Chrysler's bailout, we knew the company wasn't up to making quality cars anymore, for the "lemons" were becoming more common throughout its nationwide dealer network. Ingrid Bengis told us that her father, a Desoto-Plymouth, Chrysler dealer for thirty-seven years, insisted the family drive cars built before 1969—Valiants with indestructible engines capable of getting twenty-five miles per gallon—because the newer cars had doors that closed improperly, defective parts, poor mileage, and too many gadgets: quality debased by the company![1] Sales fell. Business was bad as Chrysler supplied its dealers with big cars when the public wanted smaller cars. The chairman didn't notice its dealers going bankrupt until October 1979, a year after Ingrid's father went under and several years after the handwriting was on the wall for all Chrysler dealers. There's some symbolism in this ordeal. It has to do with Mr. Bengis's business really being owned by Chrysler, the fact that the company "made the basic decisions on styling and pricing and model availability and dealer credit,"[2] mistakes he believed Chrysler would correct because they were gentlemen. Chrysler did not give him a hand when he went to them for help. He was their poor relation, their middleman, dispensable. The Chrysler Corporation threw him out on the dump heap as they screamed for help in Washington.

Americans who paid attention to the federal government's loan guarantee program saw effective control over operations pass from the company to the Chrysler Loan Guarantee Board, with fifty Treasury Department officials from its Office of Chrysler Finance commuting between Washington and Detroit to approve Chrysler's marketing strategy, its cost structure, its pricing policies, everything. The government had bought a car company and now it was running it. From this supervisory role over Chrysler management, some deduced that America had, in 1979, taken a significant step toward planning national industrial policy, targeting winners, getting rid of losers, and doing whatever is necessary to compete with foreign labor, goods, and companies. More thoughtful persons, such as David A. Heenan in his *The Re-United States of America*,[3] said this couldn't be: we had no national institutions to make planning work; we had no trained personnel to do the work required; none of our top corporate and political leaders wanted a national industrial policy then, nor do they want it now. Americans were worried that we were becoming more Europeanized and afraid we were becoming more like the Japanese.

The federal bailout turned out successfully for Chrysler. That company is still in business and making money. Its U.S., Canadian, and Mexican plants are still open, and its trinational set of employees are still working for the company. The Chrysler bailout was a good idea for the company, the employees, and the communities in which the Chrysler plants are located. Was the Chrysler bailout an example of how Japan's Ministry of International trade and Industry goes about its business? No. MITI is with a company in good times and bad. MITI guides a company together with its competitors in exporting 40 percent or more of the goods produced in Japan. MITI protects its own companies from foreign competition. The U.S. government didn't want to bail out Chrysler, but when it was forced into going forward with the bailout, it couldn't wait to end its oversight of Chrysler. This is how we carry out our national industrial policy.

All this, of course, is due to the import invasion. The Japanese are better at making cars than we are. They produce them $1,500 cheaper than we can. Their labor costs in the automobile industry are one-half ours and equal to our average industrial wage costs. But then we knew this in 1979, and we know this now. It's a bitter disappointment that the wages of protectionism—what the federal government insisted the unions give up in 1980 and what Chrysler gave back in 1983—are the unwillingness of both management and labor to understand the seriousness of their financial predicament. Why did Chrysler give in to the new president of the United Automobile Workers, Owen Bieber? Because he was new? Because a strike would delay the introduction of Chrysler's new cars? Because management was unwilling (or unable) to cut costs drastically? Chrysler remained protected because Japan's sales in America were limited to one car in five by a "voluntary" marketing agreement. By raising wages and passing the costs on to consumers, Chrysler perpetuates the need for protection and subsidies.

Clearly, the fix is in for a long time to come.

Protectionism Redux

Of the two major protectionist efforts disemboweling free trade—those of steel and automobiles—it is easier to speak angry words about the former, because the steel industry blatantly embedded itself in our most inner sources of power. It is harder to become as emotionally charged about the latter, because the automobile industry was careful not to demand continuous protection from Washington.

Throughout the 1960s and 1970s, the American automobile industry faced a European and Latin American industry in which government directed, financed, owned, and managed the automobile business; these government-owned business firms, or state enterprises, showed how governments reclaimed economic sovereignty,[4] and they became threats to American business. Volkswagen, Renault, British Leyland: all competed for world-market share against the Big Three, Fiat, Volvo, and several automobile firms emerging from East Asia—Toyota, Nissan, and Honda.

The rapid rise of automobile and truck production in Japan between 1958 and 1981 is well known. There were only two years of decline: 1974, because of the OPEC oil embargo and the resulting increase in oil prices, at which time world car production dropped all over; and 1982, because of persistent recession, a decline in sales in Japan, and restrictions on Japanese imports in the European Community and the United States. In 1972, Japan's automobile and truck production topped 6,260,000 units. Japan had come of age.

But the real story of the Japanese automobile industry began when Americans gave up their brand loyalty to the same makes and models their fathers and they had bought during the 1940s, 1950s, and 1960s. They bought what they could afford, since price was the other key factor in their decision whether to buy a Chevrolet, Pontiac, Oldsmobile, Buick, or Cadillac; or a Ford, Mercury, or Lincoln; or a Plymouth, Desoto, Chrysler, or Imperial. Because of

OPEC, Americans became concerned with fuel efficiency, and because of shoddy cars coming out of Detroit, Americans became concerned with mechanical reliability and quality. First the Germans, then the Japanese learned how to sell Americans the small cars and trucks we wanted.

By 1978, Japan had become the number one importer of cars for Americans. It had acquired 7.8 percent of the total U.S. market. Moreover, Japan exported 50 percent of its automobile and truck production. Goodbye, Uncle Sam, as the major producer and exporter of cars to the world.

For sweep, depth, and dominance, nothing like the surge of Japanese cars in the United States, Canada, the European Community, South Africa, and Australia has been experienced since the Big Three surged into the world after World War II. MITI helped by protecting the home market through tariffs, quotas, and limits on foreign direct investment. Our automobile companies could never get a foothold in Japan, as they did in the European Community. MITI also helped by giving assistance to the industry so that firms could modernize, expand production, and go into export markets. The sweep of this protection is so immense that one small example can reveal only the tip of the iceberg; it cannot convey the vigor of the enforcement: Foreign automobiles had to be individually inspected up to 1983, rather than receive "type" certification for entry into Japan. Japanese cars entering the United States, Canada, the European Community, and elsewhere were always given type certification to clear customs.

The potential for failure of one of the Big Three had been growing since the mid-1970s, when in successive years no amount of promotion, special deals, or gimmicks could move the big American cars. Even John Updike's fictional character, Rabbit, took on Japanese small cars as a secondary line at first, then made them his primary line in his automobile dealership in Pennsylvania. Rabbit wanted to sell as many Japanese imports as he could get. He was for free trade. However, in the 1970s, American manufacturers repudiated all the old rules of free enterprise that government and business had once accepted. The quality of the new managed capitalism is best embodied in the electrifying rescue of Chrysler, which made itself into everyone's darling (over much industry opposition among Detroit automobile executives). Chrysler changed the American economic system and the character of the automobile industry.

Chrysler is much less yet far more than a current example of state capitalism in the United States. The Chrysler rescue comes out of the economic history of America, where for two centuries two conflicting ideas have sought power: government helps business, and government regulates business. Chrysler united several streams of U.S. history: the pre–Civil War era, when government aided business in building the canals; the Civil War era, when government did the same with the railroads; the New Deal era, when government financed business reconstruction; and the post–World War II era, when government became partners with business to build up America's defenses. Only when Lockheed was in trouble did our stream of consciousness lead us to applaud another government bailout—this time for a prime defense contractor.

If the United States ever decides to adopt a formal industrial policy, the Chrysler example will become the guts of it. Any large firm with an important tax and employment base will be a target for federal government intervention. Depending on the array of political forces at any particular time in Washington, a bailout program will be enacted into law. For a limited period of time, government officials will manage the company that is being bailed out; gradually, they will return the "saved" company to its executives. The bailout program will include two essential items: federal funds to modernize and to redesign factories and products; and protection of our home market from foreign imports for a five-year period after the beginning of the bailout. Never again will a protectionist industrial policy extend for an unlimited period of time, such as two decades for the steel industry. The Chrysler bailout told us what the real limits of our industrial policy must be.

U.S. International Trade Commission

The success of protectionism in steel and automobiles is irresistible. It dominates American industry today in most matters, even among executives who should know better. A few years ago, we invented a separate administrative tribunal to hear dumping cases. The U.S.

International Trade Commission, a remake of the old Tariff Commission, is an outside, fact-finding agency that recommends whether the president should take corrective action. Governments all over the world view the ITC as representing the intent of Congress to make the antidumping law an effective means for dealing with injurious, unfair pricing practices that come from overseas. The transfer of antidumping enforcement from the Treasury to Commerce, the cabinet office that has always protected American business interests, is viewed by foreign governments as the intent of the president to be sure this law is enforced and does protect weakened domestic business firms. Such solutions make good political sense. Protectionist achievements have closed the American market to foreign-made heavy-duty motorcycles, ceramic tiles, and a host of other products. Most protectionist rules are foolish and impractical, the result of poorly devised solutions; as the Center for the Study of American Business notes, they cost each one of us $255. Many of these laws are copycats of European ones and are transplanted without thought of their roots. Admittedly, most protectionist dreams are more than European or American dreams; they are universal.

Very few free traders understand the extent to which protectionism has infected American law with notions about restricting trade. Some of these legal provisions are as follows:

Subsidized exports, 19 USC 1303, 1671 *et seq.* (1980)
Section 337 unfair competition actions, Ibid., 1337 (1980)
Antitrust considerations under the Sherman Act, 15 USC 1 *et seq.* (1973)
The Robinson-Patman Act, Ibid., 13–13b, 21a (1973)
Section 201 "escape clause" proceedings, 19 USC 2251 (1980)
Customs valuation, Ibid., 1401a (1980)
Civil penalties, Ibid., 1592 (1980)

It is the ill wind from foreign cartels, sovereign country debt, and the pressures for growth and development that drives the protectionist forces onward. Behind the compulsion of U.S. protectionists to close off America's domestic market to foreign-government–

owned firms and later to foreign-government private firms as well, was the belief—shared by free traders—that foreign business strategies (that is, foreign governments working with their own firms to dominate world markets) had perverted free trade among nations. Few foreigners even today understand the depth of feeling among Americans concerning this issue. The United States looks to them like the apple to be picked. Our free trade fervor that was so blatantly evident in the past is less visible now. But it is still there, even if steel and automobile executives do everything in their power to lessen it. The consensus for free trade is feebler, discredited by false friends, corroded by the doubts of impious souls (called fair traders), but without it, or what is left of it, America would not be what it is—the world's only government committed to free and open markets for all comers. Here's our vision confined by illusion and fear.

Then there are some governments that protect their home markets for domestic firms and, at the same time, give them a platform from which to expand internationally. These nations tend to be on the make worldwide. Japan's business strategy of close government (MITI)–business ties is a dumping strategy under Title VII of the Tariff Act of 1930, as amended (19 USC 1673 *et seq.* [1980], when there is material injury to existing industries and when the establishment of new industries is materially retarded because imported foreign goods sell here at a price lower than in their home markets. Antidumping duties can be imposed because of injury to an American industry and because of discriminatory pricing. Who can file a case before the Commerce Department and the ITC? Large firms, with staffs to put together sixty-seven cartons of information, such as United States Steel. Smaller firms, which can submit information reasonably available to them so they can meet threshold requirements for initiating a case. (Under the 1984 Trade Act, smaller firms are eligible for special assistance by the ITC.) Labor unions and trade associations—these are new petitioners—that see an injury to their members.

There is a surge provision. When there has been a massive surge in imports, the ITC can order the retroactive suspension of goods coming into the United States and assess retroactive antidumping duties. If the offending exporter agrees to cease exporting goods to the United States or to eliminate the discriminatory sales or to eliminate the injury caused by the sales, the investigation ceases. Dumping margins must be removed so that prices will be at the level of production costs in the United States.

What this law does is warn foreign exporters that the United States will protect its industries against dumped imports. What it does is require a new standard of information about equivalent goods sold in domestic markets of foreign firms and here in the United States. For a price to be legally different in the United States, it must be based on one or more of the following factors: wholesale versus retail prices—physical or technical differences, or both; quantity sales; differentials in credit terms, in selling and advertising expenses, in packaging and transportation costs, and in foreign exchanges. When the Japanese government holds the yen to an artificially low value in terms of the dollar, that's dumping. You can get a feeling of irritation talking to many Japanese businessmen because they either deny it's being done or tell you it's a government decision, not theirs. But that denial of the obvious facts lies at the heart of our irritation with the Japanese. A big reason we don't much like what the Japanese do is that they make us feel like chronic complainers; their way of doing business is as obvious as the nose on one's face and we don't want them to deny it to us but admit it and get on with the negotiations to solve the trade problems facing the two nations.

Here are the two sides of the argument. The first side says it can't be government support that makes Japanese steel and automobiles better and cheaper. Something other than protected domestic markets must account for their successes—call it entrepreneurial spirit. The same skill that makes our computers, copiers, and agricultural products sell well helps the Japanese compete. It's their skill that makes them capture semiconductor markets, that ties the Pacific Rim nations and our own West Coast to their trading system, that forces us to cite them before the ITC. Their skill will make them prosper, and so we must learn to compete with them in our own way. The second side of the argument is the intuitive reaction: "They keep us out of their domestic markets." Like the first side, it is also true. As individual firms, most American companies know firsthand the misery associated with getting through the door with MITI as the doorkeeper. With few exceptions, American executives give up—thereby contributing a part of the negative feeling toward the Japanese that goes unrecorded in our statistics. In truth, few countries, either socialist or capitalist, developed or less developed, can be blamed for their cultural biases. We usually are what we are through the shaping power of our history. One of us is *against* government in the international market and *for* free trade—or at least, we tell ourselves we are—and others are *for* government in international trade.

Maybe the answer would be best obtained by using all existing statutes against MITI and its cooperating Japanese firms; or maybe not, because we look as though we are bashing only the Japanese. We have to decide, as we did with Chrysler, whether we are impotent or whether we can do something about our troubles. But we have to decide which industry—and how much of it—and which firms are worth saving in the national interest. When the Japanese sense that the fix is in, then a wondrous thing happens: they become agreeable to our concerns, do their level best to accommodate us, and act as they should toward their chief protector. Only entrepreneurial skill counts, then, as we have seen in the rebirth of the Chrysler Corportion.

Summary

The argument: Free trade was translated as managed trade by the federal government, Chrysler, and the U.S. and Japanese automobile industries. The U.S. government has found a way to intervene successfully and save a large business firm. It did demand a quid pro quo for its intervention and protection. The United States has not adopted the Japanese habit of managed trade, through MITI's guidance, or the European and Latin American habits of government ownership of business firms. In its own way, the United States has a very limited industrial policy, directed toward international trade in automobiles, which suits the political, economic, and social realities of mid-1980s America.

Results: We have kept a third U.S.-owned automobile company afloat, but we did not regain market share lost to the Japanese. We have let the automobile industry become an agent for protectionist forces within the United States. As a captive of our own phantoms, illusions, and fears, we have created a de facto national industrial policy that saves losers rather than helps winners. We have not dealt effectively with the world as it is, and we must learn to do a better job of targeting future winning industries.

Recommendations: In learning how to target future winning industries, the United States must have a broad appreciation of what the natural North American market will be for its products. That's why we must get on with the task of developing reciprocal bilateral trade agreements. Market size must become a known quantity for American manufacturers. America's international trade policy must be based on how much market share our goods and services will gain in Canada, Mexico, the Caribbean, Latin America, and elsewhere in the world.

4
MITI

Regrettably, the Japanese live in a state of illusion about their relations with the United States. They persist in improving performance (specifically through quality circles, quality deployment, and just-in-time inventory) without regard to American fears about loss of industry, jobs, and markets. This illusion on the part of the Japanese must be understood in conjunction with another fundamental, ever-present, and sometimes contradictory Japanese trait: the "insult." The two aren't recognized as mirrors of each other. Illusion is the belief that things can go on much as before when they cannot. When something else must be done, it will be done grudgingly—without good grace and adding to our grief. The Japanese do not like to open up their home markets. The mirror image between illusion and insult, for instance, is demonstrated by their insistence on maintaining MITI as doorkeeper (keeping out all but a few foreign firms from competing with Japanese firms) and their propensity for working the backrooms of Washington to be sure no legislation passes Congress and no executive order comes from the president that will upset Japanese markets in the United States.

To be sure, hiring lobbyists and winning congressional friends is part of normal American business behavior, occasionally essential for securing proper tax treatment and government business, as well as exemption from costly regulations.

Yet the Japanese, skilled practitioners in the art of making government and business work together, trod underfoot the sacred pretenses of free enterprise and its affliction with adversarial and litigious procedures, and render its participants indignant bystanders in the passing parade of multinational business. So many successful backroom campaigns in Washington give Americans complexes, anxieties and jealousies. We think of the Japanese as leaping in to take advantage, wounding our self-respect. Japanese talk of productivity investments with large amounts of debt capital. We must use more costly equity sources of new capital. The Japanese are reluctant to admit that government is the source of these leveraged funds. They have cultural homogeneity where we do not. We cannot become more like them to beat them at their own game because we cannot create the same special government-business relationship. The Japanese sense of collective responsibility, their confidence in bringing order to the kingdom of business, but above all their inclination to see the world through the prism of their own illusions, prevents them, until the eleventh hour, from understanding that we feel insulted by their attitude. Not surprisingly, when Americans are particularly sticky about trade and investment issues, and when the Japanese know that our tolerance for the status quo has ended, they retreat into their illusions, study their choices, and from out of the blue offer the face-saving compromise all Japanese can agree to. Will they now retreat into their illusions or fire new insults?

Even if these traits describe the Japanese, they are not exclusively Japanese but also French, Brazilian, and Malaysian. What does worry Americans, and even Europeans and Asians, is Japan's single-mindedness. This might be called the predestined hard-work ethic, the will to work, the need to compete or starve, the eagerness to do all of us one better. Its compelling character is not understood. How Japanese choose what their goals will be, whether they will favor one direction over another, and who decides, have been favorite areas of study for us. We don't know much more today than we knew yesterday. Where is the source of decision? Perhaps the Japanese believe that business as separate from government is a meaningless idea. They believe that a consensus must be formed from the bottom up, and that, in fact, there is no possibility of error once all have agreed to the decision. No trade or investment dispute merits disturbing their consensus, disrupting their single-mindedness, or breaking down their illusions—so we get solace, not action until the eleventh hour.

Success

The Japanese disinclination to act quickly probably cannot be changed. Japanese consensus management, particularly in the industries that compete so strongly against our own, has been spectacular whenever their government has advanced funds to selected targeted firms, has protected their local markets, and has given Japanese executives the rationale for winning in the competition for world markets. The examples of this are well known: steel, automobiles, motorcycles, semiconductors, numerical control machines. Japanese success also may be attributed to the United States itself: knowingly or not, we are the source of much of the advanced technology Japan sells to the world and back to us. In the adoption of continuous steelcasting, the Japanese offered us the highest form of flattery: imitation; and then, they did us one better by beating us in both our domestic market and in world markets.

They are our most serious rival. What counts for them is surviving—the first oil shock, then the second oil shock, and the voluntary quotas on 70 percent of their export to the United States. Japan turns a barrel of oil at the high price of $34 a barrel into more exports. This is better than West Germany does, and much better than all other countries do. Japanese employees work, rather than collect unemployment compensation. There are no downtown Youngstowns, no vast industrial wastelands stretching across Japan. Also, the Japanese are climbing higher up the technological ladder, in electronics and computers, where we thought we had the lead for all time. They had 30 percent of our car market during the voluntary quota, and they are now striving for market share. This is getting serious. Yet it remains our prevailing attitude that they can't (Please, God, don't let them) challenge America's industrial might; our unwillingness to calm our fears, our unwillingness to do the hard things necessary to make our economy competitive again, will be the death of us. Their success is our failure.

Family

One illusion Japan has perpetuated here is that theirs is a free enterprise economy. We should be wary. What is MITI? It was the wartime Munitions Ministry which, eleven days after the war, became the Ministry of Commerce and Industry, and then became MITI, the control center for Japan's command economy. It gives "window guidance," in which entrepreneurial talent is subject always to supreme state direction.

The truth, of course, is that MITI is a Japanese family. Everyone is "in," but some are further in than others. All firms that are guided by MITI are *ie,* or "households" (written in Japanese by the graphic Chinese character of a pig under a roof). They owe a loyalty to MITI that is automatic and inescapable, a commitment for life. Back in 1955, General Electric sold to Sony the rights to the transistor. MITI forbade any American firm to produce radios in Japan. The head of the family has protected its household to this very day. In order to enjoy more harmony with the United States, MITI offers advice to American firms that wish to consider entering the Japanese market. At times, a few actually get in; most don't. MITI clings to its roles as doorkeeper and family protector.

MITI officials are central planners in the guise of free enterprisers. The difficulty of determining, with any degree of certainty, whether MITI will open the door even a slight crack to the Japanese market (an insult because the opening is so small, an illusion because the bureaucratic procedures of other government agencies—Customs and Treasury—make the crack invisible), is aggravated by some uniquely Japanese features, of which only a few Americans are aware. One is the process for commanding the economy. The current set of big Japanese conglomerates came into being when General Hideki Tojo sent Nobusuke Kishi, head of the Department of Industry (MITI), to deliver capitalism without Japanese capitalists to Manchukuo. Tojo was the military governor of Manchukuo, Japan's puppet state (the Chinese province of Manchuria). (He later became Japan's war-time prime minister and was hung as a war criminal.) Army-controlled banks gave Kishi's uncle Gensuke Aikawa, a bankrupt textile tycoon, the money to set up the army's conglomerate, Nissan (Datsun); his market share was guaranteed by the army government. During the 1930s in Manchuria and the 1940s in Japan's wartime economy, Tojo had Kishi organize army-controlled conglomerates directed by the Munitions Ministry. These conglomerate executives, who have been marinated for decades in window guidance—government-controlled finance, or guaranteed market shares at home, where there is no risk—are well acquainted with the authority of long-serving MITI bureaucrats and know that the best of these bureaucrats become ruling party politicians, and the very best prime ministers (Kishi was a war criminal "suspect" from 1945 to 1949, was prime minister of Japan from 1957 to 1960, and became president of the Japan-American Society in 1982 at age 86). They know better than to start up a new business without government approval. Even under the American occupation in 1946, Masaru Ibuka and Akio Morita did not start Sound Nippon, or Sony, without the support of Japan's Ministry of Communications.

It is not surprising that Americans have never known what was going on in Japan and that none of our post–World War II administration could really get the Japanese to change course, even when it was evident to all in the 1970s and 1980s that something had to be done about the yen-dollar imbalance and steel, automobiles, oranges, beef, chocolate, and so on. It is no wonder that Americans, experiencing all talk and no action, felt increasingly insulted by the Japanese.

One source of profound annoyance for Americans is the low value of the yen. The yen was set at 360 to the dollar, ten points under the 1949 black market rate, by a hard-nosed banker and early monetarist from Detroit, Joseph M. Dodge. He wanted the Japanese to stop importing so much from the United States; he wanted (that is, the Occupation wanted) to create jobs for the Japanese and for them to export more to the Unitd States. At 360 yen to the dollar, Japanese goods cost one-half what comparable American goods cost. The Japanese firms had money given to them in fistfuls by finance bureaucrats, and by the time the exchange rate was changed, twenty-one years later in 1971—the longest-running bargain ever—these conglomerates had surpassed American productivity, had captured our markets, and had driven us to the wall financially. What is especially galling about these historical facts is that the reasons given by MITI for doing nothing are often agreed to by consensus even at the lowest bureaucratic levels, unreached by American influence, let alone control.

Consensus

MITI is like a great river with its source situated somewhere in the past, not far from Japan's own emergence into the world, and with its outlets to the great Pacific Ocean. Nissan, Sony, Honda, Mitsui, Mitsubishi ride the middle of the river, taking the current at its swiftest. Other firms, which form the intricate network of suppliers, distributors, bankers, lawyers, and customers, swell the river to flood stage. But of those many thousands of businessmen who earn their living from sitting at the Japanese table, it might be said that be they known or unknown, all are part of the same mighty river that is breaking the levees, rushing downstream, destroying, uprooting, rechanneling, dividing up the sea for Japanese products. To a greater or lesser degree, they all take communion from the great river. Why is it, then, when the mighty stream mingles with the ocean, laps up on our shores, and builds powerful canals, there is no place for our firms to swim downstream, spawn, compete, and prosper? The Australian journalist Murray Sayle said, "There is something at the center of the Japanese system that Americans will never understand, or, if they do, will find repulsive and unworkable."[1] MITI has matched business strategies and national industrial policies in order to move the Japanese economy toward industries with higher value. MITI does not try to preserve Japan's industrial base at any given time; rather, it propels it into the future by casting off older industries—in which Japan's competitive position is declining—and pushing newer industries—in which Japan's competitive position is growing—to compete overseas.

According to Chalmers Johnson in his book *MITI and the Japanese Miracle*, MITI employed tariff and nontariff barriers to protect so-called infant industries. Let's contrast Japanese policy with American policy. We have used tariffs, quotas, voluntary marketing agreements, bailouts, and tax breaks to protect our older, declining industries. Our policies have *slowed down* change in the structure of American industry.

For example, the United States spends about $1.9 billion a year to protect itself from low-cost foreign textiles,[3] whereas Japan shifts its textile production to the less developed countries of East Asia because labor is cheaper, or moves its textile companies out of that business and into other products. Also, the United States spends $500 million per year, totaling $6.3 billion so far, in loans and loan guarantees in order to prop up its ailing shipbuilding industry. Japan's MITI, on the other hand, formed a cartel and, after consultations, scrapped over 40 percent of its capacity.

Furthermore, the United States tends to give research projects to large American firms without competitive bidding. Defense work is given exclusively to American firms. MITI gives Japanese firms equal access to research projects carried on by government and business and asks them to bid on these contracts. Of course, Japanese defense work is given exclusively to Japanese firms. Moreover, long-term financing is provided by local banks, which in turn coordinate their loans with the Bank of Japan, the Ministry of Finance, and MITI. So Japanese firms easily can drop their prices when faced with a drop in demand or too much world capacity.

Dumping: that's what the American steel industry called it. But the facts are not as United States Steel and its cohorts in the industry would have you believe. They refused to cut prices when the Japanese did. The American steel firms cried for and got protection—voluntary restrictions in 1968 and 1971, and then trigger prices in 1977. MITI compelled the Japanese steel industry to build more efficient plants, and in the 1970s, through long-term financing, Japan became the most efficient steel producer in the world. The same thing happened with automobiles and consumer electronics, and it could happen with semiconductors, high-density ceramics, robotics, fiber optics, lasers, and biotechnology.

Gridlock

Let's not pretend that the Japanese believe in free or fair trade. Instead, they believe in and practice managed trade. So adjustment must come from Tokyo. The conservative Liberal Democratic Party, which has controlled the Japanese Diet since 1955, wants Japan to succeed. Together with the powerful economic ministries, MITI officials, along with trade association executives and businessmen, coordinate their activities without the constraint's imposed by the law and lawyers. It's an old boy network from Tokyo University that governs Japan.

How do we get in touch with decision makers in Japan? There isn't anyone for us to talk to. We are mere "outside persons" in Japan. Their highly placed bureaucrats, businessmen, and politicians merge into a set of inner circles. Some circles are smaller and closer to the source of power than others. No one who is knowledgeable about the world, who speaks English, and who has served (or serves) overseas is in the innermost circle.

Murray Sayle writes that MITI is the most "insensitive component of the Japanese government. Its day-to-day policy decisions are made mostly . . . by callow young men in their 30s, swots from the top Japanese universities who know the outside world only from books in Japanese."[4] They bark window guidance (extralegal orders) at businessmen.

As we realize more clearly every day, there are thousands of nontariff barriers to imports into Japan. MITI said there were ninety nine, of which sixty seven had been eased, but these were the pennies in a piggy bank filled with silver dollars. Many of these eased restrictions have nothing to do with trade as we know it. Astonishing as it may seem, before meat can be imported from Yugoslavia that country's zoos must be inspected by the Japanese. American directors of pharmaceutical companies must submit certificates of their good health before their companies drugs can be sold in Japan. And read about this nontariff barrier (NTB). Mineral water such as Perrier must be boiled before bottled for export to Japan.

Over the years, MITI has imposed a gridlock on Japanese business; without its consent, no movement is possible. Even during periods of increased American agitation, MITI does not give its internal consent to reductions in nontariff barriers that have been agreed to by the Foreign Ministry and others. Without MITI's political commitment, nothing changes; foreign testing of products, for example, is not accepted and foreign test data are not acceptable; Japanese testing must be done for each lot sent into Japan. When MITI says no, its no sticks. The absolute authority exercised by MITI to keep out foreign goods reminds us that the barriers to imports that do exist are imposed by a national industrial policy designed to protect Japanese big business both at home and abroad as well as the shed-and-shack industries in Japan that operate under railway arches and in suburban backyards. MITI permeates the lives of *all* businessmen in Japan and, even now, our own lives and livelihood.

Take the Houdaille case. This company alleged that Japan's so-called industrial targeting was systematically destroying American competitiveness in high technology. Houdaille asked for enforcement of Section 103 of the 1971 Revenue Act, which empowers the president to deny tax credits on the purchase of goods from a foreign country engaged in unfair trade practices. Houdaille claimed that MITI siphoned $1 billion a year out of bicycle and motorcycle racing to subsidize the Japanese machine-tool cartel. The White House fact-finding committee concluded that such subsidies are spread over a vast machine-tool industry as a whole, with an insignificant amount going to robotics manufacturers competing against Houdaille. Nevertheless, the cabinet did recommend that action be taken against Japan; but MITI, through Prime Minister Yasuhiro Nakasone, made an eleventh-hour appeal directly to his good friend from the Williamsburg summit, President Ronald Reagan. The president rejected Houdaille's petition.

Or take other lobbying efforts of the Japanese. Five thousand American dealers of imported automobiles descend on Washington to defeat domestic-content legislation that would curtail the imports of Japanese-made cars. The Japanese tuna-fishing industry forced the State Department to speed up the processing of routine licenses so it could fish in American waters. The tables surely have been turned.

Let's note that the Japanese government, Japanese companies, and American professionals who work for them spend over $18 million to lobby Congress. This is more than is spent on lobbying efforts by all other foreign governments put together. And the Japan External Trade Organization (JETRO), a government-controlled business promotional group with offices is six major U.S. cities, spends another $7 million on public relations. As a result, Japan, our political ally in the Pacific, uses all forms of subtle influence to preserve its $30 billion trade surplus; high-priced American lawyers, lobbyists, and public relations agents trip over themselves to represent so lucrative a client.

One source of profound anxiety for Americans is the dilemma of how to remain master in our own house without forsaking the liberal ideals we hold to be true. The Japanese must be treated equally by our courts and administrative arms of government; all attempts at special discriminatory legislation will fail. But unlike the Canadians—first cousins who should be brothers—or the Europeans—some second, some third cousins—or the people of Latin American and the Caribbean—some close, some distant relatives—the Japanese, for the most part, are very distant relatives. What is troubling about this perception is that the reasons for the uneasiness are often set solidly in our souls and are usually unrecognized by us: the success of the Protestant missions in prewar China: the fifty-year commitment to the (Nationalist) Republic of China—Taiwan; an uneasy alliance with the People's Republic of China; the Japanese atrocities against American and Philippine servicemen during the war; the failure to find more war criminals; emperor worship; and the maddening, vexatious, irritating commercial success of the Japanese in the world. These various passions and views are difficult to influence, let alone control.

What adds to our dismay is that the Japanese seem not always to be fully aware of the passions they arouse in us. The consequences of some of their moves are sometimes, in fact, so negative as to surprise and shock them. At times Japan still appears to behave like the small, ingrown, myopic empire it used to be, a country that had to eke out a living from a resource-poor land in a world where no other power would take it seriously. At other times, overwrought by its vulnerability, it tries to be sure no firm, no group, no industry, no government, no people can impose trade policies detrimental to its own economic interests, broadly defined.

Japan has miscalculated what its role could be in the international trading community. Its illusions about what is acceptable in international trade lead to its insults of its trading partners. It cannot continue indefinitely to make this mistake because the United States is increasingly unwilling to go on as before. Time is running out for the Japanese to have unrestricted access to the American market without a reciprocal bilateral quid pro quo access to their home market.

Summary

The argument: Managed trade is what Japan's MITI offers to the world. It suits Japan's political, economic, and social realities, but a constricted outlook toward what others expect from Japan is operative. Clearly, the United States still hasn't learned how to deal successfully with Japan Inc., MITI, and the other faces Japan presents to the world. The steel industry is an example of what we should not do. The automobile industry is an example of what we can do when we do it within the framework of our own political realities. Neither of these examples shows us clearly how to accomplish our international trade objectives on a long-term basis. This will come about only by carrying out a forward-looking, reciprocal bilateral trade policy.

Results: We have not found an appropriate strategy for dealing with MITI or with Japan's national industrial policy. We don't understand the internal political forces that drive MITI and other foreign government agencies to move the international trading system away from multilateralism and toward bilateral agreements among neighboring countries. We have deemed it acceptable that countries will take extreme risks to maintain themselves within the international trading system. We have become a captive of foreign national industrial policies, and must break our bonds before it is too late.

Recommendations: Although the United States would like to open the Japanese market to American-made goods, no reciprocal bilateral free trade policy is in the perceptible future for Japan and the United States. The Japanese don't want competition at home and the Americans don't want a further increase in Japanese market share in the United States. Therefore, America's international trade policy must be based on reality rather than on hope, on the art of the possible rather than on our vision of the world in the distant future. America's foreign trade must be directed more toward our neighbors to the north and south of us and away from the dominant East–West bias that characterizes it today.

Part II
Contagion and Cures

5
Comparative Advantage

The policy of comparative advantage has a thousand shapes and a thousand ways of promoting market dominance. In Japan, it forces domestic firms to be low-price international competitors; targets industries for tax incentives, subsidies, and loans to lower their production costs; impedes the exchange of goods within sectors among the industrialized countries; refuses to integrate trade in manufactured goods into international trade; and sets up "recession cartels" to preserve the domestic market for Japanese firms when the world has excess capacity.[1] It's an interventionist policy. Japan wants the benefits but not the burdens of international trade. MITI promotes those industries it wants to grow, and lenders invest in these firms. Through certification and licensing procedures, MITI reserves to Japanese firms the growth in market demand. And when the world economy sours, MITI organizes cartels to be sure Japanese firms are the last to suffer from the recession. Borrus and others wrote that MITI's interventionist strategies encourage "the rapid accrual of production economies in the domestic market." These "lead inevitably to export drives to unload product and capture the market share necessary to justify the initial extreme investment in capacity."[2] MITI refuses to negotiate, and the barriers to trade speak for themselves. For example, since 1962, MITI has provided window guidance for the petroleum-refining industry, including construction of new facilities and setting production levels and prices. Since 1972, MITI, in collusion with Japanese petroleum firms, has monitored production costs and price increases that are administered through the Japanese trade association for petroleum products. In 1980, the Japanese petroleum refiners were sued by

Japan's Fair Trade Commission (JFTC) under the Antimonopoly Act. They were acquitted for their coordinated production cutbacks because they had followed MITI's administrative guidance.[3] In 1982, the JFTC claimed that government regulation obstructs competition in data communications, airlines, banking, and many other industries. All MITI wants to know is how far it can go in giving Japanese firms guidance to form cartels.

The JFTC does not hold cabinet rank; it is not as powerful as MITI, and it could not prevent the passing of the *Structurally Depressed Industry Law* of 1983. Under the law, MITI secures formal government intervention to prevent excessive competition and continued authority to approve recession cartels.

Failure

As we look at the policy of comparative advantage elsewhere in the world, it becomes apparent that the interventionist contagion has spread. Between 1975 and 1981 Canada's Foreign Investment Review Agency (FIRA) changed from a paper tiger into an angry bear[4] and acted as a strong barrier to foreign investment in Canada. By the close of 1981, the number of unsuccessful new business investment cases rose to 29 percent, or nearly double the number rejected by FIRA in 1980.[5] FIRA didn't want foreign investors coming into Canada and taking over local businesses. It created such a hostile environment for foreign investment that Canada saw a decline in its net capital formation and a net reduction in the number of jobs created. Many American investors—who provide 80 percent of Canada's foreign investment—gave up and never applied to FIRA for its approval; they took their investments elsewhere.

FIRA is the product of Canadian economic nationalism. It's a virus that sweeps periodically across Main Street, Canada, especially when times are good. (Canadian author Maurice Yeates says Main Street runs from Windsor, Ontario, to Quebec City.[6]) Toronto sees the Yankees coming across the Great Lakes, and Ontario fears losing its dominance in trade and commerce and federal politics. This Royal province is Canada's emotional heart. When it decides that Yankee continentalism may eradicate its favored position, and when it believes its manufacturing industries will suffer from American competition, up go the tariffs, nontariff barriers, and restrictions on foreign investments. Behind the maple leaf flag, FIRA became Ottawa's agent for Canadianizing the economy.

Canadians believed, unwisely as it turns out, that alternative domestic investment would be forthcoming to replace lost foreign investment. Instead, twelve million people, from Windsor to Quebec City, got a depreciated currency and recession's bitter pill of unemployment. The costs of economic nationalism climbed so high that a majority of provinces voted to abolish FIRA. Quebec called for free trade between itself (or Canada) and the United States. British Columbia realized that its economic interests best lay with Washington State, Oregon, and California, and it too spoke in favor of free trade. Alberta wanted to ship its oil and natural gas to the lower 48 without giving Ottawa a kickback in taxes. Its premier, Peter Lougheed, said that "the Ottawa government [Trudeau] simply walked into our homes and occupied the living room."[7]

At long last, Canadians perceived reality: in September 1982, Herb Gray, Canadian economic nationalist and pied piper to the world's interventionists, was replaced as Trudeau's minister responsible for FIRA by Ed Lumley, a friend of international trade and investment; one year later, FIRA was "defanged" and Trudeau's government called for free trade between Canada and the United States in selected key sectors.

Remember. Economics serves politics in Canada as it does elsewhere. There are Canadian-firsters as there are American- and Japanese-firsters. The fanaticism that tainted hearts and minds before could corrupt Canadians again. If they were to decide to be Canadian-firsters in the future, they might try the more sophisticated approach of the Japanese. This would not be in the best interest of Canada, the United States, or free trade. That is why both countries must get on with the business of negotiating a reciprocal bilateral free trade agreement.

The Canadians do not have a MITI, an umbrella government agency that sets and enforces the rules no matter who holds political power. Comparative advantage as practiced by Canadians gives special commercial rights to Crown Corporations—government-owned business firms, or state enterprises. These state enterprises invest in industries which, according to Ottawa (or the provincial governments, or both) have a need for a Canadian presence. The Canada Development Corporation (CDC) was established in the mid-1970s to buy back Canada from the Americans. Its most celebrated case was its controversial (in the United States) purchase of Texasgulf Sulphur, an American firm with interests in Utah, North Carolina, and Ontario, and its subsequent sale of Texasgulf to a French government–owned firm, Elf Aquitaine.[8] CDC is multinational now, with major investments in the United States. Ottawa sold some of its CDC shares to private Canadian citizens. But state enterprise capitalism, or the process of socializing losses, remains a potent North American virus that is spreading the interventionist contagion southward through the medium of this multinational government–owned business firm, CDC.

Canadian nationalists believe that the free market works against the political survival of Canada. So the dominant elites (federal politicians, Toronto businessmen, and Protestant church leaders) adopted FIRA to keep the American virus from spreading northward. Free trade without government interference cannot be permitted to gain sufficient health in Canada or an immunity will be developed against Ottawa as Ontario's meddler in the national economy.

Ottawa bureaucrats also have corrupted the meaning of comparative advantage. If they had persisted with their interventionist mania under Trudeau, if they had not defanged FIRA, if they had not begun to sell the shares of CDC to private investors, their industrial policy would have been worthy of serious GATT investigation. A reciprocal bilateral trade policy must be grafted onto U.S.–Canada trade so the interventionists never again can impede the forces for free trade between the two countries.

Reciprocity

Because protectionism is what FIRA was about, and there could be other attempts by special interests in Canada to keep Americans out of protected domestic industries, we must see what forms of protectionism FIRA charged us with and then decide whether FIRA's case against us was as strong as our case against its protectionism, as exemplified by the significant lowering of the cost of purchasing a new car in Canada because of the free-trade auto pact between the United States and Canada. When Canadian free traders were attacking FIRA's protectionism, when Canadian economists were assembling conclusive data that FIRA's efforts were counterproductive to Canada's long-term economic health, FIRA took an action similar to those of other governmental institutions which find themselves mortally threatened; it counterattacked in 1982 with an internal report entitled "Barriers to Foreign Investment in the United States."[9] The report concluded that Canadian investors in the United States must deal with a plethora of laws and regulations at both the state and federal level. The sad truth is that the United States can make the same charge about Canada's federal and provincial governments, and if our states were as powerful as their provinces, we too would have the same barriers to interstate commerce and trade that they have for interprovincial commerce and trade. Our states don't have mini-FIRAs in the capital cities, such as in Regina, Saskatchewan, taking over foreign potash firms and precluding others from coming in.

That there is some American federal legislation directly controlling foreign investment can't be denied. That our barriers are as comprehensive or all-encompassing as FIRA wanted us to believe is an overstatement. FIRA was especially unhappy with our concerns about CDC selling Texasgulf to Elf Aquitaine—a substantial public policy for us, because one foreign state enterprise was trying to sell an American firm to another foreign government–owned business firm. Yet all FIRA really could point to is how the Committee on Foreign Investment in the United States which is a federal monitoring agency, recommended to the president that we disapprove the Rumanian government's request to take over American coal mines. The federal government has done nothing to keep Canadian foreign direct investment out of the United States. In fact, we welcome such investment with open arms.

In the summer of 1980, the Reciprocity in International Investment Act was introduced into the U.S. House of Representatives as an amendment to Section 13(D) of the Securities and Exchange Act. I had first suggested reciprocity legislation in chapter 14 of my book, *Foreign State Enterprises*.[10] I suggested that reciprocity legislation should be patterned after the Mineral Leasing Act of 1920.

Foreign governments would have to permit American firms to invest in the same or similar sectors on a quid pro quo basis or their firms would be banned from investing here. I testified in favor of the 1980 bill and urged that Congress "prohibit foreign investors from buying more than 5 percent of a U.S. company unless reciprocal opportunities were available in the foreign country."[11] My views on FIRA, the automobile pact, the National Energy Policy, the sectoral free trade proposal, and reciprocal bilateral free trade have evolved over a decade of study and public discussion. The United States must make bilateral free trade work with Canada, or Mexico, and countries in the Caribbean and Central America will be suspicious of reciprocity's intent and skeptical about its potential results.

When two governments do not provide reciprocity in foreign trade and investment, the opportunities for costly protectionism are endless. We know that Canada's imposition of FIRA produced a violent reaction in the United States. American investors stopped wasting their time proposing investments up north, and after these discouragements, their pent-up anger burst into a call for reciprocity. They wanted to deny Canadian investors the right to invest in the United States until the Canadian government abandoned FIRA's nonreciprocal policy. The Canadians opened up an old wound and made it fester, and the protectionist disease ran wild on both sides of the border.

Canadian executives had a fear about remaining branch plant managers. They didn't want to report to Detroit, New York, Chicago, or Houston. They saw FIRA as the means to gain a comparative advantage over their American competitors. These Canadians don't mind taking their instructions from Ottawa; they are used to Crown Corporations and the role of government in setting up, financing, and managing commercial businesses. These executives are accountable for promoting Canadian interests both at home and abroad. These Canadian businessmen (who produce steel and petrochemicals, mine sulphur and lead, who run the air and rail lines, who take over rubber-mixing and pharmaceutical businesses in the United States on behalf of Ottawa) did an effective job in managing Canadian state enterprises. Americans got angry and pressed them.

The Canadians were unable to wrest themselves from the American viselike grip, and they had to cry uncle.

Once begun, nonreciprocal commercial behavior on the part of foreign governments and their business firms causes a thousand voices to cry out for protection. The political attack on free trade spreads. Within it is the virus of comparative advantage. It lies dormant for years; then, all at once, its interventionist contagion attacks. There is no known cure for the disease. It must run its course like a plague until the poison leaves the system.

FIRA's blatant attack on free trade is over; Trudeau saw to that. Brian Mulroney, who became prime minister in September 1984, renamed FIRA Investment Canada and charged the revamped organization with the task of bringing new investment to the country. Bilateral discussions, together with a recognition of common North American economic interests, have reduced the costs of protectionism and have ended the strained, acrimonious relations between the two countries.

Taxes

Lower effective corporate tax rates in Canada led to excessive American investment in Canadian manufacturing in the years before FIRA was established, says John D. Murray. His conclusion: Canadians have themselves to congratulate (or blame) for the amount of American foreign direct investment in Canada.[12]

In 1975, 35 percent of Canada's capital stock was owned by foreigners. Canada was then and still is the world's leading capital importer. And 80 percent of its foreign capital stock come from the United States.

Before FIRA, American investors had no fears about their Canadian investments. Canada and the provinces didn't expropriate foreign investment. The Canadian dollar was fully convertible with the American dollar, each at times stronger than the other. Canada was thought to be American except for some minor, incomprehensible differences; another Dixie or Texas, yet more reserved, like New England.

Canadians from the Maritime Provinces came down to the Boston States, as New England is known in Nova Scotia, New Brunswick, and Prince Edward Island, to study, particularly at Harvard. Trudeau's liberal cabinet—the ministers who gave us CDC, FIRA, and the National Energy Policy—had one or more degrees from Harvard. The premiers from the Martimes, along with Quebec's premier, meet routinely with the conference of eastern state governors. The four western premiers also meet annually with their counterparts, who make up the conference of western state governors. So who in the United States thought about the international boundary as a barrier rather than as a road map? Who in the United States paid attention to Canada's Main Street establishment?

Between the close of World War II and the establishment of FIRA, the Canadian establishment had given us its road map to prosperity in Canada. Both federal and provincial taxes were lowered. There were tax holidays, large cash grants, accelerated depreciation and a bonus for new jobs created. Canadian taxes were more favorable than American taxes by 15 to 20 percent.[13] These tax incentives were Canada's significant comparative advantage; they made Canada a more attractive investment climate than even the United States.

Because the United States permitted Canadian subsidiaries to defer remitting dividends, interest, and royalty payments to American parent firms, the latter could reinvest these untaxed earnings in their Canadian subsidiaries. In reality, this was an interest-free loan from the U.S. Treasury to Canadian-based manufacturing. No wonder American investors flooded into Canada! Retained earnings accumulated year after year were locked in for more direct investment. Canadian federal tax laws achieved what they were designed to do: they brought in more foreign direct investment from a nearby source, namely, the United States. Only in the 1970s did the Canadians decide this foreign investment was excessive and determine to do something about it. This is the history that led to FIRA. FIRA was a shot-gun approach to a problem that would have been better served by a rifle. Canadians wanted control over foreign investment; instead, they got a devalued currency, high unemployment, economic stagnation, and friction with the United States. Canada made protectionism work against itself. It was as if its Harvard-educated leaders had read the wrong books, listened to the wrong professors, and written the wrong papers.

The Auto Pact

In 1965, in another attempt to Canadianize the economy, Ottawa signed the United States–Canada Automotive Products Pact. At that time, over 90 percent of all motor vehicles produced in Canada were made by subsidiaries of U.S. companies, yet Canadian productivity was only 60 percent of the U.S. level. Canada had a trade deficit of $545 million in automotive parts and accessories. It wanted to improve its trade balance, increase the proportion of automobile and parts production made at home, and get out from under the countervailing duties that Modine Corporation, an American parts producer, insisted the U.S. Treasury Department impose under Section 303 of the Tariff Act of 1930.[14]

Here's what the act said. If a foreign country pays a "bounty or grant" to a manufacturer so goods will be exported, and if these goods are a dutiable import to the United States, the U.S. Treasury must impose an additional duty equal to the bounty or grant.

Bounties are remission of internal taxes; they are the drawbacks of paying a duty on imported materials that are reprocessed and then exported again. Two years prior to signing the auto pact, Canada imposed duty remissions. If manufacturers increased their automotive exports, they got a rebate of import duties on comparable automotive parts. So in 1964, Canada's automotive exports to the United States more than doubled from 1963. And in 1965 the U.S. Treasury was ready to impose countervailing duties. Instead, the auto pact was signed by the two governments. No countervailing duties by the United States. No counter-retaliation by Canada. No acrimony between Ottawa and Washington. Was this free trade? No, according to several senators who opposed the pact. Stanley D. Metzger said the auto pact simply removed tariffs for "a chosen few automobile manufacturers"[15] (General Motors, Ford, Chrysler, and American Motors). "Parts may be imported duty free only if they are going to an automobile manufacturer. . . . This is not free trade and it does not benefit American consumers."[16]

Instead of Canadian content rising as the Canadians had hoped, and instead of American sales keeping their relative share of the Canadian market as the Americans had hoped, both Canadian and American sales of the America-owned auto companies declined. Canadian sales declined by 7 percent between 1965 and 1971. Such a reversal was the result of foreign, non-North American competition, first from Germany, then from Japan.

By 1968, the Canadians wanted something done about the decline. They insisted that the "safeguards" in the pact be enforced. Canadian value added was supposed to go up by 60 percent of the growth in Canadian sales between 1965 and 1968. And there should have been an increase in Canadian production worth $260 million by the end of 1968.[17] The Americans said these were transitional figures and that the safeguards clause didn't apply after the three transitional years. If the auto pact had been a reciprocal bilateral free trade agreement, these changes in economic conditions would have been taken into consideration when the two governments made their annual review of ways to make the trade agreement work for the better of both countries.

Is what's good for GM good for Canada? The Canadians said no. They believe corporations receive the right to exist from the state. The state has the right to know about significant moves that firms plan to make before these plans are actually initiated; and the state can say no to these initiatives, can redirect them, or can join in them. This is the philosophy behind CDC, FIRA, the National Energy Policy, and other attempts to Canadianize the economy. Canadians also believe that multinational oligopolies, such as the American-owned auto companies, can and do prevent the market from operating in an industry. They want their government to guide American subsidiaries in Canada toward achieving purely Canadian economic goals: growth, jobs, and investment—in Canada.

Since 1968, the Canadians have wanted to renegotiate the auto pact. The Americans have refused. We don't want to lose more production (and jobs) to foreigners. One result of our unwillingness to make the safeguards permanent was FIRA. Yet Canada created its own need for FIRA. Its tax rates were better than American rates.

Its tariff rates were high enough to encourage American firms to invest in Canada to get behind the high tariff wall.[18] It created the branch plant syndrome in the automobile industry that led to the auto pact with the United States. When the results weren't to its liking, Canada created FIRA to show its preference for economic independence.

Canada did get more freedom of action, but at a high cost. Lost investments. A less efficient industrial sector that was financed by more Canadian and less American capital. The loss of substantial Canadian complementary investment as American investment declined. Reduced revenues to pay social welfare benefits. Ah, the price of independence in an interdependent world. In seeking to create its own comparative advantage, Canada had forfeited economic growth, industrial jobs, and capital investment. Did Canada destroy the seed corn along with the bountiful American harvest? Read on.

Summary

The argument: Canada, too, experimented with managed trade, which suited some of the realities of Canadian political life. Clearly, Canada hadn't reckoned with the chill wind from the United States. The auto pact was a very limited attempt at free trade because it dealt with the rights of four U.S.-owned automobile firms that had plants in Canada. The pact had no method for resolving disputes. Nations that are similar to Canada and that use their tax systems to promote foreign direct investment will find American firms able to take advantage of these tax breaks. We know now that too much investment by U.S. firms will lead to the creation of a government agency resembling FIRA. So the limits of reciprocity and bilateralism must be spelled out beforehand rather than later.

Results: Both Canada and the United States learned from their mistakes. We both know we are more dependent today on bilateral free trade than ever before. We both realize that multilateralism is ebbing away and that no miracles are in store for multilateral free trade and the GATT system.

Recommendations: The Canadians by themselves converted FIRA into Investment Canada and corrected many of the faults found by the Americans. The United States needs to push for the creation of a supranational trade agency in North America that could resolve some of Canada's concerns about the auto pact. This agency could be a model for the reciprocal bilateral free trade program that is so needed by the two countries.

6
Foreign Investments

Protectionism is destroying the integrity of the world's trading system. Canadian policies in the 1970s reduced the cohesion of the North American economy. These policies have become a force for disintegration, for pulling away from GATT's sacred idea of most favored nations, for ending western commitments to free trade.

Nationalistic barriers that are in place today were put there after two decades of tax and tariff policies which encouraged unrestricted direct investments by American-owned multinational firms, and by Ottawa's unease at finding company advantage was replacing comparative advantage as trade became dependent on corporate investment decisions. Canadian sovereignty over locating production, sourcing suppliers, and exporting finished goods was at bay. Canadians decided—as we did about steel and automobiles and as the Japanese did about semiconductors—that although free trade promises maximum benefits to all, over time, Ottawa must deliver jobs and income *now,* regardless of the loss in productivity and the higher costs of domestic production. Canadian politicians think that Ottawa can manage disintegration without the loss of economic well-being.

Then there are the Canadian attempts at altering existing comparative advantage. Ottawa wanted gains in automobiles at the expense of Washington. When the industry contracted, Ottawa lost past, present, and future gains.The Canadians tied themselves to the existing four American automobile companies and left no room in the automobile pact for new investment decisions by different producers. This sectoral agreement, which had been viewed as a model for future attempts at free trade across the border, divided suppliers from producers, manufacturers from retailers, and consumers in the two countries; cars still were 10 percent more expensive in Windsor than in Detroit. Sector protection made little sense in the face of changing world economic conditions. Ottawa involved itself in what and how much would be produced at Windsor, Oakville, and St.Thérèse, but it couldn't stop the shift in consumer preference for smaller, gas-efficient, quality-designed cars. Ottawa showed its power to reduce company advantage, but it was powerless to induce state-of-the-art research and development, to encourage the use of up-to-date techniques, and to foster positive balance-of-payments results that became the hallmark of Japanese industrial planning.

The pace of disintegration quickened as Canada's trade deficit increased sixfold in the decade of the 1970s. Canadian firms no longer seemed competitive, so exports declined while imports rose. In February 1980 Trudeau set out his industrial plan, which included the following:

> Subsidies and tax incentives to encourage more research, job training, and exports.
>
> Preferential government procurement practices for Canadian-controlled manufacturers to increase Canadian presence in key sectors.
>
> Direct government assistance to start up businesses and to increase the volume of exports.
>
> Stricter foreign investment controls to nullify foreign company advantage.

In April 1980, after Trudeau won control of Canada's House of Commons, the Speech from the Throne, which was prepared by the Queen's Canadian ministers, was delivered by her representative, the Governor General. In this speech, Trudeau promised immediate action on these four industrial planning measures once Parliament enacted the National Energy Policy. But his hand was stayed by the fear that the United States might unilaterally impose countervailing duties in response to complaints made under the 1974 and 1979 Trade Acts (see Sections 303(701) and 337 of the 1930 Tariff Act; the 1921 Anti-Dumping Act, revised by the 1979 Trade Agreements Act; and Section 301 of the 1974 Trade Act). Even before passage of the 1974 Trade Act, the United States employed the following protectionist measures: countervailing duties, antidumping, and safeguards. The 1974 act was a watershed. It confirmed the suspicion that our international trade policy was protectionist. The 1979 act reenforced this viewpoint by shifting responsibilities from Treasury to Commerce so the government could be more responsive to the concerns of American business. American trade policies also reduced the cohesion of the North American economy and became a force for disintegration in the world's trading system. The 1984 Trade Act was an even stronger protectionist stance by the United States.

Trade Law

Here are the remedies for unfair trade practices under United States law.

Countervailing duties: These are imposed by the United States when a foreign government pays a bounty or a grant to a manufacturer so goods will be exported and hence become dutiable imports to the United States. The countervailing duties must be an additional duty equal to the bounty or grant. This is Section 303 of the 1930 Tariff Act.

In 1979, domestic subsidies by foreign governments were defined as follows:

1. The provision of capital, loans, or loan guarantees on terms inconsistent with commercial considerations;
2. The provision of goods or services at preferential rates.
3. The grant of funds or forgiveness of debt to cover operating losses sustained by a specific industry; and
4. The assumption of any cost or expenses of manufacture, production, or distribution.

This is Section 701 of the Tariff Act, as amended by the 1979 Trade Agreements Act.

The following examples show how Section 303 is interpreted. All are subject to countervailing duties of Section 701.

Grants in aid by national governments to regionally depressed areas. The Canadian Michelin Tire case.

Government assistance for research and development when a distinction can be made between pure research and preproduction costs. The Canadian PAIT case.

The injury test: Under the 1979 act, the Tariff Court became the U.S. International Trade Commission. The ITC now was required to demonstrate that a foreign government's export subsidies had a negative impact on American industries and that such negative performance was brought about mainly by export subsidies. Material injury is "harm that is not inconsequential, immaterial or unimportant," according to the 1979 act. The ITC does not have to demonstrate a causal relationship between poor performance and export subsidies, but a casual one instead. Nor does the ITC have to show that these export subsidies are the principal reason for an industry's poor performance. The 1979 act offers American firms many reasons, some important, some trivial, for charging that foreign export subsidies are the principal reason for an industry's poor performance. Section 303 as amended in 1979 makes the United States even more protectionist.

Antidumping: When products are sold at less than their fair value, antidumping duties must be imposed. See the 1921 Anti-Dumping Act and the 1979 Trade Act. The material injury test allows the ITC to use the widest flexibility possible to find that imports have been dumped. What is less than fair value? When goods are sold in the United States at a price lower than they are sold in the country of origin, American firms can initiate a less-than-fair-value petition before the ITC. There is a technical violation of the statute when foreign companies set their U.S. import price below the country of origin price so that when the U.S. import price and the U.S. tariffs are added together, the final price in the U.S. market is competitive with the price of goods produced in the United States.

Unfair trade practices: All unfair trade practices listed by the Sherman, Clayton, Federal Trade Commission, and Robinson-Patman Acts are imposed on imported goods, too, by Section 337 of the Tariff Act and by Section 301 of the 1974 and 1979 Trade Acts. When American manufacturers lose countervailing or antidumping cases, they bring charges of unfair trade practices under Sections 337 and 301. Moreover, if foreign competitors use unfair trade practices to reduce U.S. exports to a third country, U.S. companies can bring a complaint before the ITC.

Escape clause mechanism: Section 201 of the 1930 Tariff Act permits the imposition of nontariff barriers to stop exports into the United States. Japanese and Canadian industrial targeting—industrial planning that increases exports to the United States—is a violation of Section 201. The federal government must provide offset concessions to the country involved in the complaint.

Section 337: When government-business cartels such as MITI or CDC restrict imports or exports, these actions are unfair trade practices.

Section 301: When a government's industrial strategy leads to import substitution in the foreign country or to more exports in the United States, the federal government can impose tariffs or quotas or can arrange for orderly, voluntary marketing agreements; the provision of offset concessions to the country involved in the complaint is not required.

Investment Policy

No foreign government, particularly one that feels it's a mouse living too close to an elephant, can fail to take notice of the decisions of its neighbor. This is true no matter what passionate beliefs are held by its leadership. U.S. trade law is another virulent form of the interventionist contagion, and it's the one that scares the Canadians. North American disintegration exists because there is no supranational body similar to the European Community that can be used as an official, neutral place for the discussion and solution of emerging trade and investment problems. Instead, both North American governments invent alternatives for their own national purposes, with the result that local labor, business, and consumer groups play upon nationalism's weaknesses rather than internationalism's strengths. Destructive: that's what these policies are over the years.

Add a great deal of emotion about cultural imperialism and things get out of hand. Canada's defense against its larger neighbor's trade policies has been to restrict the flow of new investment capital across the border; to make the maze of regulations so confusing that American businessmen give up; to give FIRA a stranglehold over corporate expansion. But to believe such a policy would not have a negative impact on the well-being of the Canadian economy is to turn the world upside down. The degrees of freedom available to any government are small, indeed, in an interdependent world of capital, technological, and managerial mobility.

Little known to Americans are three Canadian reports on foreign ownership of industry.[1] Canadians define foreign control as 50 percent of the shares of a company being in foreign hands; the United States defines it as 10 percent. Canadians have more foreign ownership of their key industries than their official documents report. No wonder Herb Gray's report forced the Trudeau government to act and to appoint Gray as the man in charge of a draconian FIRA.

Here's what he was told to do.

First, follow the examples in the transportation, communications, financial, and utilities industries, and restrict foreign capital control over key industrial sectors. The United States imposes the same restrictions on communications but is less concerned about transportation and financial businesses and not at all concerned about steel, automobiles, pharmaceuticals, and food industries.

Second, subsidize research and development. The United States supports defense-related research in the manufacture of aircraft, spacecraft, and telecommunications.

Third, set up a Canada Development Corporation to buy, finance, and manage commercial businesses in the national interest—mineral resources, pharmaceuticals, computers, and venture—both in Canada and overseas. The United States has no equivalent of CDC but has seen some of its domestic firms, such as Texasgulf Sulphur, become subsidiaries of this foreign government–owned state enterprise.[2]

Fourth, screen all foreign direct investments, prevent takeovers or mergers not in Canada's national interest, and do so through FIRA. The United States has no equivalent. Our interagency Committee on Foreign Investment can recommend that politically sensitive foreign takeovers be banned, but its power against the government-owned and subsidized corporations of Canada, Britain, France, Germany, and Japan is nonexistent.[3]

Fifth, develop a new industrial strategy for Canada.The United States had not addressed industrial planning and targeting in any meaningful way in the mid-1970s (and has not in the mid-1980s). The French unitary-state model could not apply to Canada, whose provinces own mineral resources and are strong politically. The Japanese dependence on close collaboration between MITI and local businessmen works in a culturally homogeneous state that has accumulated centuries of practice at consensus building and at placing the welfare of the group over individual well-being. These conditions do not prevail in either Canada or the United States, and both countries have achieved very little with regard to a national industrial strategy.

The author of the Gray report was faced with decisions taken in the 1960s to restrict foreign ownership in communications, transportation, banks, utilities, magazines, and cable TV and to use government-sponsored research as a weapon against foreign direct investment. He was also made aware of the pro–foreign investment results in the 1960s from tax and tariff policies. The report said that company advantage—what the multinationals bring to the table—does not provide the Canadian economy with a significant comparative advantage. Herb Gray's complaints against privately owned, mostly American multinationals became the world's litany, widely used in fact by European, African, Asian, and Latin American leaders to cut these firms down to size.

Herb Gray, the high priest of economic nationalism, declares the multinationals guilty. Of what?

Transfer pricing. The parent firm artificially increases the prices of supplies, research and development, and managerial expertise to its subsidiary. This reduces profits and taxable income to the Canadian subsidiary, and hence reduces tax revenue to Ottawa. The United States says the American-owned multinationals do this, too, but our Internal Revenue Service claims that our firms cost these services too low, with the result that the United States loses tax revenues. Section 482 of the IRS code says all goods and services "sold" between parent and subsidiary must be done at an arms-length price, as if the two were completely independent firms. Is transfer pricing any reason to force FIRA upon a nation?

Local debt financing. The subsidiary borrows capital locally, which gives it the ability to deduct interest from its taxable income. Firms tend to borrow in local currency rather than increase their foreign exchange exposure. It happened in France and de Gaulle complained. In Canada. And now in the United States. Is local debt financing any reason to impose FIRA upon Canada?

Herb Gray convinced the Canadians that foreign direct investment is bad and should be controlled or restricted. Between 1969 and 1972, the percentage of Canadians who thought American ownership of Canadian companies was bad jumped from 34 to 47 percent.[4] Some 52 percent of Canadians were in favor of restricting foreign ownership in 1974, the year FIRA was established.

Gray's learned treatise on foreign direct investment became Canada's philosophical rationale, its *Apologia Pro Vita Sua,* for accepting a cardinal's hat from the ancient protectionists. He handed down the doctrines of the mercantilist faith. His dogmas chipped away at the rock. Free trade's disintegration came so swiftly that Canadians thought Gray had performed a miracle. Their standard of living, their economic well-being, and their national prosperity would not decline, or so they believed. Theirs would be a long march back, a difficult penitential climb on their knees up to the top of Quebec's most holy shrine, St. Anne de Beaupré.

Disintegration

The problem of Canada's trade and investment relations with the United States stems from Trudeau's desire to be certain that America remembers who its largest trading partner is in the world: Canada. Nixon's 1971 gaffe—he said Japan was America's largest trading partner—is still taken for truth by many Americans. Canada was, is, and will continue to be America's best customer. Canada has a real existence in the North American economy, and if Americans forget it, they do so at the peril of bringing back the difficult past ten years, in which Canadian negotiators were single-minded in their quest for bilateral trade victories. Cross-border feuding became acrimonious. American negotiators were seen as too tough, too heavy-handed; we wanted Canadians to swallow every bitter pill, sip the poison alone, and cry uncle when they had enough. Herb Gray said Canada must use its economic weapons to blunt the American attack: don't expedite the sale of Alberta gas to the United States; don't spend $4 billion on American fighter jets; don't finance a steel mill in New Jersey; don't export the power of Quebec Hydro. Alberta refused to agree with the first idea and Quebec said no to the last idea, so Ottawa's nationalism was undercut in the provinces. What else is new? Ottawa nationalists in the early 1980s sought tougher foreign investment guidelines designed to discourage even those firms with the best of intentions. They overlooked Canada's critical need for more capital formation. When the American supply of capital dried up, the provinces balked. Ottawa's economic nationalism didn't work. Like its mercantilistic predecessors, Ottawa's rules were at odds with the rapid changes in the world trading system. Trudeau got what he wanted: world recognition of Canada as an industrial power; member in good standing of the annual summit meeting of the world's industrial leaders. Trudeau also got what he didn't want: an unwillingness on the part of American businessmen to invest under the rules laid down by Herb Gray and FIRA. No longer could the United States fail to take notice of the concerns of Canadians, along with those of the Japanese and the European Community.

We Americans are particularly prone to forget our own barriers to trade with Canada. At present, since 1933, the Buy American Act permits the federal government to use domestic suppliers even when their bids are higher than those of foreign suppliers. There is no equivalent federal law in Canada. However, some thirty four states and provinces have their own buy-local barriers, whereby local firms receive a 10 percent preference in their bids. Our 1979 Trade Act, Section 301 in particular, although passed by Congress to stop Japanese and European dumping, applies equally to Canadian goods. And the Canadians don't like its terms. They don't believe their prices are "unjustifiable, unreasonable or discriminatory," as the act requires the ITC to find. They also don't like the auto pact much anymore. It used to provide jobs and surpluses (in the balance of trade). In the 1980s, it did neither. Moreover, research and development is done in Detroit and decisions about the industry are made in Washington. Ottawa knows it has no leverage on this bilateral issue, and Canadians now believe, with hurt pride, as Detroit goes so goes Windsor, Oakville, and Saint Thérèse—but faster. We Americans forget that even after FIRA had been working on the problem of foreign direct investment for three years, foreign control (which was 80 percent American) remained high: 74 percent of petroleum, 54 percent of manufacturing, and 51 percent of mining. Multinationals, mostly American owned, account for 40 percent of Canadian exports; yet most of the four thousand branch subsidiaries sell only in the small Canadian domestic market, so their unit costs are high and their research output is negligible. It is this helplessness that breeds discontent among Canadians. Approximately thirty years ago, C.D. Howe embraced American investors and launched Canada toward economic prosperity. Canadians still want these guaranteed material benefits, but they want them along with political and cultural independence. According to Lester Pearson, a former Liberal Party prime minister, this is Canada's national schizophrenia. Trudeau characterized us Americans as "the sleeping elephant" and said that "our every twitch and grunt" affects American's newest neighbors. He was simply pricking us so that we would remember to pay attention to Canada also. Unfortunately, he created the great Devel Disintegrator, a machine that grinds everything to powder, a mixture most appropriate for producing chicken feed. It was a popular machine in its time. FIRA pulverized foreign investment proposals, grinding them slowly down until they were barely recognizable. For some time, Canada's FIRA spread economic dislocation and disintegration in North America, but both nations have to share the blame for its creation, rise, and "success."

Summary

The argument: Canada tried a Foreign Investment Review Agency approach to managed trade. It suited Canadians to become more protectionist in the 1970s, but their short-term program had unexpected, negative long-term consequences. Canadians know now that foreign direct investment is fungible and it will go elsewhere or stay at home as domestic investment. The United States learned the hard way that reciprocity and bilateralism means to take Canadian concerns to heart.

Results: We learned to wait out those who sought to disintegrate the North American trading system. We showed them by example how bilateral trade and investment opportunities could benefit both countries. If the Mulroney government in Ottawa can find the political will to ratify a finding bilateral relationship, then the free trade aspects of the international trading system will be advanced for at least two peoples in the world.

Recommendations: Because the United States first must obtain Canada's consent to reciprocal bilateral free trade before it can become the norm between the United States and Mexico and other Latin American countries, the United States should exclude Canada from all the remedies of unfair foreign trade practices now found under U.S. law. If this were to happen, Canada would be treated economically as if it were within the customs union of the United States and Puerto Rico.

7
National Energy Policy

Canadian decisions on trade and investment have an American, Eastern-establishment, liberal Democrat quality. Theories, suggestions, and proposed economic policies that are offered as the left's prescription for containing industry's technostructure and redirecting the affluent consumer society are enacted into law under Canada's Liberal Party. John Kenneth Galbraith, a Scot from Ontario, is the teacher. Pierre Elliott Trudeau, prime minister, Michael Pitfield, the top bureaucrat, Jim Coutts, the chief of staff, Marshall "Mickey" Cohen, the deputy minister of energy, Ed Clark, the assistant deputy energy minister, and Joel Bell, senior vice president of Petro-Canada, are all Harvard educated. Add Allan MacEachen, finance minister, of the Massachusetts Institute of Technology; and Ian Stewart, deputy minister of finance, who studied at Cornell and taught at Dartmouth; and Bill Hopper, president of Petro-Canada, who studied at Washington's American University and worked at the Arthur D. Little Co. in Cambridge, Massachusetts. The Conservatives were brought in, too. Stewart was once deputy minister of energy under Conservative Prime Minister Joe Clark. Stewart also introduced wage and price controls. In Ottawa, the Harvard brotherhood saw themselves as masters of facts, analyses, theories, and policies that would make Canadian federal interests dominant. They were pragmatists who believed in a national industrial policy, especially for creating a Canadian government–owned petroleum industry. These ministers of the Crown were interventionists. They decided which privately owned oil companies were to be bought by Petro-Canada, a government-owned petroleum company. They were not concerned whether Petro-Canada could make a takeover at a reasonable price because Petro-Canada must buy up Canadian oil companies. There would be no going back on the Liberal government's strategy for the Canadianization of the petroleum industry. Marc Lalonde, the federal energy minister, said Petro-Canada must become as large as Imperial Oil, 70 percent of which is owned by Exxon. To fund the takeovers, the Canadian interventionists placed a special tax on consumer purchases of natural gas and petroleum. Tax and Spend were the rules used by the Trudeau administration.

The petroleum industry saw its share of oil and gas production income falling from 39 percent, in 1980, to 33 percent, in 1981; the provincial share dropped from 47 to 43 percent; but the federal share increased from 14 to 43 percent. That's what was intended. The federal government skimmed $1.4 billion (Canadian) from the industry's revenues. Under the interventionists, Canada experienced a sort of tax-hungry panic—a sudden, overpowering fright in which Ottawa's energy mandarins believed the oil group would walk over them should the Liberal government show flexibility; thus, one of the world's medium-size countries, because of some misapprehension of danger to its own national sovereignty, set out unreasonably on a frantic course to secure its safety. But while the fear may be groundless, the loss of investment incentives is real, and Canadians could only hope that the Liberal government would go back to the classroom and return Canada to a more balanced, mid-continent, centrist condition. Ultimately, Lalonde was sacked by Trudeau and the Liberals were sacked by the Canadian voters.

Ottawa Insists

All those remarks by Trudeau about how the multinationals were massively favored by Canadian depletion allowances on resources, which comprised some 80 percent of their revenues, and about how they were able to write off 90 percent of offshore drilling rigs through lucrative Canadian tax breaks—Trudeau's reasons for the National Energy Policy—were seen by Alberta's Premier Peter Lougheed as "an outright attempt to take over the resources of Alberta" and to "shift an increasingly larger proportion of Alberta's oil wealth to the urban centers of Canadian banking and industry,

Toronto and Montreal." In response, Trudeau's NEP document said, "In Canada, one provincial government—not all, and not the national government—enjoys most of the windfalls, under current policies. These policies are no longer compatible with the national interest." Eighteen billion dollars. That's the difference between Alberta and Ottawa. Or roughly the cost of two oil sands plants for the province. Groveling to Ottawa can be forced by the constitutional rules over oil wells "for the general advantage of Canada" or by the national government's special powers over the economy: the member of parliament from Calgary, Harvie Andre, said on CTV's "Question Period" that the only way the federal government's actions could be enforced is with the military; Carl Nickle, a Calgary establishment figure, said separatism is better than groveling to Ottawa; and in Calgary, Lougheed went on TV and predicted a storm while armed personnel carriers of the Lord Strathcona Horse unit paraded ready for battle up and down the freeway in front of the TV station on Broadcast Hill to practice student driving. Some Albertans were alarmed by these military maneuvers of the Canadian army during a time of political crisis. After all, Trudeau had called out the army and had suspended constitutional freedoms in Quebec after the kidnapping and murder of public officials. And no one doubted his willingness to act when pushed too far. But the debate went back to economic issues, dragged along by summit meetings between Trudeau and Lougheed, and stymied by the fact that 70 percent of Albertans felt the province should share its wealth with the rest of Canada—that is, if a fair deal for Alberta could be cobbled together by the two leaders. Meaning: the ties that bind Canada together are stronger than either René Levesque, the premier of Quebec, or Lougheed thought. And Trudeau, his interventionist associates, and the civil-servant mandarins in Ottawa had the upperhand.

When NEP was carefully reviewed, Canadian links to the world price for oil were found to be broken. Oil prices were made in Canada from then on. Through a fiendishly complicated compensation charge, domestic crude (from Alberta) paid for the high cost of imported crude in eastern Canada. Lalonde "blended" the low price of Alberta crude with the higher-priced imported crude, and this average price must not exceed the price of oil in the United States or 85 percent of the OPEC international price, whichever is lower. No longer can Alberta, with 10 percent of the population, get 80 percent of the nation's petroleum revenues.

Here's how Ottawa corrected this imbalance: a federal tax on all natural gas; an 8 percent tax on all net operating revenues from oil and gas production; a Canadian ownership charge on all gas and oil consumption; and a change in the system of depletion allowances for oil exploration and production to shift the emphasis away from tax relief for big (foreign) investors and toward grants for smaller (Canadian) ones. Moreover, oil firms must give Petro-Canada a 25 percent "carried interest" in oil exploration and production in the Yukon, the Northwest Territories, and offshore in the Atlantic provinces. This means that when privately owned petroleum firms find oil on lands controlled by the federal Canadian government, that government gets a 25 percent share in the newly found oil even though the government didn't put up any investment capital. Finally, Canada wants 50 percent of the industry to be owned by Canadian government and private interests by 1990.

It wasn't just Alberta complaining. Newfoundland said it owned mineral rights offshore. Its premier, Brian Peckford, when he was provincial energy minister in 1977, demanded oil-rig jobs for locals along with 51 percent Newfoundland ownership in support industries. Texaco and the others began drilling under his terms one year later. Joe Clark, when he was prime minister, conceded offshore rights to Newfoundland, but Trudeau canceled them as soon as he was returned to power in Ottawa in 1980. With the patriation of Canada's constitution from London back to Ottawa, Peckford had to fight Trudeau in Canada's federal courts or wait for Trudeau to be forced out of office by a Conservative victory.

The oil companies also refused to go along with NEP and to be taken over by Petro-Canada. Their charge was expropriation without adequate compensation. They were stung by an NEP more stringent than they had expected. Ottawa had done a great job in financing its social programs far beyond its revenues by reaching out and capturing the revenues of the oil companies. The companies had a better hand than Trudeau; they moved their capital, people, and rigs out of Canada. When wildcatting became more profitable in the United States, it was clear that Trudeau had asked too much of NEP. How sad the conclusion that Canada damaged itself; how much better it would have been for Canadians had they let the world price force conservation at home, thereby allowing OPEC's strength to be sapped by the total resolve of the North American economy.

Stock Market Says No

Much of the early returns about NEP came from the stock market. October 29, 1980, was Black Wednesday. Bruce Lanzier, a securities analyst, with Paine Webber Mitchell Hutchins, said it was the Canadian government's objective to force down the value of oil and gas properties so Petro-Canada could buy them cheaply.[1] Canadian and American investors sold Aquitaine Co. of Canada (an Elf Aquitaine subsidiary), Hudson's Bay Oil & Gas (a Continental Oil subsidiary), Texaco Canada, Chieftain Development, Dome Petroleum, Imperial Oil (an Exxon subsidiary), Ocelot Industries, Ranger Oil Canada, and everything else. The Toronto Stock Exchange's index of oil and gas issues plummeted a record 359.86 points. The paper loss was nearly $3 billion (Canadian). Gulf Canada dropped $1.3 billion (Canadian) in two days. None of the insiders, who had met four weeks before at the Calgary oil conference, predicted the 25 percent confiscation or "carried interest" clause, said Robert Metz.[2] Petro-Canada makes no payment and does not put up its own share; instead, the affected oil companies must carry the government's share at cost, and when production begins, these firms must give that share to Petro-Canada, the government-owned petroleum firm. Dome Petroleum has a major part of its future profits tied to leases in the Beaufort Sea (Northwest Territories) and in the Hibernia offshore fields (Newfoundland). "Smiling Jack" Gallagher, the founder of Dome, Canada's third largest oil company, saw his personal stock drop $16 million (Canadian); like other Canadian-owned oil companies, Dome must finance its exploration from debt rather than profits because it is a new oil company. Gallagher said the NEP would cut back his exploration program significantly. Dome has an accumulated debt of $2.3 billion (Canadian), and it can't meet its payments while carrying Petro-Canada's interest in its exploration projects. Trudeau had thrown a lighted match into the oil patch, and the fire would take a long time to burn itself out. NEP cuts so deeply into cash flow and net income that Argus Corporation, a Toronto holding company, decided against setting up Norcen Energy Resources as its operating company in Canada and instead doubled its exploration budget in the United States to $10 million. Turko Resources Ltd., of Calgary, an integrated oil company, moved twenty of its drilling rigs into the United States. According to the Canadian Oilwell Drilling Association, 1981 exploration spending in Canada dropped by 40 percent, the number of wells drilled decreased from 9,000 to 5,400 and 50 of Canada's 576 rigs left the country. The crucial loss from NEP, in fact, was Canada's self-sufficiency—less exploration in 1980 meant fewer barrels of oil later on in the 1980s.

Wasted Years

In the foreign currency market, it's easy to discover the long-term effects of Trudeau's two-year love affair with NEP. Secure in the daily foreign exchange tables is Trudeau's record. The Canadian dollar plunged 4.5 cents since he returned to office, as if his decade-old flirtation with nationalism, FIRA, and CDC was quaint rather than threatening; but NEP was the straw that broke the camel's back, discouraged foreign investors, and ended capital inflows. What finance minister Allan MacEachen is forced to do is pay off domestic borrowing by raising more funds from overseas. Canadian banks must write down their loans to Canadian oil and gas companies that can't make ends meet because of the global oil glut and the decline in world oil prices. Betting the Canadian dollar will drop even further, corporate treasurers slow up their conversions of American dollar receivables. Such lagging means that the Bank of Canada has to push up Canadian interest rates an additional two percentage points. Yet corporate treasurers must hedge because Ottawa doesn't have the ammunition to save the Canadian dollar. Trudeau permanently altered the flow of domestic and foreign capital, and it will take years for investors to regain confidence in Canada.

None of the miraculous things that were supposed to happen from NEP did happen. The overall trend in world oil prices did not rise by 2 percent in real terms each year. Rather, it declined. Cash flow from oil and natural gas revenues was so small that no funds were available for the costly tar sands and frontier oil development programs. Economic growth faltered. The hydrocarbon-producing provinces had shrunken revenues, and Alberta had to disinvest from its Heritage Fund. Canadian industrial users and consumers had to pay roughly the same price for energy as did American and other users. Canadians obtained no comparative advantage from NEP. The decline in oil prices took away all the fiscal room that Ottawa had to maneuver through 1986. The Alsands project in Alberta, which was to have produced 8 percent of Canada's daily requirement by 1990, was terminated because of low prices and high interest rates. NEP showed that Canada—no matter how complete the varieties of bells, whistles, and levers applied from the bureaucratic handbook on how to fine-tune an industry—was incapable of forcing world events to conform to Canadian predilections. Trudeau had provided new sets of examples for traders in currency futures to speculate against the Canadian dollar. The old reality took over again, and Canadian liberals were once more the party of fiscal irresponsibility and economic mismanagement. As the foreign exchange tables filled up with news of the Canadian dollar breaking eighty American cents and dropping month by month, week by week, and day by day, an economy one-tenth the size of that in the United States felt the chill winds of nationalism riding through its more impoverished provinces. We see the unemployment lines in the Maritimes, Quebec, and elsewhere, and we know one day these "lifers" will rise up against the interventionists, force them back to their ivory towers, and start again on the long road ahead. The wasted years are the darker side of Canada's NEP experiment.

Ottawa Backs Down

The break in world oil prices undermined Canada's industrial strategy. Too many eggs were placed in the energy basket. Investment lost or postponed for another decade has been substantial; lost future economic growth has been calculated at 1.5 percent per year through the 1980s. Here are the reasons things didn't work out as anticipated.

First, the new tax burdens imposed by NEP might have been bearable in a world of rising oil prices, but they were unbearable when oil prices declined. NEP did provide grants and tax breaks for certain exploration and development projects. Still, overall tax rates rose sharply.

Second, drilling stopped in Western Canada. By June 1981, a mere seven months after NEP came into being, one half of the drilling rigs formerly in use in western Canada crossed the border at Sweetgrass, Montana, to explore for oil in the Overthrust Belt of the western United States. These are rigs owned by both Canadian and U.S. firms. Because their cash flow was being reduced by NEP taxes, the companies made a good business decision and moved their rigs where they had a better chance of making a good return on their investment. Like capital, exploration technology is mobile and goes where returns are the highest possible.

Third, no new oil supplies were brought on stream. Synthetic oil extraction from tar sands and the extraction of oil and gas in the high Arctic were stopped before they produced a barrel of oil. All these projects were on the economic margin and were cost-effective only when oil prices stayed high.

Finally, NEP set low prices for existing supplies and high prices for new suppliers. This reminds Americans of the complicated array of domestic petroleum price controls that kept prices low for "old" oil and high for "new" oil. We decontrolled prices. But the Canadians "picked out the dumbest things we've done in the U.S. in the last twenty years and copied them," said one unnamed oil-industry analyst.

Predictably, on June 1, 1982, the Trudeau government offered tax concessions to the oil and gas industry. The Canadian government sought to boost industry revenue by $2.05 billion (Canadian); these tax concessions had only a limited impact upon company financial statements. They did increase industry's share of energy revenues and reduce the shares received by the federal and provincial governments. But total revenues were down substantially because of NEP, and according to Andy Gustajtis, an analyst with Toronto-based Wood Gundy Ltd., "It's going to be a long, slow recovery for the industry,"[3]

Because American interest was being aroused by all the corporate jets flying into Ottawa, I called oil executives who routinely make Canada their beat to find out what was going on between Trudeau and the chief executive officers of American multinationals with Canadian branch plants. The hush-hush meeting took place in early November, two years after NEP came into existence. Trudeau said NEP will stay, but asked for the executives' help in getting the Canadian economy moving again. Some said Canada must make more changes in NEP; others took a wait-and-see attitude; still others said it's too late. The oil executives had redeployed their assets back in the United States or elsewhere in the world. Trudeau said FIRA will stay too. He wants American companies to do more research and development in Canada. The executives asked who was going to pay for these additional costs, for they believed the Canadian market was too small to absorb the costs of bringing new products onto the local market. Trudeau wouldn't retreat from FIRA. Then some executives asked whether the requirements for their local subsidiaries to export would be lifted. Again Trudeau wouldn't go back on FIRA. One executive asked, "How long is this socialist experiment going to continue?" Another executive was interested in whether all Trudeau's cabinet officials also were leftists, and asked why Trudeau couldn't find some good old boys from Western Canada to run his government. After some argument about whether Canadianization was socialism or worse, and after a lecture by Trudeau about not interfering in Canada's internal affairs, the executives flew back to New York, Chicago, Houston, and Los Angeles.

Back home, the executives forgot Trudeau, his control over the internal politics of Parliament, and the lack of checks and balances in federal Canada. They should not have. The Trudeau–Turner government ruled supreme until it was defeated in September 1984 at a general election. The liberals controlled Ontario and split Quebec and the Maritimes to maintain their majority in the House of Commons. They forgot Western Canada. Ontario has a third (35.4 percent) of Canada's population and produces about half (48.9 percent) of its industrial output. It produces two thirds of the country's transportation equipment, rubber, machinery, and electrical products, and more than half of its metal, furniture, publishing, and chemicals. Hamilton makes two thirds of Canada's steel. Windsor is the center of Canada's auto industry. Sudbury is one of the major producers of nickel in the world. Ontario is Royalist, the home of the Loyal Americans, those United Empire Loyalists who left the United States after the Revolutionary War. Ontario fears American domination; it believes economic penetration leads to a loss of political and cultural independence; hence, FIRA. Ontario has no oil; it wants cheap energy; hence, NEP. Ontario fears the rise of Western Canada, particularly Alberta, as a new center of industry and banking to rival Toronto; hence, the liberals' confiscatory taxes on Alberta's oil.

If you would like to know the reason that it's easy to forget Canadian realities, it may be that we think about Canada in the same way we think of ourselves. Canadians make this easy for us by going to our universities, using our products, and looking just like we do. Canadian consumer values have become so thoroughly mixed with Canadian values of national importance that it does seem odd when the folks up north insist on our putting Canadian stamps on letters we mail from Canada to family and friends in the United States; or on our having commercials edited out of the TV shows Canadian cable networks beam into Canadian houses; or on having our investments reviewed by FIRA. It also seems odd that if we have old Alberta oil supplies, the tax and depreciation rules of the Internal Revenue Service don't apply under NEP. Annoyance over day-to-day matters has blended so thoroughly with vexations over real and imagined evil in the hearts of ministers that it does not seem at all strange to hear multinational oil companies being called the source of the harmful malignancy one day and a troublesome nuisance the next.

Summary

The argument: Canada tried to remove the petroleum and natural gas sector from multilateral trade with the world and bilateral trade with the United States. This program of managed trade had disastrous consequences for Canada. Its national industrial policy for petroleum didn't work because world price trends and regional market trends changed course, and the Liberal government was first unwilling and then unable to change its interventionist program.

This failure should give pause to Americans who think a sectoral industrial policy would be easy to administer and could produce real gains for the domestic economy.

Results: We learned that the petroleum industry is a special case among a country's industries. And even though the NEP has been discredited, the Mulroney government has had to move slowly in dismantling NEP's worst features. Canada believes it is still at extreme risk in petroleum and will do whatever is necessary to protect its vital national interests. Mulroney may be forced to exclude petroleum from future bilateral accords.

Recommendations: Again because the United States needs Canada to sign on first to a policy of reciprocal bilateral free trade, we should be willing to exclude petroleum and natural gas and other sectors of Canadian industry which the Mulroney government views as striking at Canada's vital national interests. This is no more than what we do for Puerto Rico, for the sugar industry of Hawaii, and for Israel, with whom the United States has a formal, ten-year, free trade agreement.

8
Sectoral Free Trade

The nation of Canadians exists culturally inside the nation of Americans, but they are not the same nation. Few Americans know the differences. All Canadians know the similarities: the mass-consumer society of Americans is also the mass-consumer society of Canadians, and the automobiles, the televisions, the washing machines and dryers, the vacation condo, and the sports: we live in a wealthy and materialistic economy. But for a very long time now, Canadian consumers have been prisoners behind trade barriers: cars made in Windsor and transported without American customs duty to Detroit cannot be bought in Detroit and driven back across the border by their Canadian owners unless a substantial duty is paid by Canadians to Revenue Canada; in every auto parts shop from Washington State to Maine, Canadians from Vancouver or St. Johns cannot buy tires, mufflers, belts, or oil filters for their cars and return home free of Canadian duties; every American purchase is taxed. The loopholes, one by one, have been closed by careful border inspections. At one time, Canadians with American green cards could come to work in the United States each day, buy toasters, irons, radios, watches, eyeglasses, hearing aids, clothes, food on their lunch hour or on their way home. They could cross the border freely. Now they face the nightmare of red tape, regulation, and customs revenue. Goods are 10 percent or more higher in Canada because the national market is 22 million rather than 220 million. The Canadians suffer from the same economic problems as do Americans: recessions lay off workers without paying heed to national borders, and the Japanese sell low-priced, quality-made goods in demand by consumers in North America.

But Canada is a branch-plant economy, a high-cost manufacturing environment in which labor is paid less and returns to capital are lower. Canada's short production runs, inefficient and uneconomical, must be subsidized by tax breaks and high tariffs. Canada is also an economy of high social benefits, family allowances for children, socialized medicine—more utopian than in the States. It is these private and public costs that cause the Canadians to suffer from a lower standard of living and a less affluent economy than Americans.

Once, because no set of investment strategies could produce a homegrown multinational auto firm, Canadian auto workers got the benefit of producing cars for 242 million consumers. This is called *scale economies*. Canadian-produced cars were no longer uniformly 10 percent more expensive in Canada. This was the result of the U.S.-Canada Automobile Pact.

Then came the long, grueling years when nothing could prevent layoffs of embittered, unemployed workers who had no Sun Belt in their future. In those days, Chrysler tottered on the brink of collapse, and Canadian auto workers had no senators in Washington to represent their interests. They could go to Alberta and try their hand in the oil fields or be staked to a new life by the feds in the Northwest Territories.

Following FIRA and NEP, Canadians contemplated what their government had wrought, as if at the behest of Canadianization they could have economic mastery at home without paying the price in terms of reduced consumption. Though from the outside it looks as though the Canadian summer appears overnight after winter, we are misreading as badly as we did in the case of Canadian federal politics. Canadians reached their decisions differently than Americans, and occasional trips to Parliament Hill by American presidents do not help to clear up the suspicions lurking just below the diplomatic surface. This other English-speaking nation (and don't forget the French-speaking Quebeçois) had favors to grant, territories to divide, customs to enforce whose specifics were different from those south of the border but whose purpose was very much the same: win a majority in the election, pass legislation, stay in power against one's loyal opposition.

High world oil prices, double-digit inflation, and many thousands of unemployed Ontario auto and steelworkers opened up the greatest opportunity for the interventionists since the Great Depression. The willingness to let government take on the risks of major business investment is another difference considered singularly important to Canadians.

Anyone wishing to examine this proposition has only to look at how the Canadian transcontinental railroads were built, that is, one with government subsidy, and the other as a government corporation. Canadians and Americans traveled west with different cultural baggage: free enterprise was either an important but not the central idea to the making of the national economy, or it was the only worthwhile idea. Following the American example, in the 1950s and 1960s the Canadians tried free enterprise our way. They got capital, investment, jobs, prosperity. In the 1970s, they tried to do it their own way. There is more government control over petroleum than ever before. But the source of new investment capital had dried up, and it would take many years before new capital would flow again into Canadian projects.

For autumn, Canada's finest season, came again, as it always does in U.S.-Canadian relations. Reasoning prevailed, misunderstandings vanished, solutions were found to the nations' common problems, and Americans believed again in investing their capital in new Canadian projects.

Trudeau couldn't ignore his sober reading of public opinion, while Mulroney knew that the electoral market for sweeping out FIRA and NEP is very thin indeed. So Trudeau went fishing with new bait: sectoral free trade with the United States (that is, free trade in textiles and clothing, buses and subway cars, petrochemicals and specialty steel), and got Mulroney on the hook as well. When Mulroney came to power in September 1984, he changed FIRA to Investment Canada, tinkered with NEP, and pursued the Americans on free trade.

Trade Policy

Canadian trade policy didn't emerge full-blown with the election of either Trudeau or Mulroney. Here is a list of key dates in Canadian economic history which shows how Canada has gone from free trade to protectionism and back again over the past 130 years.

1854. British North American colonies get free trade with the United States.

1866. The United States abrogates Reciprocity Treaty.

1879. Canada imposes high-tariff wall against the United States to promote domestic manufacturing.

1897. Canada gains preferred access to British markets through Imperial (now Commonwealth) preferential tariff rates.

1911. Canada rejects reciprocity with the United States.

1920. Canada exchanges preferences with Commonwealth countries.

1935. Canada enters into a limited bilateral, most favored nations agreement with the United States.

1938. Canada and the United States fully restore most favored nations status. Canada permitted to retain Commonwealth preferences.

1948. Canada joins the General Agreement on Tariffs and Trade.

1960s. Canada and the United States sign the auto pact and the Defense Production Sharing Agreement.

1970s. Canada agrees to lower tariffs under the Tokyo Round. Canada consents to GATT procedures for subsidies, countervailing duties, government purchases, and antidumping duties.

1983. Canada proposes sectoral free trade with the United States in textiles and clothing, petrochemicals, mass transit equipment, and specialty steel.

1985. Canada proposes a broader free trade agreement with the United States, a form of political sovereignty and economic association within North America.

President Reagan's first U.S. Special Trade Representative, William Brock, saw the bait and flung himself on it: he immediately began to reenergize his office, build up staff, write position papers, and leak ideas to the press, until everyone forgot that the Office of the Special Trade Representative is to be abolished as an independent agency when Congress approves the new Department of International Trade and Industry.

Brock displayed America's traditional reflex reaction to free, fair, full trade proposals. Larger geographical areas, larger consumer markets, are better than smaller ones. What little sting tariffs had left would be gone by January 1987, when the Tokyo Round comes fully into force. Brock, who had negotiated with the European, Japanese, and American steel executives, saw the Canadian proposal as an easy win. He was quick to endorse it, but no one else in the Reagan administration rallied around his flag; meanwhile, Trudeau was given credit for casting an offer on a line the Americans got hooked on instinctively.

Smart politics! Trudeau a winner? No. Trudeau's liberals were losers before the Canadian voters threw them out of office. And this time the provinces were to have their say: there was Newfoundland's demand for control over offshore oil and mineral rights and Ottawa's determination to enact the Income Tax Conventions Interpretation Act that gives federal Canada the rights to the seabed and subsoil of submarine areas adjacent to the coast of Canada; both the United States government and U.S. oil firms have protested this act's retroactive provisions. Though Newfoundland lost this one, it and the three Maritime provinces are demanding far easier access into the United States for their fish, forestry products, potatoes, blueberries, iron ore, and zinc. Then there is Quebec. It favors free trade. Textiles, clothing, tanning, and footwear employ 20 percent of the Quebeçois; 60 percent of its exports go to the United States. Quebec prefers a full customs union with a common external tariff for both nations; Ontario does not. The Royal province benefits from the Canadian economic union by supplying the domestic national market. It agrees to sectoral free trade when there is no other choice for making specific Ontario products competitive—automobiles under the auto pact and specialty steel under Trudeau's sectoral free trade proposal. Western Canada, expressing its historical concern about the cost of the Canadian tariff, wants to broaden the number of duty-free goods beyond agricultural machinery and implements and oil and gas equipment to include mass transit equipment made in Manitoba (and also in Quebec), costly consumer goods, such as textiles and footwear, made in Ontario and Quebec, and other manufacturing industries as well.

Now the sectoral free trade proposal balances out regional needs, gives Ontario its Royal veto and, in the midst of the public's slight shift to the right, almost lets Canadians know that their thirty-five year quest for self-sufficiency is a journey with no end in sight. Few industries (food, beverages, and paper products are exceptions) export more than they import. Many industries (such as plastics, rubber, and machinery) import more than they export. Trade deficits remain; trade surpluses are not within view.

Americans must review what Canada expects from free trade and what the United States should demand in return for opening up its vast internal market. Brock's reflex reaction is not good enough for us, because not only does free trade *cost* us jobs and income (in steel, autos, and heavy-duty motorcycles); it also *gives* us jobs and income (in agriculture, computers, and pharmaceuticals). And, in our desire to do what's right, we forget to balance our own regional needs with the national interest. The reason we forget is not that we haven't thought clearly about what sectoral free trade means. Sectoral free trade is a modest expansion of the auto pact. It is not reciprocal bilateral free trade in which all sectors of the economy are open to free trade unless specifically excluded by Canada or the United States. Let's see how sectoral trade works today between the two countries, and let's try to understand what bilateral free trade might mean for each of the sectors discussed below.

Trade Practices

Agriculture and food processing—dairy, poultry, milk, eggs, turkeys, and chickens are subject to domestic supply management in both countries.[1] Food grains and oil seeds are subject to international price competition. Trade in cattle and hogs is duty-free between the two countries; there is one North American livestock market. Canada wants to increase its self-sufficiency in fresh peaches, fresh and frozen broccoli, asparagus, spinach, celery, onions, tomato paste, cauliflower, peas, and grapes.[2] These products and frozen french-fried potatoes, corn, peas, and blueberries, as well as specialty beers, are targeted as having the highest export potential. Canada has set up a Crown Corporation, Canagrex, to push agricultural exports in the United States.

Argue as we must, both nations will go their separate ways because agriculture and food processing touch too many special interests for both. Too bad. North America needs a common agricultural policy to ward off further inroads being made by the European Community, Japan, and Australia. Instead, each country passes its own legislation (the U.S. Meat Import Law and the Canadian Meat Import Act)—without consulting the other—and non-North Americans excess meat is diverted from one market to the other.

Fish and fish products. The United States is Canada's single most important market for cod, haddock, ocean perch, and flatfish.[3] Canadian access to other non-U.S. markets is limited by tariffs and nontariff barriers (quantitative restrictions, licensing, state trading, health and sanitary requirements). Canada wants more sales in the United States. What's the quid pro quo? Here's one Canadian sector that could be traded for one in which we are interested.

Forest products. Tariff-free trade in lumber, pulp, and newsprint does exist between Canada and the United States.[4] However, both Canadian federal and provincial governments provide stumpage-fee subsidies that are now subject to U.S. countervailing duties. The U.S. International Trade Commission found these fees to be a bounty subsidized by the Canadian government. Under reciprocal bilateral free trade, Canadian lumber would be treated as if it were U.S. lumber, and Canadian stumpage fees would not be considered an unfair trade practice subject to U.S. countervailing duties.

Metals and minerals. Because Canada is the world's largest exporter of aluminum, nickel, and zinc and one of the major producers and exporters of asbestos, molybdenum, gypsum, and platinum, it has sought to raise the level of processing domestically and to buy back these mines from foreign ownership. These decisions by Trudeau, CDC, and FIRA led to America's lack of sympathy over steel. Both countries live in a world where 75 percent of world capacity is government-owned or controlled. Washington has placed border restrictions (trigger prices) and the states have insisted on Buy American policies for steel. Metals and minerals are one of the crucial products for reciprocal bilateral free trade.

Energy. After NEP, what can one say? Canada imports coal from the United States to generate electricity in Ontario which is then exported back to the United States. Canada's iron and steel industry gets 40 percent of the coal. Mulroney may not be able to deliver this industry to reciprocal bilateral free trade.

Petrochemicals. Here's something the Canadians want. They have three internationally competitive petrochemical complexes in Alberta, Ontario (at Sarnia), and Quebec (at Montreal). Western Canada wants to export more to the United States and to the Pacific Rim countries. Give them sectoral free trade in petrochemicals (ethylene, glycol, synthetic resins, molded and extruded plastic parts).

Textiles and clothing. We know what we want in this category. Ninety percent of our textile and clothing imports (and those of the European Community) from developing countries are covered by restraint agreements. The Canadians know what they want, too. Ninety percent of their clothing imports and 7 percent of textiles imports are subject to quantitative restrictions.[5] However, they export 50 percent of their coated fabrics and industrial textiles to us. They want a North American market so their textiles will have free access to the United States at the expense of the developing countries and without the restrictions of the ornamentation clause in the U.S. tariff schedules. Let's agree to do this, too.

Electrical machinery and equipment. Canadian export success lies in doing custom work in the heavy electrical equipment sector for power generation (Grand Coulee Dam). Canadians are annoyed that 50 percent of the U.S. electrical utility market is eliminated because of the Buy American policy.[6] This type of equipment is not subject to the GATT Agreement on Government Procurement. Let's include these products under reciprocal bilateral free trade.

Machinery and equipment. All major industrial countries export a substantial portion of their production and import a substantial portion of their needs: 30 and 13 percent for the United States; 50 and 65 percent for Canada.[7] Canada's industry was built behind high tariff walls and through Commonwealth preferences.

Also agricultural machinery, pulp and paper equipment, and some heavy metalworking equipment have duty-free access into the United States; the rest pay modest tariffs. Because the 1979 Tariff Act requires an injury test before countervailing duties must be applied, Canadian goods are virtually free from border penalties. The Canadians worry about our Foreign Sales Corporation (FSC), Buy American efforts, and concessional financing from America's Export-Import Bank as three means to boost U.S. exports at the expense of Canadian exports. Let's ease their minds and put these under reciprocal bilateral free trade.

Automotive products. Canada wants more Canadian Value Added (CVA) in the production of cars and parts for the two countries; it wants research and development shifted to Ontario; and it wants to raise tariffs on foreign auto-parts suppliers to plants in North America. Royal demands from Ontario have no weight when the United States is against these suggestions. If Ontario joins the movement toward reciprocal bilateral free trade, then we can give Ontario more CVA in the production of cars.

Urban transportation equipment. We don't have a substantial export capability in buses, light-rail trolleys, and subway cars; the Canadians do. But our Surface Transportation Assistance Act requires domestic content on urban transportation equipment financed by federal and state funds. We have Buy American, Minority Business, and Small Business requirements also. So Canada's Bombardier must produce its Flyer buses in the United States before it can sell them competitively to municipalities. The Canadians want these requirements changed. Let's change them under a reciprocal bilateral free trade agreement.

Aircraft. "Rough balance." That's what the Canadians get under the Canada–U.S. Defense Sharing Arrangements. They are treated as if they were American firms in supplying wings, parts, guns, avionics, and defense electronics. Here is bilateral free trade at work already.

Ocean and shipbuilding industries. Neither Canada nor the United States is competitive, but both subsidize their industries.

Electronics. Here Canadians should join with Americans to negotiate worldwide reciprocity for telecommunication market access by all exporters so that the flow of transborder data will not be impeded. These joint negotiations with the rest of the world should be part of our reciprocal bilateral free trade pact with Canada.

Royal Veto

The scoresheet. Canadians have given us a road map for negotiating reciprocal bilateral free trade. Americans need to study that map more carefully and then decide whether we can travel on the same road with the Canadians. I think we can. Both sides agree that free trade is best in the abstract but fair trade will do—and if neither is possible, well, both of us will take managed trade under some form of reciprocal bilateral trade.

It's not clear what managed trade means. Now it's what we have, a crazy quilt of tariffs, local content requirements, injury tests, and countervailing duties. Businessmen must pick their way among the regulations, decide what they can do, and pray that neither side accuses them of violating the border's trade barriers.

Autumn has come to U.S.–Canadian negotiations concerning reciprocal bilateral free trade. Free trade is spoken about more freely now; the free traders are heard more often because they know they must complete their work on the free trade agreement before the winter chill sets in. Even while these discussions are going on, Ottawa and Toronto churn out NEP and Investment Canada regulations. Nobody can turn the protectionist machine off completely. Washington waits under the deep blue autumn's-end sky. The Americans wonder whether anything will happen: they call Ottawa and get the answer "Wait and see." Is a North American market alive or dead?

During 1986, the Americans and the Canadians will make several proposals. We believe NEP must go. But how can Mulroney give up so much for textile and clothing workers in Quebec and Ontario, for petrochemical workers in Alberta, Ontario, and Quebec, for mass transportation workers in Manitoba and Quebec, and for specialty steelworkers in Ontario? Americans want one North American energy market. They want natural gas from Alberta and electrical power from British Columbia and Quebec. When Canadians say NEP stays, Americans sit on their hands, help Newfoundland, fight to keep the Canadian feds out of the continental shelf.

Some of us congratulate Quebec's Parti Quebeçois for its commitment to a full customs union no matter what Ottawa thinks, and there is no getting rid of the French, their language, and their desire to be out from under the Royal thumb. Western Canada continues to wonder whether the costs of the Canadian economic union are worth its benefits, and all consumer goods cost 10 percent more, so all households do with less. And Ontario awaits another benumbing winter, when all Canadians will rush to Ottawa to be sure their safety net is in order because of the taxes levied on the Royal province.

Summary

The argument: Bilateral free trade is coming to Canada and the United States. It's coming because we are developing a better understanding of what is and is not possible in Canadian-American trade relations. It's coming because Canadians don't want to assume extreme risks in their international trading anymore. It's coming because the perceived interests on both sides of the border favor bilatral free trade over multilateral free trade.

Results: Americans have begun to learn how to carry out the beginnings of an effective trade policy with one neighboring country.

Recommendations: In the negotiations over reciprocal bilateral free trade, each sector of importance to Canada and the United States must be examined with care. Most should be subject to bilateral free trade after a short transition period. Those sectors that cannot be subject to bilateral free trade because of political, economic, and societal realities in both countries should be traded off one by one in a reciprocal fashion so that neither country will have too many sectors still protected. Neither country should let any sector of the economy push its leaders into making extremely risky international trade decisions, as Canada did with petroleum under NEP or the United States does with sugar. In this way, the vital national interests of both countries will be protected.

Part III
Realities and Results

9
Managed Trade

Nations will fight to the bitter end before they give up their export subsidies, safeguards, border taxes, and other disruptive market practices. Interventionist nations tend to be very protectionist, even when they are members of common markets, customs unions, free trade associations, and GATT, the General Agreement on Tariffs and Trade. Daily, from Monday morning through Friday afternoon, Europe's protectionist animal, the European Community, goes about its dirty work and sets support prices, buys excess output, and dumps or destroys agricultural products; sets production quotas, pays out subsidies, rebates value-added taxes, and negotiates "voluntary" export restraints with foreign nations on industrial goods. The European Community manages a mandatory price cartel for steel. It imposes quantitative import restrictions against textiles and clothing, quartz watches, hi-fi equipment, television tubes, color TV sets, motorcycles, forklift trucks, light vans, passenger cars, machine tools, and so forth. When the European Community finds that foreign imports have caused material injury, it authorizes import restrictions as safeguards for the member states; when the European Community finds that foreign imports are selling in Europe at prices below those in effect in the domestic market of the importers, it imposes antidumping remedies such as additional or countervailing duties. The European Community's power comes from the member states. In the 1957 Treaty of Rome, the European governments, in Article 113, told the European Community to set their common commercial policy—in other words, to do their dirty work for them. They had in mind getting control over world trade policy to benefit Europe at the expense of Japan, Canada, and the United States. All three of these nations protested to the ten member states, whose response, in so many words, was as follows: "The European Community is our regional arrangement for expanding intra-European trade. Are you against Europe? Against our unification? The European Community represents us at GATT. And anyway, all these measures used by the European Community to protect Europe's markets are legal under GATT."

This is true. Two thirds of the voting members at GATT are the European nations and those African, Caribbean, and Pacific countries (ACPs)—the former colonies—that are tied to the European Community under the Lomé Convention. Nothing gets done at GATT without their collective approval, and the ACP countries vote the way the Europeans want them to vote for fear of losing access to the Community's markets. Over the years, the following products have been included in their protectionist activities:

> Textiles. The Europeans refused Japan most favored nations status until the mid 1960s because Japan was flooding their markets. Together with the United States, the Europeans signed the 1962 Long Term Agreement to restrict the flow of low-cost cotton goods from less developed countries. In 1973, that agreement was replaced by the Multifibre Agreement, which covered cotton, woolen and synthetic fibers, fabrics, and made-up clothing; and the MFA permitted the less developed countries to increase their textile sales by 6 percent annually. The European Community makes unilateral mandatory changes in the quotas open to the ACP countries. The United States negotiates voluntary bilateral changes with its LDC textile suppliers from Asia. Although textiles and clothing have never been subjected to mandatory tariff reductions and removal of nontariff barriers under the 1960s Kennedy and 1970s Tokyo GATT rounds of worldwide trade negotiations, the European Community can and does do what it wants to protect its older, outdated, underfinanced industry. No wonder Canada wants to come under the American umbrella and is pushing for sectoral free trade for textiles and clothing.

Sugar. When the European Community decided to raise price supports for domestic beet sugar and give the rest of Europe's sugar market to cane producers in former colonies (Protocol 3 of Lomé), it decimated Brazilian sugar exports. The European Community's action is consistent with GATT's Article XXXVI. The United States gives out quotas for its domestic markets to friendly countries, too.

Citrus. The European Community gives preferential treatment to Mediterranean citrus: fresh grapefruit, fresh lemons, orange juice, and grapefruit juice. Spain and Israel are immediate beneficiaries; Somalia (a former Italian colony in Africa) benefits under Lomé; the United States and Brazil see their export earnings reduced. The European Community's citrus policy violates the most fundamental principle of GATT, most favored nations.

These are agricultural or primary products as defined by GATT Article XVI (3). Most countries refuse to adhere to this article; those that do adhere to it make a major exemption, for example, the price stabilization programs of the Community's Common Agricultural Policy (CAP), or the U.S. price support program and other assistance efforts. Because of these factors, the "equivalent equitable shares" provision of XVI (3) can't be enforced. By the stroke of a pen in Brussels, countries gain or lose market share and the displaced country finds it impossible to prove a causal relationship between a loss in business and the Community's enforcement of import restrictions on agricultural goods. Since the displaced country can't prove economic injury, it can't demand a quid pro quo.

It is hard to read the history of the European Community's restrictions on agricultural goods without thinking about the mountains of food piling up in warehouses across rural Europe. It is hard to forget how the monetary compensatory amounts and the green currencies were used to protect European farmers from the ravages of currency fluctuations, more efficient producers in North America, and Latin American and Australasia, and from the need to further unsettle Europe and move the rural poor to prosperous German, French, and Benelux cities. What Europe wanted was high incomes for farmers, who became affluent behind the Community's protectionist CAP; that's not what the United State expected when it gave its complete support to the formation of Europe's common market. American trade negotiators get a feeling of irritation talking to their Community counterparts, and that irritation lies at the center of America's problem in dealing with the European Community. A large part of why we don't much like CAP is that it reminds us of our guilty feelings about our price supports for commodities and dairy products; the Europeans eye our payment-in-kind program and don't need to say anything. Some of us are convinced that they are guilty—simply because they try to dump their cheese here or sold grain to Russia when we embargoed it after the invasion of Afghanistan. They tell us to look at ourselves, and stop demanding they be purer than driven snow. Both perspectives, in different ways, are correct. On the one hand, it clearly can't be chance that made the small-scale family farms of Europe prosperous. Something other than back breaking work must account for their success—call it CAP. CAP—the Community's way of paying high prices for inefficient, intensive farming—has made European farmers prosperous beyond their wildest dreams. It's CAP that forces the Germans and British to pay for Irish, French, and Italian luxuries, that keep out cheaper American farm products, that subsidizes European agricultural exports, that forestalls enforcing GATT Article XVI. CAP must be altered before protectionism will wind down. On the other hand, the official American reaction—"Things can't go on like this anymore"—makes sense, too. As the breadbasket for the world, we want to sell our food for the best price possible. But if we can't, at least we want the less developed countries to have a fair shake at selling their food so they can earn foreign exchange to pay for our manufactured goods. It's an interdependent world, not a European-ACP world. In truth, none of us, neither high-cost nor low-cost producers, can be blamed for our agricultural trade practices. We usually must do what our farmers want because they are so numerous and so powerful and because we feel good about helping people who work the land. And most of us are protectionists—or, at least, we do what we have to do. A few of us are disciples of free trade.

National passions about protectionism can help explain why

most governments spend a lot of time arguing over export subsidies, dumping, safeguards, material injury, border tax rebates, duty drawbacks, hidden taxes or *taxes occultes,* countervailing duties, and so on. The conviction that protectionism results in trade-enhancing programs like CAP and value-added taxes (VAT) or the Foreign Sales Corporation (FSC) can lead the milk-toast bureaucrat to become a fighter for national favor over multilateralism. If protectionism results in mandatory market share requirements for foreigners (15 percent under the Burke-Hartke bill of the 1970s; the same 15 percent demanded by steel today), then why not keep foreign goods out altogether? This way of thinking is free trade's misfortune. Unfortunately, the European and ACP protectionist nations form a two-thirds majority in GATT, and for them the need to get in the ring and fight is a source of great exhilaration, creating a powerful constituency for more definitive trading rules. It's hard to argue with the less developed countries, who want their own rule-making regional trade associations and special deals under GATT with the European Community. They are just following in the footsteps of the Community and ACP, the U.S.–Canada auto pact, Japan's subsidy of offshore, lower value-added plants in its Co-Prosperity Zone, and South Africa's special trade relations with the other nations in southern Africa. Not only do the less developed countries understand; they're also basically right. For all our free trade principles, though, we are more in favor of protection whenever someone else can produce the goods better and cheaper, disrupt competition in home markets, and beat our firms at their own businesses. If foreigners deliver goods cheaper in domestic markets, we rush in with antidumping measures, countervailing duties, higher tariffs, or some other remedy; if we can't prove a causal relationship, we slap on quotas and tariffs anyway and pay the offending country compensation (GATT Article XIX, European Community Safeguards, U.S. Section 201). And this sort of forced action illustrates the way we think of protectionism nationally and internationally. The cause-and-effect arguments and the arguments about export subsidies can go on endlessly (while farmers get rich, steel executives keep their perks, and politicians keep oil prices low), but the results are undeniable: free trade is sickly, and all of us (Do we really believe in it, or are we just paying lip service to it?)

are unwilling to do anything about it. We need a national commitment growing out of a willingness to cooperate on a reciprocal bilateral basis, and a better understanding of how the world worked so well in the 1950s and 1960s. We can, of course, go on as we are. We can let steel executives dictate national trade policy as they did in 1979, when they wrote into American law that the federal government can't work out a settlement with a foreign government unless the American steel industry agrees to withdraw its complaint about unfair trade practices. Or we can recognize that steel caused its own trade failures and force upon the industry a long-term industrywide adjustment. Once we agree to break steel's stranglehold over our freedom to maneuver, then we must insist others do the same. And we could even start to think about where the logic of free trade leads: to a willful, deliberate decision to end protections for farmers, steel executives, and textile manufacturers.

Maybe this lesson is best understood by looking at the United States itself. It's the largest common market in the world. It has no internal trade barriers. It is a success story. The European Community is on its way to becoming a similar success story. The Community has not reduced all of its trade barriers, and it still has ten national currencies. But the wondrous thing is, if you end trade restrictions sector by sector, form a free trade association, put up a common external tariff, and form a common market, then those nations that give up one of their national prerequisites, namely, the ability of government to protect local industries, can enjoy the benefit of lower costs, greater productivity, and increase economic prosperity. That's what free trade is all about.

Tokyo Round

Throughout the post–World War II years, GATT members have entered into rounds of trade negotiations to reduce tariffs, to slow down the increase in the number of nontariff barriers and to settle disputes about subsidies, government procurement and the place of common markets in GATT. These rounds occurred in the 1950s (the Dillon Round), the 1960s (the Kennedy Round), and the 1970s (the Tokyo Round). Multilateral free trade was the watchword in the 1950s because the United States was its champion. During the

1960s, the European Common Market and similar customs associations began to push for less multilateralism and more bilateral agreements. The United States was excluded from these trading arrangments. So in the 1970s we sought to make several changes in the GATT trading system, a list of which follows. Many of these changes dealt with a small part of the problems facing GATT's multilateral trading system. On the whole, the changes did not come to grips with the protectionism that controlled the European Community, nor did they resolve the fundamental problem facing GATT—that is, the world's drifting away from multilateralism toward bilateral free trade. The United States was unable to stop this drift during the Tokyo Round of trade negotiations. Now the United States must design a whole new trading system for itself, one that I have called a reciprocal bilateral free trade approach to the exchange of goods and services worldwide.

On April 12, 1979, the Tokyo Round of trade negotiations under GATT was completed with the readiness for government signature of twelve agreements called the *procès-verbal.* Each agreement tells how to resolve a trade problem.

Standards Code. The technical specifications for imported goods must be the same as those required of domestic goods, so-called national treatment for imports.

Government procurement. Ministries and semiautonomous and state-owned commercial enterprises must not discriminate between national and foreign suppliers in the purchase of equipment, spare parts, and supplies. This is an agreement among Austria, Canada, the European Community, Finland, Hong Kong, India, Jamaica, Japan, Norway, Sweden, Switzerland, and the United States. It applies to federal and state or provincial governments in North America and member states of the Community.

Countervailing duties (Article VI). Injury must always be present when subsidies are granted by the exporting country.

Antidumping duties (VI). Injury must always be present and evidence must be presented on the volume of dumped imports and their effect on domestic prices, and the impact on domestic producers. These duties are levied only against low-priced goods.

Export subsidies (XVI). Only primary products from farms, forests, or fisheries are eligible for subsidies so long as the exporting country does not gain more than an equitable share of the world export market. The preceding three years are the base. Export subsidies for minerals are excluded.

All other subsidies (XVI). These cannot be used when they cause harm to the export trade of other nations.

Bovine meat. The International Meat Council recommends solutions to trade problems for live animals and meat, whether fresh, frozen, or salted.

Dairy products. The International Dairy Products Council imposes minimum prices of exporters and processing requirements for skimmed milk powder. Five less developed countries (Argentina, Egypt, Honduras, India, and Mexico) agreed to specific safeguards: protection of local industry and maximum prices.

Valuation for customs purposes (VII). To introduce a fair, uniform, and neutral system of customs valuation, the following valuation methods can be used:

• Invoice price must be used. If it is unavailable, then use

• Transaction value of identical goods sold under fully competitive conditions for export to the same country of importation. If this cannot be done, then use

• Transaction value of similar goods. If not possible, use

• Resale price of actual, identical, or similar goods. Or importer can choose

• Computed value of material and manufacturing costs, profits, and expenses.

• Intrafirm sales. The burden of proof that the transaction is at arms length is on the firm.

Import licensing procedures. Foreign exchange must be provided on the same basis for goods requiring and not requiring licenses. New exporters from developing countries get special consideration on filling quotas of licensed imports.

Developing countries. The LDCs get preferential treatment with the industrial countries, and the LDCs may grant special concessions to one another without giving them to all other nations. The LDCs don't have to abide by most favored nations requirement.

Safeguards. These are for balance-of-payments purposes and must be reviewed by GATT under Articles XII and XVIII.

Safeguards for development or infant industry purposes (XVIII). LDCs may use higher import duties to expand or set up new factories.

Civil aircraft. This is an agreement among Canada, the European Community, Sweden, and the United States on all civil aircraft, engines, ground flight simulators, and all parts, for the purpose of eliminating duties. Government subsidies (military research and development costs) and concessional export credits are subject to the GATT codes on subsidies and countervailing duties.

The U.S. Trade Act of 1974 gave the president the authority to enter into the Tokyo Round multilateral trade negotiations (MTN). These agreements were ratified by the U.S. Trade Act of 1979. They deal with tariff reductions and nontariff barriers. These agreements update GATT trade law on customs valuation, import licensing, technical standards, and export subsidies, including countervailing measures, safeguards, and government procurement. These agreements also offer special preferences for the less developed countries.

The European Community disagreed with the less developed countries over the safeguards because the latter thought, and not without substantial provocation, that they would be the subject of the safeguards imposed by the Community. The European Community also disagreed with the United States over export subsidies because the latter thought, again not without substantial provocation, that the subsidies are just more protectionism when used by the industrial members of the European Community.

The European Community's variable subsidy program for agricultural products, the lack of a systematic injury test under U.S.

countervailing legislation, and all other uncertain measures for excluding exports will be given closer scrutiny so that fairness can be introduced into the trading system. Neither the Japanese nor the European Community are willing to pay the political and social costs of mass rural migration to cities so that American farmers can have an easier time exporting across the oceans. Both remain highly protective of their domestic agricultural markets.

By November 1982, when the ministerial meeting in Geneva took place, eighty-seven countries had become members of GATT. Sixty of these were less developed countries, and another thirty were applying GATT decisions to their commercial policy. When the 1982 meeting was over, the world's trade representatives agreed to clarify the safeguards, the differential and favorable rules for the less developed countries, the rules for trade in agricultural products and in textiles and clothing, the export credits for capital goods, and the trade in services. The European Community dissented on future negotiations over these matters but agreed to study them for another two years. They are still under study by the Community and the less developed countries. The Reagan Round of trade negotiations for the 1980s has yet to begin.

Protecting the Past

Measured in terms of the willingness to resolve outstanding GATT problems, the European Community has become more protectionist as its common market has matured. All food imports are controlled, and internal food trade among the ten member states is regulated by the CAP and the green currency system. Japan is equally protectionist about food imports. And the European Community, Japan, and the United States prefer to keep farm income up rather than subject the agricultural sector to the discipline of the free market. There is an international consensus that agriculture cannot be subject to normal trading conditions under GATT.

On the other hand, there is no international consensus that steel cannot be subject to normal trading conditions under GATT. Yet both the European Community and the United States control steel trade. The United States used voluntary controls against the European Community and Japan between 1967 and 1974, instituted quotas in 1976 and trigger prices in 1977, gave the steel industry the power to block agreements in 1979, and in the 1980s let steel's complaints against Japan, the European Community, and the less developed countries become the basis upon which agreements are reached between governments. The Community began to control steel in 1977 by limiting exports from Japan, issuing surveillance licenses as a nuisance barrier (the United Kingdom), charging anti-dumping levies against Japan and Spain, controlling imports from nonmarket economies, and setting price and quantity controls or voluntary production controls on Community suppliers. By the 1980s, when demand for steel was down, mandatory and reduced production controls were imposed on Community steel producers, and each was guaranteed its existing market share of a much smaller total market. The Community now managed a steel cartel whose main producers were owned by the governments of the nation-states. The steel producers were told what to do; they were not allowed to dictate terms to the government, as is the case in the United States.

Managed trade has become as prevalent in the European Community as it is in the less developed countries. For example, all textile trade is controlled by protectionistic measures. In fact, one quarter of the European Community's manufactured imports and one half of its total imports are controlled.[1] This is the same as for the less developed countries. The European Community must give special assistance to textile and clothing manufacturers or face the disruption of rapid import growth from low-cost ACP producers.

Shoes: both the European Community and the United States restrict the import of shoes from the less developed countries and nonmarket countries. Cars: voluntary controls over Japanese exports to the European Community and the United States were put in place, too.

Managed trade, which made its debut in the 1960s and became 40 percent of the trade among market countries by 1974, emerged in the 1980s to control 50 percent of trade among the European Community, Japan, the United States, and the rest of the world.[2] This excludes the socialist nonmarket countries. If oil is excluded, the figure would be 20 percent lower. The U.S. total is higher for manufacturers. The Japanese published figure does not accurately reflect Japan's compulsive industrial policy between government and business. As the LDCs enter into world trade more aggressively, they increase their import controls while the industrial countries slap on additional restrictions. The sovereign-debt crisis of 1982 (Mexico) and 1983 (Brazil) means the external trade of debtor nations is even more closely managed than before. Why managed trade at this time in the world's history?

Simply put, managed trade, according to the Cambridge Economic Policy Group of the United Kingdom, helps governments make structural changes in their national economies at a pace faster than the one at which relative price changes occur in free markets. Managed trade—cutting back imports, increasing domestic employment, manipulating the exchange rate so exports are cheaper, earning a balance-of-payments surplus—means to break all the GATT rules. Managed trade is an argument for national planning and controls over all sectors of the economy.

And the Tokyo Round has moved the world farther down this road. The European Community, Japan, and the United States got these regulatory codes on industrial standards, on government procurement, on safeguards against imports of particular goods, on trade restrictions by the less developed countries. The LDCs obtained infant industry protection under the generalized system of preferences; this ended most favored nations status for the industrial countries in the LDCs, a once-sacred GATT principle relegated to the dustbin of history along with free trade.

The Tokyo Round, the multilateral trade negotiations, the Trade Act of 1979: products with so many negatives. The LDCs want to impose a new international economic order on the world, restructure trade, and shift its economic benefits to themselves. The costs of more controls result day by day in greater loss of benefits. For a while, domestic intervention, that is, breaking the GATT rules, achieved success in external trade. Now, when all nations do it, some sincerely and some for revenge (as in the case of the OPEC oil producers), the world suffers from instability, autarky, and stagnation.

Managed trade means it is better to protect the income of steel or textiles rather than raise the total income of the nation, the industrial countries, and the world. It means more detailed controls over sectors, firms, and employees because government never gets it right for all the players. It means permanent control, permanent protection, permanent government intervention.

Unsettling the United States

The European Community won the Tokyo Round.

Fortified with new internationally approved protectionist powers, the European Community's tradition of government intervention, sector by sector, is becoming the world's standard. The European Community's practice of approving privately controlled industrial cartels is fast becoming the common practice around the world. The European Community's philosophical ally is Japan. Although Japan practices a different form of government intervention, it, too, prefers managed trade. Japan concentrates its energies on product development, domestic market protection, and export market dominance. It agrees to "voluntary" export quotas when it is challenged for having gone too far in dominating foreign markets. These two allies are dividing up world markets between them and splitting North America in half. The Pacific Coast is Japanese territory. The eastern seaboard belongs to the European Community. The Midwest belongs to neither at the moment. No wonder Canada (especially Ontario) wants protection under Uncle Sam's umbrella.

Managed trade means the unsettling of North America, the closing down of factories in one region, the establishment of new ones in other regions. Skilled workers from the Frost Belt move to the Sun Belt in the quest for work. Capital flows to Houston and Los Angeles to take advantage of the higher returns from Japanese-sponsored foreign direct investment and the distribution of Japanese–made goods. There is no substitute for success. We take up Japanese managerial practices, try out quality circles, close executive dining rooms, and do our morning exercises, which we all need, overweight as we are, before making motorcycles, trucks, and other items designed in Tokyo. We may find all of this to our liking.

The Europeans don't offer anything as new or different. Their model of managed trade is something from the past, dressed up in the clothes of the European Community and sold as the model for the 1980s to Latin America, Africa, the Caribbean, and the Pacific.

However, unless the common markets, free trade associations, and customs unions in these regions develop a lot more intraregional trade, their agreements will not flourish. So don't expect the European Community and the less developed countries to give up their export subsidies, safeguards, border taxes, and other disruptive market practices.

Read on to learn how to live with managed trade.

Summary

The argument: The European Community experimented with managed trade, too, which suited the realities of European economic life. Clearly, the United States still hasn't learned how to deal successfully with the European Community. The concept of managed trade as defined by the European Community under GATT must be countered by the United States with a bold, forward-looking strategy, that is, reciprocal bilateral free trade.

Results: The European Community has skillfully exploited the GATT trading system to its own advantage. The Community has tied its former African, Caribbean, and Pacific colonies to itself through bilateral agreements under an EC-Lomé banner. The 1979 *procès-verbal* that was signed by GATT members underscored to the world the dominance of the European Community in the settlement of disputes among GATT members.

Recommendations: The United States should pay less attention to GATT and more attention to its bilateral trading arrangements with neighboring and friendly countries. The United States should move quickly to negotiate reciprocal bilateral free trade agreements with Canada, Mexico, and other Caribbean and Latin American countries.

10
GATT

The United States got a bad deal from the Tokyo Round of the multilateral trade negotiations. Here are the rules the European Community and the less developed countries forced upon us, and here's what we must do to stop the dry rot in our external trade.

Export Subsidies

The new rules are called export subsidies. You know them by their effects on trade and investment. There is a nonexhaustive list attached to the Tokyo Round Agreement (Articles VI, XVI, and XXIII) because many are unaddressed, by choice of the European Community.

Border taxes: the European Community and the United States argue over whether border taxes should be indirect (paid by the consumer) or direct (paid by the producer). The Community uses indirect taxes, especially the value-added tax. VAT is remitted to the payer when the goods are exported from the Community. The United States has complained about this VAT border tax. The United States uses direct taxes and forgoes or remits a portion of the tax due on earnings from export sales. From 1972 until 1984, the United States forgave taxes due on export earnings under its Domestic International Sales Corporation (DISC). Owing to the prodding of the European Community, GATT declared DISC an illegal export subsidy because it is a direct-tax rebate on exported manufactured goods. DISC was ended and replaced in 1985 by the Foreign Sales Corporation (FSC). The FSC gives American firms a 7 percent tax reduction on their earnings from export sales. DISCs were located within the Unitd States, but FSCs must be located outside the customs territory of the United States and Puerto Rico. Presumably, FSCs will be GATT-legal because they conform to the territorial principle for border taxes that the European Community has imposed upon GATT.

Hidden taxes on capital equipment, services, and fuel (the GATT term is *taxes occultes*) are eligible for border tax adjustments, too. Most countries rely on these indirect or hidden taxes. They are a burden on U.S. external trade.

Duty drawbacks (or refunds of import charges): When these are incorporated into the product, they are not export subsidies. Yet duty drawbacks when hidden are the most sophisticated *taxes occultes*. Out-in-the open *and* hidden duty drawbacks are shifted forward to the consumer; in LDCs, where the exchange rate is fixed, or in the United States, where the exchange rate stays artificially high because of the actions of others (Japan and West Germany), the cost disadvantage to the exports of the less developed countries and the United States is substantial. Duty drawbacks are pernicious.

Permissible duty drawbacks include quantitative import restrictions for balance-of-payments and development purposes, as well as substitution drawbacks to reduce the price of domestic goods going into exports. These are used in import substitution schemes to reduce the cost of capital, semifinished goods, and transportation. None of the less developed countries wants their exporters to be at a cost disadvantage, even though these countries are far from the markets.

The argument over duty drawbacks is as old as GATT, and the United States is partially to blame. In 1960, when the declaration was made giving effect to Article XVI (4) and duty drawbacks, the United States issued a reservation. It obtained permissible duty drawbacks for exported processed products (for example, confectionery candy and cake decorations) from primary products (in this case, sugar, chocolate, and flour). The United States wanted to be sure domestic primary products were used as ingredients for producing exports.

All of these are permissible border tax adjustments. They are supposed to have zero impact on trade. Some do; most don't. The argument for free trade is that there are no grounds to reward the earnings and savings of foreign exchange from any specific sector, industry, or firm. Therefore, taxes should not be rebated for goods that are exported. Exports are not free goods but must be subject to taxes. Managed trade is the opposite: There *are* grounds to reward the earnings and savings of foreign exchange from a specific sector, industry, or firm. The rewards can be high, medium, or low. Multiple exchange-rate systems are used to reward winners and cut back on losers. VAT and FSC are examples of these rewards given to exports and not to domestic goods.

There is a connection between an overvalued currency and export subsidies. The inability to devalue the currency forces a nation to reimburse its exporters for lost sales. This applied to the United States in 1983, when its currency was overvalued by at least 10 percent. It should have subsidized its exports to Japan by the same amount until Japan brought its currency into line with world expectations. Clearly, the United States did not take advantage of the GATT rules.

Export subsidies are simply a way for countries to correct distortions in their external trade that are caused by other countries. From the Tokyo Round, the less developed countries obtained the capacity to earn more foreign exchange, diversify their exports, and accelerate the rate of growth of their exports. They intend to do this through export subsidy programs. Here are some examples: tax credit certificates for raw materials and fuel (15 percent of the value of the exports is rebated and this can be used to pay income and sales taxes); special credit facilities; or regional funds for social welfare.

GATT rules, Article XVI. When can countervailing duties be imposed because of export subsidies? Export subsidies should not cause harmful effects on other nations (XVI [2]). Nor should export subsidies be used to gain more than an equitable share of the world market (XVI [3]). Nor should export subsidies be used to sell goods for less than the price charged in the home market (XVI [4]).

This is important because it says dumping is not permitted. But then, in the 1970s, few nations accepted XVI (4); they went ahead and dumped their goods at will. The United States retaliated. It shifted dumping enforcement in 1979 from the Treasury, which always could find a good reason for not doing anything about dumping, to Commerce, a friend in court for American business.

Can XVI be made to work? The intractable problem is the difficulty of proving causation between a subsidy and a harmful effect on trade. GATT should force the subsidizing nation to justify its subsidy and the importing nation to show the harmful effect on domestic markets, or the competing nation to show the harmful effect on its external trade.

Article XVI is suffering from "trade rot." This is an article that has been rejected as an empty gesture by the world trading community. It must be given life. Or, export subsidies in all their forms must be rejected. That's a worthy goal for the United States.

Safeguards

Safeguards, escape clauses, makeshift arrangements, and government assistance to help an industry in decline internationally (Article XIX) are all part of the new rules, too.

The precedents are American. Our 1942 Trade Agreement with Mexico has an escape clause, that is, a legal way of abrogating the agreement. President Truman, by Executive Order 9832 on February 25, 1948, made escape clauses mandatory in trade agreements. Congress enacted such clauses into law in 1951 through the Trade Agreements Extension Act.

Article XIX comes into force when the importing country wants to raise its reduced tariff because of unforeseen developments such as the Japanese dominance of the U.S. motorcycle market, that have caused serious injury to domestic producers. The burden is on the exporting country to prove that the safeguards imposed by the importing country don't meet the conditions of GATT. Otherwise, the importing country may impose its higher tariffs or quantitative import restrictions. The importing country is required to provide compensation to the exporting country when the former can't offer a convincing case of injury.

Voluntary export restraints are substitutes for XIX. Exporters agree to these voluntary restraints on exports because they prefer them to mandatory quantitative import restrictions. Examples:

steel, automobiles, consumer electronics. New and different suppliers are excluded from these markets as the exporting and importing countries keep out new entrants to the industry. These are also known as orderly marketing arrangements and they must be linked to adjustment assistance by the importing country.

Safeguards must be imposed on a nondiscriminatory basis against all supplying countries; hence, the preference for voluntary export restraints in textiles (the Long Term Agreement and the Multifibre Agreement). Safeguards have been imposed unilaterally, while the United States and Canada impose them bilaterally through voluntary restraints.

The United States has learned to get around XIX by requiring voluntary export restraints from Japan and others. We should pay attention to the demands for changes in safeguards; these will come up at the next round of trade negotiations, and we don't want to get a raw deal again.

Border Tax Adjustments

Border tax adjustments lay the groundwork for a countervailing duty war between the United States and GATT (and, by extension, other nations). The Tariff Act of 1930 defines a bounty or grant, and the courts have ruled that a rebate of excise or sales taxes upon goods exported to the United States is indeed a bounty or grant under the act. This principle was laid down in *Downs* v. *United States* (1903) when the U.S. Supreme Court sustained the imposition of a countervailing duty under Section 5 of the Tariff Act of 1897. In *Downs,* Russia gave a rebate of excise taxes on sugar exported to the United States but did not do so on sugar sold within Russia. This was a border tax adjustment subject to a U.S. countervailing duty. *Downs* was reaffirmed in *Nicholas and Co.* v. *United States* (1919) for whiskey and gin. *Downs* gave birth to the countervailing duty statutes passed by the Congress in 1930.

Tax remissions on exports are bounties or grants. This is a settled principle of American law. Another settled principle is that a law of Congress has precedence over a trade agreement (Article VI of the U.S. Constitution). Thus, GATT Article IV (4), which forbids antidumping duties by reason of exemption from taxes, conflicts with the 1930 law of Congress, and GATT must yield. Even the remission of *taxes occultes* (Italian Law No. 639 granted a remission of registration, stamp, and mortgage taxes) is a bounty or grant and is subject to countervailing duties. The remission of value-added taxes by the European Community can be considered a bounty or grant, too. Here is the war between the Community and the United States.

GATT rules, which are European Community directives, permit only destination principle border-tax adjustments on indirect taxes, for example, the value-added tax. These rules place a double burden on the United States. First, the United States relies heavily on direct taxes. Second, imports must be taxed at the same rate as domestic goods and exports must leave the United States tax-free; a compensatory tax must be placed on imports, and rebates must be given on exports. Something must happen at the border. And it must take the form of a consumption tax, which the United States doesn't want.

In 1974, Congress in that year's Trade Reform Act (Section 121 [a.5]) called upon the president to change GATT Article IV (4). It is possible that this anomaly will continue for a long time. The 1979 Trade Act did add an injury test before countervailing duties could be imposed. This modification in American law was the result of the Tokyo Round and the multilateral trade negotiations.

The United States had to accommodate both the European Community and Japan on border tax adjustments.

DISC Becomes FSC

GATT said DISC is a discriminatory income tax under Article XVI (1). GATT believed DISC is a form of income support that subsidizes American exports and injures the domestic products of importing nations.

In 1962, the United States enacted "sub-part F" of the Internal Revenue Service Code and began taxing income currently (instead of deferring income until it was repatriated) of American shareholders of controlled foreign corporations.

In 1972, the United States enacted DISC, the Domestic International Sales Corporation, Sections 991 to 997 of the IRS Code, and exempted it from federal income tax. One half of its earnings was deemed distributed to its shareholders and was taxed as dividends. Under these rules, the net effect was that 25 percent of DISC's earnings was tax-deferred and not subject to interest payments for late payment of corporate income taxes.

GATT considered DISC a violation of XVI (1) and XVI (4). DISC was an illegal subsidy in GATT's eyes. The Carter administration agreed to submit to Congress legislation that would revise DISC so it would conform to GATT. The Reagan administration submitted such substitute legislation, the Foreign Sales Corporation, and the Congress passed it in 1984. The Congress had accommodated itself to European (GATT) wishes.

So GATT is perishing slowly. The European Community, Japan, Canada, and the less developed countries have caused the free-trade bark to fall off the world's trading system. Dry rot is very bad on export subsidies and border tax adjustments. The United States has found it difficult to nail or glue the free-trade bark back onto GATT. Decomposition is beginning on safeguards, too. The Tokyo Round encouraged more spoiling. GATT is a museum piece ready to be shown to a disbelieving public about how the world's trading system was once organized. When you visit GATT, look at what it does. It confirms what its two-thirds majority is thinking about managed trade. There are codes of conduct ready to be imposed on the United States. These GATT codes will tell us what to do. Is that good?

Standards Code

Japan's emergence as the international competitor for both the European Community and the United States forces them to study the ways in which national technical standards, implementing regulations, testing procedures, and certification procedures effect distortions in their trade with Japan.[1] The standards are hard to quantify; yet, if the market is large enough, importers do make adjustments in their products. The problems with Japan's technical standards are these: first, they diverge a great deal from American and European national standards; second, American and European certification procedures (such as those developed by the Underwriters Laboratory) are not acceptable in Japan; third, Japan insists on certifying every batch separately that is imported rather than the total amount of goods imported with the same characteristics, trademark, and brand name. All of these actions by Japan hamper trade. They also protect Japanese manufacturers behind an impenetrable nontariff barrier. Foreign manufacturers find the process too costly, so they forgo exporting to Japan.

The Agreement on Technical Barriers to Trade, the so-called GATT Standards Code, applies both to agricultural and industrial goods but does not apply to goverment purchases.

Here are the questions for which the United States will have to provide provable answers when it makes a complaint against a foreign technical standard:

Is there protectionist intent?

Does the measure go beyond what is "necessary"?

Is there discriminatory intent in setting the standard, testing the product, and certifying the import?

Does the national standard deviate unacceptably from the international standard? Does the national standard go beyond what is needed for national defense, public safety, and protection of the climate and the environment?

How unwilling has the foreign government been to harmonize its standard with the international norm?

Is the foreign government still insisting on design specifications instead of on performance results?

Private commercial firms refuse to give up their blueprints and design specifications because they know these will be copied. The Japanese still insist on designs and drawings. Moreover, the less developed countries want them also so that technology can be transferred to them without the firms receiving long-term royalty payments. The United States will have to be extremely vigilant in this regard; otherwise, it will find the technology created by its firms duplicated elsewhere and then protected by nontariff barriers, such as national technical standards.

Japan is going to be very reluctant to change the way in which it handles foreign compliance with its national standards. Japan belongs to no regional common markets, free trade associations, or customs unions. The Standards Code presumes countries will work together to forge technical standards suitable to themselves individually as well as collectively; these standards will then be forwarded to the appropriate international organizations, if such organizations exist for the products covered by the standards. Over time, these regional standards will become the international norm.

The United States comes to the discussion over technical standards at a disadvantage. It, too, belongs to no regional trading associations. However, its current primary interest is to open up the Japanese market for American goods, and therein lies the danger. While we beat the Japanese over the head about their technical standards, the European Community and its faithful ACP allies—the Lomé countries— will implement the Standards Code in a way not to our own liking. They want it to reflect their protectionist leanings by keeping out products with American standards.

Common Markets

One day in 1947, GATT gave up its unconditional most favored nations principle. The principle means that any trade advantage given to one GATT country must be given to all other GATT countries unconditionally and immediately. It's an American idea (and a Canadian idea). We agreed to Article XXIV—for the sake of our European allies, of course. It permits common markets,[2] free trade associations, and customs unions to abandon the most favored nations principle, conducive to a world in which any group of countries could form a regional trade association and discriminate against American products. Musty misconceptions fill the discussions about "liberalizing substantially all the trade" (XXIV [8] [a], [b]), and the sweetly dispensed drivel about Nicaragua—a GATT member that has a relatively small volume of trade with other GATT members—and the explanations given for why Nicaragua and its partners in the Central American Common Market did not have to meet this requirement immediately, if ever, seem now an artifact unworthy of further study. The European Free Trade Association (EFTA) shook GATT politics even more. EFTA's insistence that its bilateral agricultural agreements were an integral part of the members' free trade agreement and that these agricultural decisions must be considered in calculations of whether "all trade has been substantially liberalized" forced GATT to back off and cease demanding an annual report on "progress." Our agreement to Article XXIV has long since condemned us to the silence of the damned; because we must live with them in our external trading lives. The Latin American Free Trade Association (LAFTA) permits bilateral agreements between two of its members. The Arab Common Market has an extensive list of exceptions. The Caribbean Common Market, under Section VIII, permitted special marketing arrangements to help members dispose of surplus agricultural production in a hurry. The New Zealand/Australia Free Trade Agreement covers only 50 percent of the goods trade. America is impatient with GATT's inability to decide that these common market agreements are in violation of XXIV. Regrettably, the United States has no choice but to go along with them. In an unhappy corollary, GATT threw up its hands at agreements between market and nonmarket (or socialist) countries and among nonmarket countries. Common tariffs have different meanings in nonmarket economies. When a market economy lowers its tariffs to a nonmarket economy, the market economy suffers a unilateral disadvantage because it doesn't know what the costs and prices are in the nonmarket economy. Later on, GATT refused to find economic cooperation agreements among a few developing countries (so-called South-South arrangements) outside the scope of XXIV. India, the United Arab Republic (Egypt), and Yugoslavia, three nonaligned countries, did not propose to form a common market, customs union, or free trade association. The goods traded freely among themselves were an insignificant portion of their total imports and exports, and they didn't give these exemptions from customs duties to other less developed countries. Their cooperation agreement was purely a preferential arrangment for themselves. They should have sought a waiver of Article I (1), the most favored nations article and the most basic principle of GATT. That GATT neither condemned them for their act nor asked them to request a waiver shows the extent to which putrefaction has set in at GATT.

Regional agreements, on the whole, tend to be trade diverting. They don't expand trade; instead, trade is shifted from cheaper overseas producers to less efficient producers in member countries. Regional arrangements tend to misallocate resources. Their appearance everywhere in the world, their use as links between less developed countries and industrial countries through which the Lomé Convention gives its Africa, Caribbean, and Pacific members special trading deals with the European Community, reflects the developed world's willingness to buy time in the never-ending battle to improve the lot of the LDCs. So on November 18, 1979, GATT gave the LDCs a specific exemption to Article I: they can give differential and more favorable treatment to one another. GATT recognized the new international economic order proposed by the LDCs. Resources would be diverted to them under the rules of GATT, particularly those countries allied with the most successful regional common market, the European Community.

The European Community speaks for its members at GATT. It is a party to the agreements on export subsidies, antidumping and countervailing duties, customs valuation, and other matters. The European Community has a separate legal identity and is subject to public international law. The GATT articles and codes can be applied within the European Community only according to Community law, and any remedies demanded by third parties must be in accordance with the rulings of the Court of Justice of the European Community or the courts of the member states.

The ten member states like GATT rules when they suit individual countries. But when these rules don't suit the members, the problem becomes a Community problem: the buck gets passed on to Brussels for a long discussion and unadvertised burial, and all that really counts is forcing GATT to give up, or the United States, or Japan, or whoever is challenging a member country of the European Community. In the world of European steel, which has a ramshackle legal house, the European Coal and Steel Community has separate responsibilities from the European Community. It is not clear which intra-European organization is bound by Article VI,

GATT's antidumping code, when it comes to negotiating a common commercial policy for European steel and an international policy for steel among the European Community, the United States, Japan, the less developed countries, and others.

The thing about the most favored nations article, though, is that it ended some time back, and it's not likely to return. Or, rather, while most favored nations lives within the European Community or between the United States and Canada, it's hard to imagine Lomé giving up its special deals with the European Community or the Caribbean nations giving up its deals with the United States. The trading system is irrevocably different. And while GATT did approve of a new enabling clause for "differential and more favorable treatment," the change means the less developed countries (in or out of regional customs unions) don't have to seek a waiver of Article XXIV, which they never sought anyway. For one thing, the European Community, together with the LDCs, has imposed collective responsibility for social welfare on the international community, so the resources of the industrial countries (the United States included) are available for use by all peoples. When the less developed countries look at the industrial countries, they often complain about their unequal status and say they must be treated better or else. And if this is not enough, they've managed to make us feel guilty about their economic backwardness.

Since the trading system is not going to return to those simpler days of yesteryear no matter how much we prefer most favored nations, the question becomes how to cope with the system we actually have to work within. Say for the sake of discussion that we accept the less developed countries' argument that they are indeed backward and need special deals to put them on a par with us—for instance, "differential and more favorable treatment." The first way to better their lot is to give their agricultural goods free access to our markets, because that's what they have the most of; and that's what we restrict the most with quantitative import quotas (on sugar) or dumping duties (on orange juice concentrates). This method doesn't appeal to many Americans, particularly the sort who want to sell you high-cost cane and beet sugar from the United States or who want to keep their south Florida in groves until a developer takes it all away from them with an offer they can't refuse. But, worthy as this profit-minded objective may be, its salability is questionable. It is difficult to see how the LDCs would want to go back to being suppliers of agricultural commodities when they tasted the fruit of selling steel, alumina, and other higher-valued items. Now they will want our nontariff barriers dropped as well; now they will want our technical standards relaxed; now they will want our governments to buy their small arms, planes, and other defense systems. If we care about the world, we must give the less developed countries a more than equal opportunity to diversify their exports; we must buy their products, good, bad, and indifferent; we must let them use export subsidies without challenging them under antidumping laws of the United States. We expect one thing from the less developed countries—that they join and subscribe to the GATT articles. This would mean that Mexico, for example, must give up its pretentions to unreconstructed economic nationalism. Differential and more favorable treatment means the less developed countries accept full participation in GATT and the reciprocal exchange of concessions and advantages envisioned by GATT. The new enabling clause permits a higher set of tariffs to protect LDCs as they develop economically, but it does presume these tariffs will come down over time and the reduced tariffs will be applied to goods from all GATT countries on the same basis of most favored nations. Additional protection can be gained by joining in regional trade associations. Nevertheless, those less developed countries that make good progress are expected to graduate from a status of maximum protection to one of less protection and then to one of full compliance with GATT.

Graduation would impose hope instead of facts. Graduation won't work, because the less developed countries won't give up their special preferences and the GATT system probably won't be changed. At best, graduation gives the less developed countries a stake in the GATT system of international trade regulation. We can have their participation within agreed-upon rules or outside of them. So we are in bed with the less developed countries and the European Community and Japan and everyone else. We must pay more attention to what they do inside of GATT, the European Community, and the other regional trade associations. No longer can we hide behind our Constitution and say that international rules conflict with congressional law and GATT must give way. It's an old American argument—a cop-out, others say. And it has caused dry rot in GATT, too.

Summary

The argument: Multilateral free trade is ending among western nations, especially between the industrial and less developed countries of the world. It's ending because the nation-state members of GATT prefer common markets, free trade associations, customs unions, and bilateral trade deals. It's ending because even the last champion of multilateralism, the United States, prefers bilateral agreements.

Results: we are beginning to understand that GATT has a chance to be an international instrument for equity and rationality in world trade. We are beginning to think through a trade policy that would make GATT an effective instrument for America's emerging reciprocal bilatral free trade policy. We are groping for the formula used so successfully by the Europeans.

Recommendations: The United States should pay less attention to GATT disputes because generally they are resolved in favor of the European Community and the ACP countries. The United States should not encumber its proposed reciprocal bilateral free trade agreements with the legalisms now found in the GATT system.

11
The European Community

Letter from Geneva:

It has been several years now, and trade distortions due to differing trade regulations and standards are still very real, as these are approved by governments the world over. Examples of these are Belgium's nitrogen content for fertilizer and California's minimum fat content for avocados.[1] The Japanese government's decision to certify domestic automobiles for emission controls once a model passes the test but require each foreign automobile to be certified separately has not made the Germans feel better. A May 29, 1981, report in *Die Zeit* estimates that the forty-one technical regulations imposed by the Japanese increase the cost of the VW Golf by one-third in Japan.[2] GATT Article III says governments have an obligation to give foreign products treatment that is no less favorable than that accorded to domestic products in terms of technical regulations; yet testing and certification are applied for the purpose of hampering imports. Are these requirements reasonable? Are they legitimate in terms of national policy toward public safety and health? And if they discriminate against foreign products, can the escape clause—GATT Article XX—be used to protect national standards and regulations? To do so, these technical rules must not be arbitrary or impose unjustifiable discrimination or be a disguised restriction on international trade.

The Standards Code applies to agricultural and industrial products but not to services (Article 1.3) or to government procurement (Article 1.4) or to technical rules already in force (Article 14.26). Technical rules must be written in terms of performance rather than design specifications (Article 2.4). International rules must be used where they exist (Article 2.2).

Among corporate executives, these international rules on standards are seen as becoming binding precedents with the force of law. A powerful international force (the multinationals) has been outmaneuvered by another powerful segment (the GATT community). The corporate executives know that the way in which they are treated by world organizations is an important subject, but the anger they feel about it is mainly misplaced. What they should do is either get in on the ground floor when the agenda is set or face up to regulations they don't like.

Corporate executives listen to diplomats present speeches about the responsibilities of transnationals. Diplomats tell them that they should not think of World Codes as some vague list of expectations written by do-gooders but rather plan to implement these rules through national legislation. Pharmaceutical executives who were bruised by the infant-formula milk complaint now know to get involved in the World Health Organization. Executives must realize that World Codes are as important as federal and state legislation. They know what it is like when their products must pass Underwriter Laboratory tests and then additional "quality assurance" requirements are imposed, and then, when the goods arrive in foreign ports, the lot has not been precleared, and suddenly out of nowhere comes the dictate that each item must be inspected individually. That annoyance, that bitterness, is as good as an example as any of why getting involved is so important. They should prepare pro forma World Codes as part of their corporate responsibility, with everything they want revealed so no diplomats will have to wonder whether their own negotiations are helping or harming multinational corporate advantage.

Executives want to sell their products to the U.S. Department of Defense, to national telephone monopolies, to government-owned hospitals. Their desire to be included in government procurement represents a healthier bottom line, fattened profits. No leap of imagination other than good corporate sense is required to know that government sales for aircraft, avionics, telecommunications, trucks, and a host of other items range from 50 to 100 percent of many national markets in the United States, Canada, the European Community, and elsewhere in the western world and in Japan. Executives should know that the Government Procurement Code of GATT does not prohibit preferential government procurement. In fact, government procurement is exempted from the rule of national treatment and it may be strengthened by subsidies of domestic products (Article III, 8 [a], [b]). It makes sense, then, that the $400 billion government procurement market is subject to nontariff barriers. Providing and taking away access to domestic government procurement are the means by which economic power moves, after all; fear of losing market share is what economic power runs on. If governments want to give special access to nonmarket countries—as West Germany does to East Germany and as the European Community does to Yugoslavia—then they can do so without being the subject of a complaint. If governments want to insist that their national companies be favored, then domestic bidding procedures will get a preference, 6 percent on the average, for all United States products and 50 percent for defense products. Observing what governments do, executives will know that only 3 percent of total government procurement in both France and the United States was supplied by foreign producers.[3] The impulse to give up on government procurement is understandable—the idea seems mechanically simple free of ambiguity. The need to get in on the ground floor is critical, difficult to do, and subject to many false starts.

Here are the rules under the government procurement code. For the developed countries:

> Services are not covered. Equipment leasing is not covered. Only industrial and agricultural products are covered.
>
> The value of the contract must be at least SDR 150,000 (or $150,000).
>
> The buyer must be a federal government agency listed in the annex to the code. The code does not apply to state (provincial) or local governments.

Rules for the less developed countries:

Developed countries have a responsibility toward the less developed countries. The former must provide the latter with technical assistance (Articles 11, 12.7, vis. Article III [8], [9]), and the former must set up information centers (Article III [10]).

Less developed countries are exempted from international standards when these do not meet their trade and development needs (Standards Code Article 12.4).

Less developed countries are not expected to give reciprocity (Government Procurement Code Article III [3]).

Less developed countries that get "tied aid," from the U.S. Agency for International Development, for example, can give American suppliers preferential contracts (Annex).

Less developed countries may require foreign suppliers to incorporate domestic content as an offset transaction (Annex).

Rules for both:

If both the developed country and the less developed country are members of GATT, that is, signatories to Article I and grantors of most favored nations tariffs, then the Standards Code applies to all nations, not just the two countries involved. These agreements are called multilaterals.

If the less developed country or nonmarket country is not a member of GATT, their agreements with the developed country are called bilaterals. The textile agreement, some agreements under the Standards Code, and all agreements under the Government Procurement Code are important only for the bilateral arrangements between the two countries involved.

On April 12, 1979, the European Community authenticated all the Tokyo Round agreements except those which applied to tariffs or products subject to the European Coal and Steel Community Treaty, and signed the *procès-verbal*. Under Article 113 of the

Treaty of Rome, the ten member states gave the European Community power to set commercial policy for Europe. Its supranational diplomats set rules for executives—on standards, government procurement, weights and measures, labor law, and agricultural subsidies; it's a ring fence around the European Community rather than the national barriers that used to exist in Europe. But as I read the letter from Arthur Dunkel, the director general of GATT in which he enumerated the multiplication of bilateral treaties and his reasons for forming a seven-member panel to study how to restart the move toward multilateral trade, I remembered the charge of the United States about GATT's inability to resolve trade disputes fairly. The United States won a rare first-round victory in its complaint that exports of pasta by Italy were unfairly subsidized. The verdict was weakened and delayed at the next stage. Angrily, the United States insisted that clear-cut verdicts must be inescapable in the future or it would conclude more bilateral agreements. And I remembered the harshness of America's charges that the European Community has manipulated the GATT dispute procedure to benefit Europe against the United States, Canada, Japan, Australia, and other developed countries. I thought of all the Lomé countries from Africa, the Caribbean, and the Pacific that are tied to and dependent on the European Community, and I know how the European Community won control over GATT. I wished corporate executives paid more attention to commercial-policy decisions made in Brussels for these become decisions on trade disputes in Geneva. It's the diplomats in both European cities who are contemptuously, laughing a thousand-decibel laugh at the ineptness of corporate executives. The diplomats know that the corporate executives don't understand how to fight back in GATT or at the European Community.

Dominate

"It is Europe, not the U.S., which dominates world trade movements," says Anatole Kaletsky, economics columnist for the *Financial Times* of London.[4]

Europe accounts for 24 percent of total worldwide imports (excluding trade within the European Community), the United States 15 percent, Japan 9 percent. Market conditions in Europe have a greater impact on import prices than do monetary conditions and interest rates in the United States. Although many prices are denominated in dollars and although the dollar was strong through the 1981–1983 period, dollar-denominated prices for imports were not sacrosanct when currencies within the European Monetary System had their values changed to reflect new conditions in Europe. No more did the European countries fall under the spell of the dollar illusion, and the European Community became the greatest single influence on the world trading system.

The Community's policy is to keep GATT under its thumb, corral the world's protectionist forces so they will work in Europe's favor, and promote freer trade within the European Community.

Europe also dominates trade between the United States and the Community. Almost one quarter of America's exports go to the European Community; it's Europe's prices (including subsidies, grants, and bounties), standards and technical regulations, and directives on government procurement that determine how much is sold, what products can be sold, and whether American farmers and manufacturers make money in exporting to the European Community. Europe's share of America's import market is about 12 percent, and during the era of the strong dollar, European Community penetration of American markets increased dramatically.

Common Commercial Policy

European Community authorities announced agricultural support prices, bought excess output, and then destroyed or dumped this food. No competing imports were allowed into the Common Market by the European Community.[5]

European Community authorities established a mandatory price cartel for steel. Here, too, the Community set production quotas, paid out subsidies, authorized national subsidies, and negotiated voluntary export restraints with the United States and other foreign steel-producing countries. European Community authorities also set quantitative import restrictions against textiles and clothing, quartz watches, hi-fi equipment, television tubes, motorcycles forklift trucks, light vans, passenger cars, machine tools, and many other products.

In 1982, the European Community approved 288 import restrictions for France and Italy. The European Community program is, of course, protectionist[6]—proof positive that every group of countries must set up a supranational commission whose only duty is to protect the domestic producers of member states and allow them to set up cartels. The United States might as well set out to reduce the millions of pounds of butter and cheese stored by the government or to solve the noncompetitiveness of steel by getting Canada to join in a North American Commission. (The United States, for that matter, might get Mexico to join so wheat stockpiles might be sold off.) It should go without saying that covering up national restrictions through supranational efforts will not make free-trade multilateralism work or cause anyone studying trade decisions to mistake the European Community for any other regional protectionist association—except, perhaps, GATT. For many years, the only result of the European Community's effort has been to show other nations in Africa, the Caribbean, and the Pacific (Lomé countries) and in Latin America (LAFTA countries) how to use supranational protectionism as a means to hide the many national hands behind quotas and other import restrictions. But angry complaints are useless nonstarters. What else should American officials be doing? We—the Americans who are out of work—don't have much choice. Keeping out European (and Japanese and Latin American) steel would ensure that United State Steel's Southworks (near Chicago) will stay open for a little while longer. Another year, maybe two. Even if all the appropriate new technology were put into our mills, they still would be noncompetitive if labor rates remain $10-to-$15-an-hour higher than overseas rates. By letting the European Community practice protectionism, we are admitting there is a problem and we are responsible for solving it. We realize that the European Community's answer is no answer, and we realize somehow that what we have been doing is not right either. We realize also that we should change things around so that European steelworkers are laid off at the same rate as American steelworkers.

Instead American steelworkers have been laid off at a faster rate than European steelworkers. Somewhere in that equation the supranational European Community Commission sits.

Common Agricultural Policy

Like Cassandra, the European Community prophesies evil without being believed by the United States, and we later find their prophecies to be true. We have rows with the European Community over the Soviet gas pipeline and carbon steel exports in 1982, and more rows over dairy products, corn gluten feed, specialty steels, and unitary tax in 1983. Throughout the year, Brussels, and the European national capitals with it, observe Dirty Work Week, which is highlighted by the European Community's taking on unpleasant responsibilities that are too touchy to handle in Paris, Bonn or Rome, which results in the European Community becoming Europe's most protectionist animal out to please Europe's agricultural, steel, and other lobbies. Price increases under the Common Agricultural Policy (CAP) must continue, say the ten ministers of agriculture and the European Community, without regard to the budgetary implications, because to talk against CAP is to talk against Europe, the ideal, the dream, the vision, never quite realized by the European Community.

Not unusual is the European Community's proposal to impose a standstill on the imports of American cereal substitutes, principally corn gluten feed. It comes as a by-product from the manufacture of agricultural sweeteners, and it has become an immensely popular animal feed in Europe. This would create a larger domestic market for the European Community's cereals surplus. Cereals *surplus.* Once the European Community's cereals prices had been aligned with world prices, production costs would fall. Costs would fall by getting rid of the surplus, so Europe imposes a standstill on lower-cost corn gluten feed from the United States.

A few hundred miles away, in Europe but not in the European Community, is Geneva, headquarters of GATT. GATT represents the world, but the European Community, together with Lomé, controls its voting power. GATT issues directives, or joysticks—decisions favoring those in control and against those who attack its favorites. GATT blasts America back to Canada by giving the European Community what it wants—permission to impose a standstill—with limited compensation for the United States. And GATT felt it "did good."

And from that moment on, whenever we looked at the European Community, we saw that even during Dirty Work Week, Brussels never slept. The European Community wants to tax all oils and fats and raise seed oil prices, expecially soya exports from the United States, so as to boost butter and olive-oil sales of European Community producers. While the United States cut production through payment-in-kind (PIK) and other programs, the European Community increased production, kept producer stocks high, and maintained prices higher than those on the world market. America disciplined its agricultural markets; the European Community did not. Rather, the latter resorted to export subsidies. So the United States was forced to subsidize its grain exports to Egypt and take that important market away from the European Community.

Very noticeable is the European Community's unilateral action to abrogate existing GATT agreements and to impose upon the United States new GATT understandings. Without a doubt, the European Community is retaliating for the United States' decision on specialty steel with restrictions on agricultural commodities. Both strategies are ineffective and duck the real problems associated with producing too many of these goods in the United States or in Europe.

Sugar Policy

While it isn't nice to scold old friends, it is especially unpleasant to have caught them with their hands in the till. Since 1975, the European Community decided to create a surplus in sugar for itself. It did this by spending money on export subsidies, by refusing to join the club of producers and consumers called the International Sugar Agreement, and by working with the Lomé Convention countries to be sure Protocol 3 (the European Community's commitment to import 1.3 million tons of cane sugar annually from the developing African, Caribbean, and Pacific countries) is enforced. The European Community's common sugar policy that made us grieve for our free trade friends came in the form of European Community supports for Community producers, interlined with import levies and export subsidies, a steady, somehow reassuring river of internal guideline that erodes principles, policies, and positive regulations down to where they've rechanneled the stream into eddies and have set an internal price above free market prices, established reserves for the domestic Community market, and subsidized the dumping of surplus production overseas. The European Community did not say that its sugar regime—a system of escalating price inhibitions on production above the requirements of self-sufficiency—was created at the expense of European Community taxpayers, who had to bear the cost of disposing surplus beet sugar from northern Europe and surplus cane sugar from Italy and the French Overseas Departments (Guadeloupe, Martinique, and Réunion), and at the expense of non-European exporters, who had to compete with more dumped European sugar. Not until sugar scarcity hit Europe in 1975 did the European Community negotiate a security of supply contract with Caribbean Commonwealth sugar producers, and not until three years later, with mounting sugar surpluses and growing support costs, did it become evident that the European Community, this protectionist beast, had overreacted to what was obviously a short-term, temporary shortage in the world supply of sugar.[7]

Moderation in producing goods, but certainly not food. By its very dependence on nature, food comes to market in abundance and scarcity. You can, for example, have a little and a lot within a few short years; but you can have a lot more of some food items when government subsidizes prices, imposes production quotas, and dumps exports. Cane sugar can be produced more cheaply in the tropics and beet sugar needs government assistance to be competitive at home in temperate climates, and when government goes beyond mere subsistence to raise prices to excess so producers' income will rise substantially, then producers switch crops to take advantage of better prices—for example, from cereals to beet sugar. In the spirit of surfeit, the European Community had created such a surplus in sugar production that producers' income in less favored areas of the Community would be seriously affected by reducing production quotas, cutting support prices, and opening up the domestic market to more cane sugar from Lomé producers.

These European Community proposals for the 1980s guarantee

Lomé producers their 1.3 million tons but hide the fact that the Community's surplus comes from excess beet production and that this excess is due entirely to the European Community's misreading of market conditions in 1975. It is this excess Community production which has caused instability in world sugar prices and the failure of the International Sugar Agreement to stabilize these prices. About 90 percent of ACP cane sugar goes to the United Kingdom. Since the European Community instituted its high support prices for beet sugar, the United Kingdom has increased its domestic beet sugar production and closed three of its six cane refineries; to make matters worse, consumption in the United Kingdom has fallen by 15 percent. ACP producers are worried about their guaranteed market, but the European Community wants its votes at GATT and will continue to pay a sugar price subsidy for these votes. Beet sugar production will have to be curtailed, and if the European Community joins the International Sugar Agreement, the European Community would have to accept an imposed export limitation.

As GATT weighs Australian and Brazilian charges against the European Community's export subsidy program for sugar, it must decide whether the European Community failed to provide adequate information (Australia's charge under Article VI [1]) about the extent and nature of these subsidies, their estimated effects, and why such subsidies were necessary in the context of the world sugar market; also it must decide whether the European Community reduced the export earnings of developing countries (Brazil's charge under Articles XXXVIII and XXXVI). The GATT panels reached the following conclusions:[8]

> First, the European Community system of granting refunds on sugar exports is a subsidy subject to Article XVI.
>
> Second, the European Community failed to prevent production from increasing, and neither the exportable surpluses of sugar entitled to export refunds nor the amount of refunds granted as reduced by the European Community.
>
> Third, the European Community's share of world export trade in 1978 and 1979 had increased, so the Community received more than an equitable share of the world trade in sugar because of the use of subsidies.

Fourth, Community exports displaced Australian exports in China. No clear relationship was found to exist between the Community exports displacing Brazilian exports in a third country.

Fifth, Australian sugar exports may contract further when Australia's bilateral agreements expire and subsidized Community exports take their place.

Sixth, both Australia and Brazil had obligations under the International Sugar Agreement, and these agreements resulted in a contraction in their sugar trade.

Seventh, the GATT panels could *not* reach the conclusion that an increased share of world export markets for sugar resulted in the European Community "having more than an equitable share of world export trade in that product" in terms of Article XVI (3).

Eighth, the panels did conclude that the European Community's refunds for sugar exports depressed world prices and caused damage to Australian and Brazilian interests in terms of Article XVI (1).

Ninth, the European Community system was a permanent source of uncertainty in world sugar markets and a serious threat in terms of Article XVI (1).

Tenth, the European Community did not collaborate with Brazil, as a developing country, to further the principles of Articles XXXVI and XXXVIII.

These ten conclusions are illuminating because they lay bare the contradiction that underlies all attempts by GATT to resolve a trade dispute against the European Community. At the heart of the contradicition is that at the Working Party level, the European Community said the first seven conclusions of the GATT panels had vindicated the European Community. Australia argued that conclusions eight and nine showed the European Community had breached Article XVI (1); the European Community system of sugar subsidies caused or threatened serious damage. It is now possible, so says the European Community, to bend Article XVI in such a way that all subsidy systems relating to agricultural commodities are compatible with GATT, but the European Community clearly wanted something else. It did not merely want GATT to affirm its sugar export subsidy system but also wanted GATT itself to affirm whatever the European Community wanted to include under GATT. The European Community wanted GATT to exercise its right to decide and at the same time to forgo that exercise in favor of the European Community's will—to be both independent and not independent—and this means to hold the European Community blameless in all matters affecting internal European Community decisions. Thus, the European Community wanted the Community to be the decision maker, yet not be seen as making decisions; to rule in Geneva without public knowledge, yet also to be seen as going through the process of GATT panels, the Working Party, and the GATT Council; to control an international organization without suggesting to other nations that they were subordinate members. The European Community's tragedy in this respect is the familiar one of chickens coming home to roost—so, making others angry, they gang up in other forums, complain loudly, and threaten corrective action. The dilemma is one from which the European Community cannot escape until Europe's agriculture, steel, and other lobbies are forced to take a world view of their commercial interests.

Throughout the discussion of the Working Party, the European Community showed how prone it was to the evils that flow from these "chickens." And the European Community continued to insist its vision of the right way was the only correct vision. The European Community sought to scatter the seed of co-responsibility: the cost of exporting sugar produced in excess of internal consumption would be paid by Community sugar producers. To hear the European Community tell it, it would subsidize only that amount of exported sugar equal to the amount imported from Lomé. The Working Party rejected these notions because they contained no built-in limit to either the amount of sugar to be exported or the amount of export refunds. The Working Party concluded it was an open-ended system, a source of uncertainty in world sugar markets.

The main problem with the European Community's GATT policy, however, lies not in its goals, with which it is hard to quarrel, but in the fact that it is the European Community that champions refusal to limit or end its subsidy system under Article XVI (1)—the same as Article 25 of the United States draft of the Havana Charter, the International Trade Organization—and in accordance with a 1957 GATT precedent under which the United Kingdom ended its subsidy of egg exports after a complaint from Denmark, Belgium, Germany, the Netherlands, and Sweden.

The European Community's sugar system for the years 1981 to 1986 differs from what was wanted by the Working Party. Instead of a reduction in sugar beet production, Community quotas were redistributed to those areas best suited for beet sugar production. The co-responsiblity levy was set at a lower level, and the self-financing aspect of the European Community's system was rejected by the European Parliament, which suggested that money be taken from the value-added tax and be given to sugar beet producers. The European Commission rejected the Parliament's recommendations just as it had rejected those of the GATT Working Party. It is the kind of failure exhibited by the European Community that destroys confidence in all world institutions. In order to "win," the European Community had to give something other than lip service to GATT principles; it had to make itself subject to GATT decisions. The European Community's failure to do this is the reason that protectionism, much to everyone's unhappiness, is driving free trade off the boards. The European Community is simply fighting the right battles in the wrong war. The European Community should be fighting the right war for open markets and for no nontariff barriers. There are the crucial battles, and the ones that Europeans and others are unwilling to fight. Ultimately, European Community policy in trade is circumscribed by the same insurmountable lobbies that doom American, Japanese, and other efforts. All of us are quite properly unwilling to put down loud domestic voices. They have become aroused and are unwilling to take direction in the cause of a better world economy. For some time now, the protectionists have been rejecting the attentions, friendly or otherwise, of free traders, GATT officials, economists, and other would-be missionaries, and have been taking their affairs into their own hands.

Summary

The argument: Multilateral free trade is ending between the European Community and the rest of the world, especially with the North American countries. It's ending because the nation-state members of the European Community prefer their Common Market to all other trading arrangements and they will use the GATT to ensure that their views prevail. It's ending because the European Community has done great damage to the spirit of multilateralism and to the willingness of the United States to uphold this spirit in the face of actual Community policies.

Results: We know that GATT, under the domination of the European Community, can't function as we first thought possible. We have come to recognize GATT for what it is: a protectionist animal that does the bidding of the European Community. We are beginning to suggest to our neighbors north and south that bilateral trading agreements will work to the advantage of North America as they did for Western Europe.

Recommendations: The United States should review the trade practices of the European Community and decide which of them have a place in a North American free trade area. The United States should not encumber its proposed reciprocal bilateral free trade agreements with the legalisms now found in the European Community.

12
Preferential Trade Agreements

World protectionism is like a great river with its source situated somewhere in the distant, almost impenetrable foreign markets not far from each country's own monuments to full employment, surplus accounts, and growth without inflation, and its terminus ever before us, just over the next set of ranges, just as soon as one more group of producers gets what it needs to be competitive at home no matter what the consequences are overseas. England in the post-Napoleonic period and the United States after World War II rode the middle of the river, tamed it for their own use, and forced others to contribute their own efforts toward making it flow freely, without dams, levees, or other restrictions. A few countries, some inconsequential, others like France under de Gaulle, tolerated because of political considerations, put up a few barriers, but these were swept away as the whole world prospered from the river's mighty flow of goods and services among market countries. But those few instances of barricade building grew into many as the river swelled, changed course, and rechanneled itself. Why is it, then, that in the swell of free trade, channel markings changed, then the river itself accepted the restrictions imposed on it by MITI, FIRA, the European Community and GATT. It's only by looking at what the European Community, Canada, and Japan have done that we can see just how far the river named for free trade came to be known as the great river of managed trade and protectionism. The events that really opened my eyes were the European Community's Mediterranean policies in textiles and citrus. I won't bother to review all the world discussions over multifibre arrangements and the bilateral agreements between the European Community and individual less developed countries (or between the latter and the United States). My view is that such deals slowed down the conversion of both European and American mills to more modern, more competitive plants because their domestic markets were protected. My feeling is that they should not be protected anymore.

"Doing away with protection is politically unrealistic." When you see that written in the popular press, you will know for sure that the authors don't know a great deal about the European Community's Mediterranean policy; in fact, they know less about it than they do about Australia's policy toward Papua New Guinea. As anyone with even a slight familiarity with the European Community will tell you, the latter has ringed itself with protective trading pacts: Lomé ACP countries and the Mediterranean. And the United States is about to do the same with its Caribbean Basin Initiative and sectoral free trade pact with Canada. To stop the United States' drive toward special North American trade arrangements calls for an end to special European Community–Mediterranean arrangements. So, as it must be, the willingness of the European Community to grant the industrial products of Mediterranean countries free access to the Community's Common Market is the European Community's contribution to their industrial development. The yellow light of caution blinks here, too, because the European Community has maintained quantitative import restrictions against the Mediterranean's most important industrial products, textiles and clothing. This troublesome difficulty has stood in the way of even tighter linkage, but the European Community accepts blame without a great deal of worry; you see, it's just the way politics work their way through the European Community.

Now, to set the record straight, and to put an end to the half-truths, I will tell you about the textile policy of the European Community toward the Mediterranean. I am afraid it's a simple story, entirely devoid of exciting, secret schemes. The European Community is the most important export market for Morocco, Tunisia, Cyprus, Israel, Malta, and Turkey. In terms of textiles, Morocco ships 10 percent, Tunisia 18 percent, Turkey 15 percent, and Malta 40 percent to the European Community. So the European Community's import policy has a major influence upon these countries. Because only Egypt and Yugoslavia are signatories to the Multifibre Agreement, the European Community has exchanged notes of understanding with the other countries, in which they have agreed not to exceed the agreed-upon import quotas and the European Community has agreed not to apply the safeguard clause. It is the European Community's intention to grant the Mediterranean countries a preferential status. Here's how it's done.

> First, through administrative consultation, the quota system is managed among the European Community, the member state, and the Mediterranean country.
>
> Second, a great deal of flexibility is permitted. "Savings" between different product categories or different years ("carry over") or to the next year ("carry forward") are okay.
>
> Third, in the case of sudden surges, there are no fixed limits for textiles imported in small quantities (or no "basket extractor mechanism").
>
> Fourth, reimports of outward processed products are okay, too.
>
> Fifth, the Mediterranean countries have preferential growth rates for their imports, about 1.5 times higher than the rates for Multifibre Agreement countries. But in this case, the Lomé countries enjoy free access to the European Community, and if their exports go beyond the European Community's "ACP line," an internal European Community ceiling on ACP imports, the Community is free to impose the safeguard clause of the Lomé Convention—for example, against the import of T-shirts and sweaters from Mauritius.

The record shows that the European Community has granted the Mediterranean countries preferential treatment, but not free market access. That may come in the future.

Multifibre Agreement-I

I know that Europe has been faced with a crisis in its trade policy for several decades in steel, shipbuilding, electronics, motorcars, cutlery, footwear, and most notably in textiles and clothing. Well, I love to shatter Europe's illusions; so has the United States. We insisted that the flow of low-cost cotton goods from the less developed countries be restricted under the 1962 Long Term Agreement. The Long Term Agreement protected older, out-of-date, underfinanced mills on both sides of the Atlantic Ocean. Eleven years later, it was replaced by the 1973 Multifibre Agreement; MFA-I covered a wide range of cotton, woolen, and synthetic fibers, fabrics, and made-up clothing. It permitted a 6 percent annual growth in overall textile sales so that developing countries could expand trade in an orderly fashion without disrupting the markets of the developed countries. Hailed as the best the liberal tradition of managed trade could offer, MFA-I was scrapped in 1977 for a more restrictive covenant, MFA-II, that protected the interests of the developed countries. The European Community signed both agreements under Article 113 of the Treaty of Rome, which gives it the authority to establish a common commercial policy for the Community, with the Community understanding that the GATT-approved agreements would not go into effect until the bilaterals were agreed to between the European Community and individual less developed countries.

The liberal 1973 MFA-I came into being first as the oil crisis hit. The older textile industries were faced with both a decline in demand and a growth in cheap imports. Of course, Europe couldn't compete, especially France, Belgium, and Italy, and later the United Kingdom and Ireland. The latter two countries became European Community problems when in 1970 they joined the Community and made Europe more vulnerable to cheap imports from British Commonwealth countries. Only Germany and Denmark, the two countries that made rapid technological changes in textiles, were able to compete with the flood of goods from Brazil, Egypt, India, Pakistan, Taiwan, Hong Kong, and South Korea. The end of MFA-I arrived with the loss of 500,000 European jobs in textiles and 750,000 in clothing and with Europe's synthetic textiles industry operating at 30 percent of capacity.

The less developed countries envied the European Community for being able to ram through a tougher MFA-II, with bilateral orderly marketing agreements between the European Community and individual developing countries. The European Community picked the agreements off one by one, and only the strongest major cotton producers—Pakistan, India, Egypt, and Brazil—were able to negotiate better deals, to the consternation of Britain and France. How the less developed countries preferred the old deal, their 6 percent annual growth rate for all products, loopholes for cottage industry products, their freedom to ship what they wanted into the European Community! Whenever new synthetics were available from the less developed countries, they were considered "most sensitive products" by the British—some 61 percent of British imports—and no growth was permitted. This was a major blow to India, Singapore, and Hong Kong.

Let me tell you the facts about what happened to Europe's synthetic textile industry. In the first place, because there was too much capacity, the European Community gave the world orderly marketing agreements, called voluntary, but not voluntarily imposed by the importer on the exporter. And these have jumped the Atlantic to become a United States weapon, too. And then the European Community gave the world cartels—an old European habit, updated for synthetics and later for steel. These normally contravene Articles 85 and 86 of the Treaty of Rome, which prohibit restraints of trade and competition, but they can be authorized under Section 3 of Article 85 for exceptional circumstances. Maybe we weren't watching carefully. But the Europeans were building a protectionist regime right under our noses. They were eroding free trade, in itself a disorderly process, and undermining the stability of the international trading system.

Textiles and Clothing Policy

The European Community's policy toward its clothing industry is one of protection against foreign imports and the maintenance of internal competition. During the 1970s, it turned out to be safeguarding jobs because that's what it's member states wanted.

> *Belgium*. Interest-free loans to maintain 90 percent of the workforce employed in the clothing industry. These loans must be refunded before profits are distributed to shareholders. Belgium

proposed a safeguard plan that called for an even more restrictive MFA.

France. Assistance given to firms that agree to restructure, and value-added taxes are used for regional economic development programs.

Germany. No direct subsidy schemes. But textiles and clothing, along with iron and steel, nonferrous metals, and pulp and paper enjoyed the highest effective protection rates of any sector, at averages of 21 percent in the early 1970s.

Italy. Government acquired bankrupt and failing industries, helped them modernize in terms of quality and creativity through its Sistema Moda, and set up the Wages Integration Fund to maintain jobs. The latter program was unacceptable under Article 92-1 of the Treaty of Rome.

Netherlands. Subsidies and assistance channeled to firms to improve productivity and product quality.

United Kingdom. Many programs since 1959 to revive a hopelessly declining industry, and one of the key countries in restricting imports even more under the MFA.

Multifibre Agreement-III

In December 1981, MFA-III was agreed to, and it covers the years 1982–1986. Forty-one countries (the European Community signed as one signatory for its member states) are signatories, and it covers four fifths (or $80 billion) of world trade in textiles and clothing. It defines market disruption as "a sharp and substantial increase in imports . . . and where products are offered at prices substantially below those prevailing for similar goods of comparable quality in the market of the importing country." Neither technological changes nor changes in consumer preference are to be considered. MFA-III is a standstill agreement.[1] It protects the biggest producer of textiles, the United States, and the largest importer and exporter of textiles, the European Community. It does not give the non-Lomé, non-Mediterranean less developed countries a chance to expand their textile and clothing exports to the European Community. No magic of the marketplace is permitted to work for the less developed countries under MFA-III.

The truth is that from the Long Term Agreement through MFA-III, the European Community alone, the United States alone, and both together have circumscribed free trade in the textile and clothing market. Or, to be more exact, neither was willing to pay the political price in lost jobs, declines in regional economies, and the export of direct investment overseas. Only the Japanese followed a consistent industry policy toward textiles and clothing. They shipped the production of cheap textiles to Taiwan, Korea, and elsewhere in Asia. The Japanese concentrated on producing the higher value-added products; of course, they kept control of the overseas mills. So they made money both at home and abroad selling a full line of textiles and clothing to the European Community and the United States. By the time we and the Europeans realize what the Japanese have done, it will be too late. The textile complaints from the less developed countries are, in part, Japanese complaints. This is a sweeping indictment of European and American politicians, who are unwilling to take the heat for unemployment decisions. Now they are faced with difficult choices for steel, automobiles, and other products. Will they follow the Japanese model.[1] Don't bet on it.

Mediterranean Policy

European Community policies toward the Mediterranean countries have taken on a preferential quality. Goods, products, and even services that could be produced in Europe have been given over to Mediterranean basin countries. Protectionism is rampant. Special tariff reductions, cooperation in capital flows, transfers of technology, and critical aid for economic development all are designed to displace American exports to the European Community in favor of goods produced in the Mediterranean.

"Interim" preferential protectionist agreements with Morocco, Tunisia, Algeria, Cyprus, Egypt, Lebanon, Syria, Jordan, Malta, and Israel. "Association" preferential protectionist agreements with

Portugal, Spain, and Turkey that have led to full European Community membership for Spain and Portugal in January 1986.

Are they consistent with GATT's most favored nations cornerstone principle? Article XXIV exempts customs unions and free trade associations from most favored nations, and it exempts interim agreements when they lead to membership in these common markets. The Mediterranean agreements do not meet the conditions set forth under Article XXIV, but they follow the precedents set between the European Community and its former colonies under the Lomé Convention. The United States believes that these interim agreements with the Mediterranean countries are disruptive to its own exports. So for citrus products, the United States negotiated with the European Community a reduction of the most favored nations duty on oranges during our peak growing season. This, too, is an interim preferential agreement in violation of Article XXIV and most favored nations.

The European Community–Mediterranean agreement displaced trade in favor of preferred countries for fresh oranges, grapefruit, and lemons starting in the early 1970s, and later on for orange juice and grapefruit juice.[2] The United States lost market share in the early 1970s but regained it in the later 1970s. Israel gained at the expense of Brazil. In the 1980s, Brazil paid its orange growers an export subsidy to sell concentrate to the United States and the European Community. This subsidy was found to be a bounty by the U.S. International Trade Commission, and Brazil was forced to raise prices. However, as a consequence of Brazil's export subsidies, Brazil captured 80 percent of the world market for orange-juice concentrate sales notwithstanding the ex post facto application of American trade law by the ITC.

The world seems to be experiencing a sort of subsidy nightmare—a delirium in which bureaucrats use tax money to support noncompetitive industries—and the world's autarkic countries, by virtue of some special magic wand, present themselves as free trade giants in the imagination of the world's statesmen. But while the giants may be illusionary, the economic disasters are real, and the world can only hope that somehow the spell will be broken—that in the minds of the men in power, the actions of little protectionists and the survival of an open trading system will become disentangled and that export subsidies will shrink back to their best use—thus returning the world's economy to a more open, less managed condition.

Summary

The argument: Right now, before our very eyes, multilateral free trade is ending because the European Community, the United States, and Japan have placed national advantage over multinational competitiveness. All are guilty as charged. Even the United States' adherence to the dogma of multilateral free trade has been patchy. Still, the dogma is the norm in our public thinking, even though our institutions have had neither the will nor the ability to make multilateral free trade become a reality. This is the state of affairs in which we live. So we must build upon a new dogma and create institutions that can make bilateral free trade work.

Results: We know that all the special multilateral sector deals, such as those for textiles, sugar, citrus, and so on, are not working to further multilateral free trade. We know these agreements pile up hugh surpluses that must be paid for through the taxation of consumers.

Recommendations: The United States should open its markets to the products of the less developed countries without the many restrictions imposed by the European Community on the import of these same LDC products. This would reduce the need for the LDCs to take extreme risks in trying to maintain themselves in the international trading system. The United States should learn positive lessons from how badly the European Community behaved toward the less developed countries.

Part IV
Prospects and Problems

13
Lomé

All that stuff about European colonialist dogs and sly French (substitute British, Dutch, Belgian, Italian) bureaucrats and greedy business bloodsuckers—some prime ministers and presidents from the Lomé countries really talk that way. Americans historically haven't paid much attention to the African, Caribbean, and Pacific states, and we weren't there in 1976 when the nine member states of the European Community with all their former colonies and other less developed countries (Ethiopia, Equatorial Guinea, Guinea-Bissau, Liberia, and the Sudan) ratified Lomé. Preferential trade agreements with no timetable for forming a more complete free trade association were improper under GATT rules in the mid-1970s; yet Lomé was seen by its participants as the means for Black Africa to stand together and work with the developed countries of Europe in a new partnership, while at the United Nations Conference on Trade and Development (UNCTAD), attempts were being made to set down rules for a new international economic order in a charter of economic rights and duties of nation-states. Much of the debate over UNCTAD, vital and timely though it surely was, dragged along, caught in a net of inflammatory rhetoric and unbelievable boredom that marks so many international trade conclaves. But the Lomé Convention riveted the attention of the world. Lomé was intended to be a breakthrough agreement whereby the new international economic order could shift from confrontation to consensus. Black Africa—through its Organization of African Unity, a regional group Americans pay little attention to—said it wanted financial and technical assistance, special trade arrangements, a scheme to stabilize export earnings, and additional bargains to give all less developed countries a place of greater equality in the world's economic and monetary system. And then, at Kingston, Jamaica, in July 1974, in the midst of the negotiations, the European Community made four historic concessions to the ACP countries. It agreed to give up reverse preferences; minimize obstacles to the free access of ACP goods into the Community; widen Stabex, the stabilization program for ACP agricultural exports; and help the ACP countries to industrialize.

It was clear then that the European Community had made a fundamental change in how it would handle its relationship with the less developed countries. The European Community suggested to the United States and Japan that they do something similar for Latin America and Asia. Only Japan responded by recreating its co-prosperity area that now encompasses most of the Pacific Basin.

The ACP countries saw Lomé as the means by which their ex-colonial masters could help them accelerate their economic and social development. French-speaking statesmen said something stern, and the English-speaking statesmen, who are London-trained Fabian socialists, read from their Marxist-Leninist copybooks; references to social classes, socialist realism, and capitalist aggressors punctuated their remarks, and many of them continued to complain during their francophone colleagues' speeches (when Americans call international trade conferences inflammatory and boring, it is these speeches they refer to). ACP's concern for its economic development is the reason that stress is laid on free access to the European Community for almost all ACP goods (except those covered by the European Community's common agricultural policy). The impossible was made possible—94 percent of ACP products subject to the common agricultural policy got European Community exemptions from duties and free access to the Community's Common Market; for the other 6 percent, ACP products are given preference over those from other countries, and as the ACP countries diversify their agriculture, other farm products will be given special preferential arrangements. The European Community will not impose quantitative restrictions, nor will it enforce with rigor its rules of origin. Products with more than 50 percent value added by two or more ACP countries will be treated as coming from a single customs territory and will be free of duty. K.R. Simmonds said the European

Community's agreement to abandon reverse preferences, something which the United States imposed on its trading partners in the Trade Reform Act of 1974, was considered to be the most important feature of Lomé.[1] Both GATT and UNCTAD applauded. ACP countries agreed to give European Community member states most favored nations treatment, but not if most favored nations involved other less developed, non-Lomé countries. The European Community was an ex-colonial master, they said. Now the European Community keeps the products of the less developed countries out of its vast common market, they said—and certainly the European Community, as paymaster for the nine member states, must share the wealth. The European Community, they said, must spend its riches on the creation of the new international economic order, for this is the duty of the developed countries.

It wasn't just trade and commercial cooperation that were important; the European Community agreed to stabilize the export earnings of ACP countries for their twelve primary products (groundnuts, cocoa, coffee, cotton, coconuts, palm and palm kernel products, hides and skins, wood products, bananas, tea, raw sisal, and iron ore) through a system of commodity-tied compensatory financing. The least developed, landlocked, or island ACP countries have significantly lower "activation thresholds" and "dependence thresholds" than do the more developed ACP countries, and the former receive less from the Stabex Fund. Even with the solid Black African front, the haves do better than the have nots. How sad that even the European Community must forget the real basket cases. How much better it would be for everyone if the European Community had found the formula to help all the poor nations. The European Community agreed to forgive the interest-free loans from Stabex, even from the better-off ACP countries.

In Protocol 3 to the Lomé Convention, it's easy to discover the long-term effects of post-colonial economic fragmentation on ACP sugar producers. Secure on account of the 1.375-million-metric-ton annual quota exported to the European Community, the ACP countries obtained a Community assurance to purchase their cane sugar at a freely negotiated guaranteed price, and if the two parties couldn't agree, then ACP cane sugar would be subject to the common agricultural policy, as if it were sugar produced in Europe and eligible for the Community's high protective prices. What many ACP citizens envision in their reverie of yesterday is the mother country taking care of them. Free, but not free of its former colonies, the European Community comes to the table and haggles over price. The former colonies want a secure, long-term resolution to their sugar problem. Yet during the years after Lomé—as the European Community first misunderstood the extent to which there would be a shortage in sugar and then subsidized beet sugar producers to secure Europe's supply—European intentions per se became a matter of concern for these emerging states, no longer sure who was master, who was servant, but insistent there be more balance in the relationship. The European Community showed that it had other ways—different and equally burdensome—of shaping trade patterns; the European Community provided new information for future negotiations with ACP. But the argument over sugar evinced the old reality, and Europe was once again acting as a colonial master in Black Africa. As the signatures were affixed to the sugar protocol, a product of export importance to most ACP countries, the European Community realized it was destined to be Africa's paymaster—from Brussels, now—until the former colonies were able to walk by themselves. The sugar protocol is the darker side of the ACPs' dependence on the European Community, and it keeps coming back to haunt them.

The less developed countries' interest having been aroused by all the advance publicity, they looked at the agreements for more industrial, technical, and financial cooperation between ACP and Community, which were to be the prototypes for UNCTAD. Industrial cooperation—an agreement to help create infrastructure, establish new manufacturing firms, do research studies, and promote technology transfer—was not as specific a European Community commitment as was hoped for by the ACP countries, but it came as close as possible to what the less developed countries could expect from the developed countries in the mid-1970s, and it made the less developed countries regroup themselves for a further assault on GATT through the Tokyo Round discussions, which concluded by binding not only the European Community but also the United States and Japan to giving the less developed countries what they wanted as outlined under UNCTAD. Financial cooperation, an agreement by the European Community to give $3 billion in grants, "soft" loans, risk capital, and Stabex funds, and another $390 million in hard loans, all with a 3 percent effective rate of interest, was considered generous by the European Community and niggardly by the ACPs. Technical cooperation, an agreement to help the ACPs with rural development, personnel training, and market and sales promotion, was designed to increase intraregional cooperation among ACP countries. The European Community is the ACPs' most important commercial partner. The Lomé Convention was a landmark for the European Community with regard to the establishment of external policy goals. It introduced a common development policy. It pushed the world to a "redefining of relations between rich and poor countries, between producers and consumers of raw materials, between industrialized economies and primary producer economies . . . the vital issue of our time."[2] That's the large claim made by the European Community.

If you would like to know why America has not done much about the less developed countries problem, the answer may be that we think about it in the same way we think about our daily problems—that is, about where to shop or how to pay for a new household appliance or what to wear on Friday night or which bank is best for our meager savings. The concerns of daily living have clouded our vision of what we can do now that we no longer conquer continents, races, and peoples for their betterment and ours.

Lomé-I

The UN Group of 77 less developed countries (which includes Latin American and Arab countries) viewed Lomé-I as an attempt by the European Community to split the Group of 77 apart. On the face of things, this view about the European Community's motives could hardly have been more different from the view held by the nonsignatory developed countries; the United States saw Lomé-I as a threat to its economic interests, especially its preference for multilateralism. The ACP countries believe the following: aid administration is cumbersome, Stabex pales behind the International Monetary System's compensatory financing facility, and all EC-ACP cooperation programs have been slow moving. Yet Lomé-I is the model for North-South arrangements, a stabilizing economic institution, and a source of world order. According to G.K. Helleiner, the ACPs don't expect the European Community to give up its safeguard clauses vis-à-vis ACP exports, but they do expect the Community to be constrained in their use.[3] It is particularly important that when the European Community ceases to offer an agreed-upon trading benefit, the ACP countries are to be compensated, just as under GATT and 201 decisions made by the United States. Instead, because the ACP countries have signed an agreement with the European Community, the latter threatens to impose voluntary restraints or worse upon the former without consultations. (The European Community refuses to support ACP desires to establish sugar-refining and textile industries because both would compete with dominant European interests; so much for industrial cooperation.) And the ACPs wants the European Community to follow the American practice and add ACP value added to European value added when goods are reexported back to the European Community—this is the U.S. border industry program with Mexico. There is also a common, if unacknowledged, lack of infrastructure: unavailable export credit on competitive terms, lack of adequate forward exchange credit, no insurance, inadequate transportation. Without improvements for intra-ACP trade, reductions in freight rates between the ACPs and the European Community, and the granting of permission to Stabex to process raw materials for export (sugar and textiles again), very little will change in terms of the barriers that the European Community has put up against ACP products.

Although the Group of 77 held to its view, it was possible, after three years, to see the presence of ACP imports into the European Community as marginal (documented by ACPs' 7.5 percent share of Community imports) and to see that third states (India, for example) enjoy more favorable import trade with the European Community under bilateral arrangements.[4] Though the ACP countries are significant textile suppliers, the ACPs want the European Community to keep its domestic market open for future exports of textile products, especially cotton and manufactured cotton products, instead of buying them elsewhere or subsidizing production in the nine European member states. In a similar vein, the bitter complaints over the difficulties in obtaining import licenses for rum (Protocol 7) and the inadequate distribution and promotion of bananas (Protocol 6), when trading conditions deteriorated worldwide for both products, began to take on a fault-finding character, with the ACP countries expecting more from Lomé because the Group of 77 saw more in it than really existed: preferential sale of surplus agricultural products from the European Community to the ACPs, systematic trade promotion, cooperation in the production of processed goods, protection of European Community markets for ACP semimanufactured and manufactured goods. The European Community, in turn, was reduced to hiding behind the oil-induced recession, GATT Tokyo Round negotiations, and UNCTAD discussions—a face-saving strategy that made the ACPs feel they were going to lose their competitive advantages and their 7.5 percent market share.

Under Stabex, those who thought commodity prices could be stabilized outside a world fund were wrong. It almost goes without saying that those who suffered most from commodity prices not keeping up with the inflation in prices for manufactured goods were the poorest ACP countries—those that had the least diversification in their economies and the smallest stake in the struggle over refining cane sugar, processing cotton, and manufacturing textiles between the European Community and the ACPs. The European Community agreed to add seven new products for Stabex (vanilla, cloves, pyrethrum, wool, mohair, gum arabic, ilang-ilang) to the stabilization system. The ACP countries want to develop processing industries for bauxite, copper, leather, sisal, timber, and cocoa under Stabex. The Group of 77 was somewhat discreet in its comments on Stabex because they saw it as the model from which UNCTAD could propose a worldwide common fund under the auspices of the United Nations. The opportunity to get the developed countries to transfer resources to the less developed countries, we were meant to understand, came first. The sugar protocol (3) contained the seeds of ill will because the price was supposed to be negotiated annually. The European Community was forced to guarantee to the ACP states the same revenue it guaranteed to beet sugar producers in the Community; it did so grudgingly and unilaterally, imposed storage charges, redefined intervention prices, and changed the en-tire price structure. It is not entirely clear what the European Community expects to gain by provoking the sugar controversy with the ACPs, nor does it matter. From the ACPs' anger, it was obvious that those who could least afford to lose their European Community market were being threatened by their former colonial protector.

It turns out, in fact, that one of the chief differences between the Group of 77 and the ACP countries was that in the world of Lomé the views of Black Africa about the need for a transnational code of conduct and international standards for accounting dominated the discussion, while in the Group of 77, as different nations formed pressure groups—first the Latin Americans, Asians, and Africans, and then the Caribbean and Pacific peoples—the developed countries could play one off against the other. Some of this difference is reflected in the radical proposals made by the ACPs. The Group of 77 struck a more moderate note with an image of responsible negotiations concerning special non-most favored nations rules for the less developed countries and concerning the graduation of less developed countries to full participation in the most favored nations rules of GATT. The experiment was over, ACP nations suggested, and the Lomé advances in North-South economic relationships represented by cooperation in industrial, financial, and technical areas would make possible a progressive transfer of resources to the less developed countries—a world envisioned by the ACPs, the Group of 77, and UNCTAD. Lomé-I ended with an explosion of the world's trade policy bureacracy (make work for unemployed Fabrian socialists, radical leftists, and Marxist-Leninists), an overlapping of national, regional, and international institutions and frustrations over the slow progress made in economic development by the less developed countries. In what seemed a caricature of their true reason for being, the ACPs were even pushing the new world economic order.

Lomé-II

In theory, Lomé-I is a grand success for the ACP countries because they have a special preferential relationship with the European Community. In fact, Lomé-I did not provide the ACPs with a significant redistribution in resources, an abundant Common Fund, or escape from safeguards—a new form of protectionism employed frequently by the European Community. The ACPs faced a new reality, in which UNCTAD V (Manila) was a failure and the Tokyo Round was deadlocked. In this new reality, the special preferential relationship was to be valued above everything, and no one else's views were to intrude—not those of the Group of 77 or UNCTAD. All of these parties, who are caught up in the consequences of decisions that they had no part in making, are left to respond as best they can to the signed protocols. Lomé acts; they only react. But in matters of economics, trade, and finance—and especially in these international matters—*re*action, by its very nature, is feeble. The power to create a special preferential trade relationship is the power to create a compelling new reality. Trade itself creates strong ties that may have little to do with the wisdom of lack thereof in regard to forming the special relationship, and these ties are likely to dominate business and government decisions about the Convention as a whole. When the protocols (on sugar, rum, bananas) are already in operation, the overwhelming impulse is to rally to their support, and, almost by implication, to the support of the cause for which they were drafted. The time when debate about a trade agreement might count is before it goes into operation, when alternatives still lie open. But now those who might prefer something different must live within the framework of the Convention, its protocols, and annexes. Then, unable to change what is already history, they are consigned to work on the "margin" as bureaucrats who must make it work no matter what they believe. Lomé-II illustrates the dilemma. Its European Community negotiators sought to consolidate Europe's access to raw materials and get guarantees for its overseas investments. And that's what the European Community got. But the ACPs, of course, wanted much more and had to settle for a lot less. The EC-ACP signatories of Lomé-II moved from "gamble to policy"; in effect, if local groups dared to challenge the protocols as protectionist interlopers, they were enemies to what Europe, Africa, the Caribbean, and the Pacific had deemed important.

Of course, under any preferential trade agreement, which is what Lomé-II still is, however few benefits the European Community may wish to grant ACP countries, bureaucratic decisions remain a powerful force—one before which even important textile and clothing merchants and sugar refiners have bowed. In Lomé-II, however, not only were the merchants not consulted beforehand but they were kept in the dark about the negotiations because the EC-ACP bureaucracy, in keeping with tradition, had made up its mind what to do. Keeping businessmen in the dark strengthens the bureaucracy. It builds a superior knowledge. Businessmen, of course, deal with the implementing regulations—they can hardly do otherwise when their goods can't cross frontiers without conforming to rules of origin, safeguard measures, and quota restrictions—but their complaints have little effect on what the EC-ACP bureaucracy decides. Much, much later, when all the decisions are added up (it turns out, for example, that contrary to the advance notices of the ACPs, few changes were made in the most important protocols of the Convention), the information, though it may reveal the facts about what was accomplished in 1979, has somehow become a part of the bureaucracy's superior knowledge. It has all the dullness of another government form and cobwebs of records stored for time and eternity. By then the Convention goes on, and the businessmen, unprepared as they are for the requirements of another bureaucracy, have become mere puppets on a string in the accomplishment of their own business.

Here's what happened under Lomé-II.[5]

Trade cooperation. All ACP products, with certain exceptions, enter the European Community duty-free. But then 75 percent of total ACP exports to the European Community enter duty-free under most favored nations, and 95 percent of ACP manufactured exports enter the European Community duty-free under the Community's generalized system of preferences. Lomé-II gives the four major ACP beef exporters (Kenya, Swaziland, Botswana, and Madagascar) a guaranteed quota of thirty thousand tons for five years and gives Caribbean rum producers a higher quota. Rules of origin have been made more lenient for the poorest ACP countries. Lomé-II does not change the sugar protocol, the safeguards provisions, and the rules of origin for most ACP countries: three items of critical importance to ACP.

Stabex. The list of eligible products is increased from thirty-four to forty-one. Both the "activation" and "dependence" thresholds have been lowered to 6.5 percent below average earnings over the preceding four years (2 percent for the forty-seven poorest countries). Grants will be made to the poorest countries, and interest-free loans spread over a seven-year payment period will be made to the ACP countries. Lomé-II ends the requirement that repayment be made as soon as there is a "good" year for export earnings.

Minex. Here's something new. Because the European Community is heavily dependent on Africa for minerals, it wanted to guarantee its supply. The European Community will spend $370 million to protect the export earnings of traditional producers of copper, cobalt, phosphates, manganese, bauxite and alumina, tin and iron ore (which is transferred from Stabex). The European Community will provide financial and technical assistance to help the ACPs explore for and mine new ores that can be sold to Europe. Minex meets the aspirations of key ACP countries that were left out of the Stabex system.

EC-ACP cooperation. Energy is one area targeted for greater industrial cooperation. Agriculture is a new area for cooperation, and if it proves to be successful, it will be helpful to the ACP countries, whose economies are primarily agricultural. More financial and technical cooperation is also provided. Seven billion dollars are to be spent between 1980 and 1985; some of it is earmarked for Stabex, Minex, regional cooperation, and emergency aid; the bulk of it goes to the poorest countries in the form of aid.

Every preferential trade agreement gives something both sides want. Lomé-II protects the domestic trade of the European Community through the sugar protocol, the safeguards provisions, and the rules of origin. For this, the European Community subsidizes Stabex, Minex, and cooperation agreements in agriculture, manufacturing, and social services. These are items the ACP countries wanted.

Behaving rather like a spoiled child, the ACP countries cried for more and made a beeline for protective support from the Group of 77 and UNCTAD, where they learned, among other things, that the special provisions granted by the Tokyo Round to the less developed countries were all they were going to get from the developed countries. This time.

Results

I'm beginning to believe that Lomé forces some special direction on the world's negotiations over trade. Lomé imparts the knowledge that cooperation between developed countries and less developed countries is possible. What is Lomé? How does it impart a special purpose? Here are some of the things Lomé has accomplished:

> Got the European Community and ACP bureaucracies to sit down regularly and hammer out solutions.
>
> Pushed more ACP goods into Europe.
>
> Forced the European Community to reconsider its expensive common agricultural policy for beet sugar.
>
> Put European Community money behind helping the social and economic development of the ACP countries.

Lomé is almost a decade old. Its discipline—outlined in the two conventions—is the Lomé Way, a process for making different groups of countries work together for the common good. Its way is powerful.

How does Lomé do it? It pledges cooperation for the future while forgetting the past. The Lomé bureaucracy is in control. The Group of 77 and UNCTAD are watching to see whether Lomé will go from success to success. Lomé has captured the hearts of bureaucrats around the world. Lomé.

Summary

The argument: Bilateral trade has come to Lomé and the European Community. Bilateral trade reduces some of the turbulence wrought by the desperately striving ACP economies that are at extreme risk in international trade. Bilateral trade without full reciprocity supports the agenda of the relatively well-managed, developed European Community economies. Bilateral trade without full reciprocity prevails because there exists no force of concept, authority, or perceived interest that will alter these realities.

Results: The United States has a role model in Lomé for perfecting its reciprocal bilateral free trade agreements with Canada, Mexico, the Caribbean countries, and other Latin American nations.

Recommendations: The United States should make several concessions to the Caribbean and poorest Latin American countries. First, it should give up reverse preferences. Second, it should minimize the obstacles to free access of Western Hemisphere goods into the United States. Third, it should include Western Hemisphere agricultural products in its farm programs. Fourth, it should help the Caribbean and poorer Latin American countries to diversify their exports. If Canada, Mexico, and the richer Latin American countries enter into reciprocal bilateral free trade agreements with us, then they too should offer the Caribbean and poorer Latin American countries the same concessions.

14
Graduation

According to the Lomé Convention, "products originating in the African, Caribbean, [and] Pacific States should be imported into the European Community free of customs duties and charges having *equivalent effect*... and the European Community shall not apply to imports of products originating in the ACP states any quantitative restrictions or measures having an *equivalent effect*" (my italics). Equivalent effect gives ACPs a margin of trade preference greater than for other less developed countries, but it also forces ACPs to protect their special relationship at all costs. The European Community worries about trade deflection when goods from other less developed countries slip into Europe through the ACPs, and it sees its carefully managed common external tariff unraveling before its eyes like a ball of yarn. Some of these separate difficulties come together for the European Community under the safeguard clause in attempts to restrict cotton textiles from the Ivory Coast, Madagascar, and Mauritius. They export significant volumes, at least 1 percent of the European Community's imports; and European Community restrictions are an extreme measure with high political costs for Lomé and other less developed countries. So rules of origin are the better instrument of trade policy imposed by the European Community against ACP products. ACP countries are still economically tied to their former colonial powers and still feel compelled to sell their narrow range of exports of primary products to the European Community, as we would expect. We note that coffee, copper, and cocoa account for about 40 percent of the non-oil exports of ACP countries to the European Community; that Ivory Coast accounts for one third of the coffee imports; Ivory

Coast and Nigeria account for 80 percent of the cocoa imports; and Zaire and Zambia account for almost all the copper imports. The list of ACP countries that are industrializing—where the share of value added in manufacturing is between 20 and 40 percent of total value added in commodity production—implies more industrial activity than really exists, because their mineral processing is for their domestic markets and not for the European Community. These eighteen industrializing ACP countries depend on opening up the European Community's textile export markets to diversify exports, expand manufacturing, raise incomes, and expand economic growth. Since intra-ACP trade is limited (4.5 percent of nonoil exports) and is unlikely to grow, because effective regional cooperation is lacking, the ACP countries come to Lomé demanding emphatically that their manufacturers be treated on equal terms with those of the European Community, the European Free Trade Association, and the Mediterranean countries. The ACP countries want tariff- and quota-free entry into the European Community for ACP manufactured goods; capital from the European Development Fund; subsidized loans from the European Investment Banks; and the transfer of technology and know-how through industrial cooperation between the two trading blocs.

The most important problem facing the Lomé trade preference system, according to Matthew McQueen, is "origin," the question of how much local content in ACP exports is enough to give them a European Community tariff preference.[7] The origin of goods is one of those issues that are complicated by today's multinational effort to produce inputs in several countries, assemble in still other countries, and sell the finished products in all possible markets. There are always shifts and changes in the location of production, and Lomé faces a string of excellent questions, both redundant and new, like freshmen students without the hope of tutoring by the European Community. Local ACP content must go through substantial transformation. Substantial value must be added in the production of goods within ACP countries, and it must occur to such an extent that there is a tariff jump in the Brussels Tariff Nomenclature (BTN), now known as the Nomenclature of the Customs Cooperation Council (CCCN). The ACP questions make clear to us not only how insistent the European Community is that there be a significant change in the character of goods, that is, a move from one four-digit tariff heading to the another, but also how many of the ACP goods are not given the benefit of equivalent effect because no tariff jump (no "substantial transformation") occurred. Sewing on buttons is not significant work to the European Community, even though it means income to the ACP poor. The ACPs recount, but in less than diplomatic terms—the kind of Community bureaucratic pettifoggery it impatiently dismisses as "nouveau colonialism."

It is, however, the European Community's A and B lists supplementing CCCN that draw blood. If there is a tariff jump but the European Community puts the ACP products on list A, then by Community definition no substantial transformation has taken place. To get on the good list, B, the European Community requires that a minimum value be added and a minimum amount of processing be done by the ACP exporting country; some processes (simple mixing and assembling) are excluded from getting products on list B. These two lists give the European Community the upper hand in trade negotiations. The imagery of colonialism's worst face comes to the fore when ministers of sovereign ACP countries must argue their case for B-list status with faceless Brussels bureaucrats. The ACP at first feels itself to be the industrious child and then, as it renegotiates Lomé without obtaining better terms, the young adult—headstrong but perforce still friendly—required to make more pressing reforms. The ACPs like to acquire pocketfuls of miscellaneous deals, and they watch over Lomé negotiations with a vigilant eye. They are much too impatient, much too demanding to wait indefinitely for origin to cumulate across ACP countries so that products can move from list A to list B. Instinctively, like an adult ready to make his mark on the world, the ACPs demand a derogation from the rules of origin. Sometimes derogations are given to the twenty-three least developed countries to keep them quiet and to support the EC-ACP bureaucracies. A system of trade preferences must be protected, and, in the ACPs' view, Lomé will have a long struggle with the rules of the European Community that do not apply equivalent effect to ACP products.

In a time described by the Tokyo Round as indulgent to trade preferences for the less developed countries, the European Community took lists A and B seriously, for it saw list A both as the guardian of sensitive European industries (textiles, footwear, leather products, electrical and electronic goods, optical and photographic goods, toys, and musical instruments) and as the protector from emerging, competitive African, Caribbean, and Pacific industries. There is a wealth of examples, always illuminating, about required levels of value added and processes deemed suitable for developed countries that possess a wide range of manufactured goods, strong flows of materials, and large domestic markets. For textiles, the European Community demands a multistage operation in which qualified garmets (for list B) must start from raw cotton or yarn and not from textile fabrics. The ACPs (from an UNCTAD study on harmonizing the rules of origin under the generalized system of preferences) point out how difficult it is to meet these demands. Matthew McQueen shows that only Nigeria, with its population and resource base, can meet the European Community rules for list B on its own.[2] Moreover, ACP products destined for export must have more intermediate imported goods if they are going to be competitive, because ACP labor doesn't have the skills to produce advanced technology cheaply. The Community's origin rules are important because they protect its manufacturers from ACP competition. The rules go beyond their proper role of preventing trade deflation. They remind ACP countries that the European Community is unwilling to abide by Lomé when the latter doesn't suit the European nations and that equivalent effect won't be provided for ACP goods when sensitive products of the Community are threatened. Again we see that the European Community is a thoroughly protectionist animal. Its active world is truly the Treaty of Rome; its ancillary world is its trading agreements with the European Free Trade Association, the Mediterranean countries, and Lomé; and its forum is GATT.

We Americans fail to realize that European Community rules of origin permit European multinationals to provide goods for and set up factories in ACP countries to the exclusion of other multinational firms. The European Community has built in a bias for European technology, resources, capital, and management. This is tied trade. It forces ACP countries to do business with European cartels and inhibits the growth of ACP industries.

Multilateral free trade is buried under the European Community's rules of origin for Lomé.

Equivalent Effect

At the same time of Lomé I and II, the European Court of Justice was defining equivalent effect for the ten member states of the European Community. The Court interpreted Articles 30 to 36 of the Treaty of Rome. From its cases have come Brussels Directive No. 70/50. The following government regulations, which have the equivalent effect of quantitative restrictions, are prohibited.

> First, measures that lower the value of the imported product.
>
> Second, measures that subject imported products to conditions that one different from those laid down for domestic products and that are more difficult to satisfy.
>
> Third, measures that only subject imported products to conditions about shape, size, weight, composition, presentation, identification, or putting up that are different from those for domestic products and that are more difficult to satisfy.
>
> Fourth, measures that only hinder the purchase by private individuals of imported products or that give preference to domestic products.

This is the Court's *Dassonville* formula. It comes from Case 8/74 (1974) ECR, 837, *Procureur du Roi* v. *Dassonville,* in which Belgium made it more difficult to import Scotch whiskey via France than via the United Kingdom. Here's what the Court said: "All trading rules enacted by member-states which are capable of hindering directly or indirectly, actually or potentially, intra-Community trade, are to be considered as measures having an effect equivalent to quantitative restrictions."

The European Community was speechless. Here's the interpretation of the Court's decision:

> "All trading rules" pertains to production and manufacturing, marketing and distribution among member states for goods, services, industrial, and intellectual property. "Buy French" or "Buy British" are prohibited.
>
> "By member-states" includes the European Community itself.
>
> "Capable of hindering" means that member states can't prohibit imports even temporarily. It doesn't matter whether rules are insignificant.
>
> "Directly or indirectly" is a per-se prohibition of all discriminatory measures affecting interstate trade, whether they are Community or member state rules or both. The effect on interstate trade is decisive.
>
> "Actually or potentially" means that Community and member state rules can be prohibited even when they have not become operational.
>
> "Intra-Community trade" means that Community trade must be free of member state restrictions.

But!

According to the European Court of Justice, the "reasonable measures" clause of Article 36 of the Treaty of Rome permits member states to impose measures having the equivalent effect of quantitative restrictions, whether these be for economic or other reasons. Scarcity, balance of payments, national defense, and human, animal, and plant protection are valid reasons. However, derogation from the principle of free trade with reasonable measures under Article 36 can be carried out only if Community rules exist (the so-called harmonization process). Such derogation is permitted between domestic (or Community) goods and imported (non-Community) goods when public health and safety are involved. Inspections for the public goods are always understood to have the equivalent effect of quantitative restrictions, are always justified, can be discriminatory, and can be carried out by member states as long as the border checks don't frustrate the Community's common commercial system.

René Barents concluded that the "reasonable measures" clause does not cover economic policy; the following are not permitted: unfair competition, fiscal controls, reducing consumer protection, public health and environmental controls.[3] This is the Court's *Cassis de Dijon* formula. It comes from Case 120/79 (1979) ECR, 649, *Cassis de Dijon* (*Rewe*), in which Germany required an alcohol content of 25 percent for liqueur. French fruit liqueur must have between 15 and 20 percent alcohol. Germany banned *Cassis de Dijon* because it failed to meet the minimum alcohol content. Here's what the Court said: "There is therefore no reason why, provided that they have been lawfully produced and marketed in one of the member-states, alcohol beverages should not be introduced into any other member-state." The member states were speechless.

National laws may be applied only if they protect certain narrow, national interests; they cannot be applied when a Community measure exists, when they affect interstate trade, and when their purpose can be accomplished by other means. When a member state makes it more difficult for importers to obtain a certificate for importation of goods that are already in free circulation in another member state, the former has put into place a measure having the equivalent effect of a quantitative restriction. Article 36 must be interpreted as narrowly as possible, since it constitutes a fundamental exception to European Community law.

And!

Again according to the European Court of Justice, equivalence is what counts. This is the *Fietje* Case 27/80 (1980) ECR, 3839, in which the Dutch government prohibited the sale of a German alcohol drink because its label about alcoholic content was in German instead of containing the words "likeur" or "liqueur," as required by Dutch law. The Court held that a labeling requirement is not justified where the imported goods already have a label containing at least the same information in a form which the consumer could understand equally well.[4] This means that real products from member states can be sold anywhere in the European Community, and it gives European consumers a wider preference and range of products to buy. It also forces the European Community in the direction of greater harmonization.

Citizens of the ten member states were speechless.

With little fuss, the European Community imposed equivalent effect on interstate trade among the ten member states but took reasonable measures against the goods of nonmember states, particularly goods that compete successfully against sensitive products of the European Community. That the European Community is not living up to its obligations under Lomé is obvious. That the European Community is backing off from its commitments to Mediterranean, North American, and other GATT countries is obvious, too.

Differential Treatment

Out there on the trade frontier, smack up against the great or ghastly unknown, it can get, oh, so very hot. Sometimes the temperature is measured in heated words. (Sometimes there are polemics and diatribes.) Stay out there long enough and it's a sure bet you'll begin to see flames. Flames that come out of all mouths. Flames from everywhere. These last few years, the developed world spent a lot of time with the dragons of the new international economic order—the uncharted wilderness of seeking to graduate the LDCs. And we've seen the flames. For example: To phase out differential treatment in trade for less developed countries, and require that they compete under the generally applicable rules of the GATT trading system means to end their infant industry protection and the preferential access they receive in markets of the developed countries. You end subsidies on exports of nonprimary products; their quantitative restrictions for protective purposes on imports; and their ability to impose exchange controls on current transactions and engage in discriminatory currency arrangements; and you insist that they offer reciprocal concessions for negotiated tariff reductions. Right away, as unmistakably as an excitable Brazilian refusing recompense, graduation linkage between special treatment for LDCs and its phasing out for the most advanced LDCs becomes the divisive issue of the 1980s. How, we ask the Brazilian, did he expect the least developed countries to export more and create new industries if they couldn't sell without restrictions to the middle-income markets—like Brazil?

"Brazil [substitute Mexico, South Korea, Taiwan, Singapore, India, Nigeria, Ivory Coast, and others] must upgrade itself first," he said, and for a second we understood his selfishness. But then he launched into a long and devious spiel about the injustice of "equal treatment of unequals" and the inappropriateness of GATT's most favored nations principle and its rule of reciprocity, including the noninterventionist role for government in international trade and payments. By the time he was done, we heard him say that trade must become Brazil's engine of development through the active efforts of government to redistribute world resources in favor of the less developed countries, and we were reduced to asking, "Are you serious?"

"Yes," he said, "we are, and we expect our differential treatment with respect to export subsidies to continue, too. We won't subscribe to an outright ban on export subsidies for nonprimary products (GATT Article XVI [4]). We mind if importing countries offset our export subsidies by imposing countervailing duties (Article VI) because they have experienced material injury." (The United States did just that against Brazilian oranges and Brazil agreed to raise the price of its oranges delivered in the United States to compensate for the export subsidy.) "We want special protection for our domestic market. We want special access to your developed markets."

A roomful of diplomats, trade negotiators, and hangers-on listened respectfully as Brazil cried out for inclusion within Lomé. Developed nations must do positive things to help the less developed countries export their products to Europe, Japan, and North America. The group spoke in tongues (an extended family of aroused adolescents, from an aroused Latin America right up to a bemused Pacific Rim) and gave a recitation about how GATT makes no provision for graduation. Instead, GATT recognizes the differential treatment of less developed countries in Article XVIII (Governmental Assistance to Economic Development) and Part IV (Trade and Development) comprising Articles XXXVI through XXXVIII.

> Article XVIII gives special dispensation to countries "in the early stages of development" to use tariffs and quotas to protect

> infant industries or to defend the balance of payments. What are the criteria for country eligibility? None. When has the article been invoked? Rarely. No GATT case law exists. So graduation is, at best, only implicit in Article XVIII.
>
> Part IV consists of commitments made by the developed countries to the less developed countries. Are the less developed countries defined? No.
>
> Article XXXVII (4) is a commitment by less developed countries "to take appropriate action in implementation of the provisions of Part IV for the benefits of the trade of other less developed contracting parties" insofar as such action is consistent with their individual development, financial, and trade needs. The more advanced less developed countries have commitments toward the least developed countries. So graduation is hinted at.

In 1971, the GATT signatories granted two waivers of the most favored nations principle to permit preferential treatment of trade by less developed countries:

> One. The less developed countries could extend preferential trade among themselves by signing a special protocol. This protocol did not show they could graduate out of these special privileges.
>
> Two. The individual countries could apply the generalized system of preferences to the less developed countries. The generalized system of preferences does include graduation principles. The less developed countries themselves do not graduate, but certain products or portions of their external trade in such products do. For example, the European Community gives reduced tariffs until the product quota is filled; then all other products above the quota are subject to regular most favored nations duty. The United States eliminates a less developed country's generalized system of preferences when that country's exports exceed 50 percent of total American imports of the product or exceed a predetermined dollar ceiling.

In 1979, the Tokyo Round endorsed an enabling clause for graduation, so all the GATT codes (government procurement, standards and technical regulation, subsidies and countervailing duties, and safeguards against "market disruption") except customs valuation include differential treatment for less developed countries, along with the graduation principle that the codes will become increasingly applicable to the less developed countries as their development progresses.

The less developed countries are forced to sign the subsidies code whether they like it or not, because if they don't, they immediately become subject to U.S. countervailing duties on their subsidized exports to the United States. The United States does not have to apply an injury test to impose countervailing duties against those LDCs that refuse to sign the subsidies code. Even big-mouth Brazil signed and agreed to phase out its export subsidies so it would not be subject to U.S. countervailing duties unless material injury against a U.S. industry could be proved (Brazilian oranges, 1983).

But the less developed countries are not forced to give up quantitative import restrictions or other measures of equivalent effect. There is no carrot-and-stick approach to compel the more advanced LDCs to liberalize their trade practices and open up their home markets. Most of the discussion about graduation is inflammatory, overly emotional, diabolic, and singed with bitterness, so it is of little use in forcing advanced LDCs to give up some of their preferential treatment.

When the Brazilian monologue ended, the developed countries sidled up to a bar in GATT's Geneva headquarters and put the less developed countries through their paces. "Trade not aid," they burbled dutifully. The developed countries' diplomats carefully selected the next round, an unblended malt whiskey, real Scotch, from Scotland, and then leaned back to hear the Brazilian say, "I can only drink the real thing here because my government keeps out Scotland's best with high import duties, quantitative restrictions, and other measures of equivalent effect—indeed, the cruelest fate of them all."

Countries that have graduated in the post–World War II period: Japan, Israel, Ireland, Greece, Spain, and Portugal. (Greece, Spain, and Portugal became the tenth, eleventh and twelfth member states of the European Community, respectively. Israel has a comprehensive bilateral free trade agreement with the United States. And Japan has become one of the big three industrial powers in the world.)

Market Share

More difficult than graduation, perhaps, but no less intractable is the Third World's rise as a steel power—a prototype of the new world that will be here tomorrow. Within ten years, the less developed countries have doubled their capacity. Indonesia produces seamless steel pipe for its own oil and gas industry, and by so doing, has devastated the traditional markets of Japan, Europe, and the United States. Even worse, more than 40 percent of the steel imported into the United States comes from Brazil, Mexico, Argentina, South Korea, Taiwan, South Africa, and Spain. Third World producers are highly competitive, and this challenge can be met only by modernization and greater efficiency in the United States' steel industry.

When we talk with our Brazilian colleague, we find that his government-owned steel firm, Siderbras, owes $7.7 billion externally—the equivalent of $1,000 for every ton of steel it produces—and $10.9 billion domestically. Its debt is a millstone. And because Brazil is hopelessly overborrowed, it has to live with a domestic price structure averaging 40 to 50 percent below world prices. Given falling domestic demand, rising world output, and the need for foreign currency—to pay off its staggering debts—Siderbras offers an 80 percent dumping margin on Brazilian imports to the United States (according to United States Steel).

As far as steel producers from the LDCs are concerned, this is the time to gain market share. They cannot wait for the European Community to open up Lomé to the Latin American and Pacific Rim countries. Instead, they intend to displace the European Community and Japan in the American market. Then they will be able to trade this card for guaranteed access to the United States through the Caribbean Basin Initiative and a wider hemispheric preferential trade pact. Lomé's influence is long-lasting and grows yearly, no matter how the European Community treats the African, Caribbean, and Pacific countries.

Summary

The argument: Bilateral trade between two regional trading groups is not free of problems. More similarity exists among members of the European Community than among ACP countries. As the United States crafts its own bilateral trading agreements with Canada, Mexico, and the Caribbean countries, each agreement must be different and must serve the best interests of the nation involved. Canada should enjoy a comprehensive reciprocal bilateral free trade regime with us. Mexico should have access to markets and capital without the imposition of graduation under the generalized system of preferences. The United States should guarantee investments (and jobs) in Mexico. The Caribbean countries need special help from the United States and Canada because they are so poor. This includes stabilization funds and the relaxation of barriers on trade in sugar and other basic crops. The Caribbean Basin Initiative must be amended to correct its deficiencies for the Caribbean countries. Other Latin American countries that seek bilateral free trade with the United States must commit themselves to help the poorer nations of the hemisphere.

Results: The United States has an opportunity to learn from the mistakes of the European Community and do a better job in making bilateral free trade work for the benefit of the less developed countries.

Recommendations: Reciprocal bilateral free trade means the United States guarantees market share to those countries that agree to open up their domestic markets to our goods. It means that the United States does not guarantee market share to those countries with which it has no formal bilateral agreement. Therefore, the market share of the U.S. market currently controlled by the Europeans and the Japanese should be reduced, and that share should be redistributed to the Canadians, Mexicans, and nations in the Caribbean and elsewhere in Latin America.

15
Debt

At the International Monetary Fund (IMF), the distinction between trade and payments is based on the principles of less developed country graduation and differentiation among LDCs. Industrial countries are refraining from imposing restrictions on payments and transfers for current international transactions, and from engaging in discriminatory currency arrangements or multiple currency practices; and most of the payments system in "legitimate" hands swaps lines of credits with skill and discriminate practice. Thus, the IMF debate on LDC debt grows more heated. Graduation comes about by subscribing to IMF Article VIII.[1] Consider Brazil's insistence on maintaining restrictive and discriminatory payments practices—IMF Article XIV—while its domestic economy grows and develops. One's instant reaction to the news is, of course, outrage, for it is hard to see why Brazil (or Taiwan, South Korea, or Turkey) should be protected indefinitely. Undoubtedly, as the years dragged on, the advanced less developed countries had fallen into their own routine, spending the months at whatever tasks are called for by their bloated government bureaucracies—mini-devaluations, mainly—watching for drops in exports that meant the local currency was misaligned. At the proper moment, they would give favored exports a very cheap local-currency dollar rate and see sales overseas explode, because a country can manipulate its exchange rate successfully whenever its trading partners do nothing—don't retaliate. And then in the 1970s, that way of life ended, their hopes crushed under the weight of the worst payments crisis they had known in the post–World War II period. After the anger passed, the Article VIII countries began the long and difficult process of recycling petrodollars: short-term Arab oil money that was filtered through the privately owned multinational banks became long-term investment capital for new industry, modern transportation, communications systems, and alternative sources of energy. But as the debt crisis flashed around the world, it became clear that debtors borrowed too much and lenders lent too much, and that the world economy had slowed so much that the debt once carried easily by the LDCs had now become like lead on their shoulders. The IMF, together with the United States and its allies, was forced to reschedule the debt of the less developed countries: how, we asked, could the Mexicans have so miscalculated the price of oil that they acquired a debt of over $90 billion? And many of us are perplexed at each new crisis announced by Brazil, Argentina, and Venezuela: which country should we allow to go under in order to show them all that they must get their houses in order? But this impulse is tempered by the reality of an interdependent world. Nations don't default. Countries must extend their debt, and the IMF must reschedule the debt of the less developed countries. What can be done with the Latin American countries when no one is willing to let Poland default? Those communists are enemies, dangerous and perhaps true believers; so what? Demands to force default shift quickly into demands for more careful lending policies, which leads to demands for stricter accounting rules. The less developed countries are not searching for graduation; instead, they are gripped by blatant nationalism, Europe's pre–World War I mania, which makes them unwilling to give up any particle of their independence to multilateral or bilateral institutions unless they can control these institutions for their own purposes. Brazil and all its autarkic comrades in the Third World and elsewhere, including Lomé, are playing a statist game we don't recognize for stakes we cannot measure, and it's useless to insist they follow our rules. The existing payments system—unjust, structurally unsound, and none too steady—has some virtues: it allows for a transfer of resources and for the calculation of who will lend and who will pay, and it provides a forum when rescheduling becomes a necessity. At the very least, it gives us liquidity and a sense that the world will go on. Insistence on graduation rips away the facade—it is hard to imagine that Brazil will relinquish its Article XIV status. As we lose the ability to force graduation, we must be careful about granting any more preferential trade agreements. Perplexity becomes befuddlement: we want to do something about graduation, but what?

Conditionality

We spent the 1970s and early 1980s stabilizing the balance of payments of less developed countries by working through the International Monetary Fund—the world's credit institution for countries in financial difficulties—which manages the Compensatory Financing Facilty (CFF), the Buffer Stock Financing Facility (BSFF), the Extended Fund Facility (EFF), the Oil Facility (OF), the Trust Fund (TF), the Supplementary Financing Facility (SFF), and various other subsidy schemes—programs that are not designed to promote graduation. Heavy users of the IMF in the 1970s were India, Argentina, the Philippines, Chile, and Pakistan; these five accounted for 29 percent of the total drawings by less developed countries from the IMF credit facilities. By the end of 1982, 80 percent of the commitments of the IMF were going to countries with per-capita income of less than $300,[2] in other words, to the poorest, least developed ACP countries. The IMF shifted its use of credit facilities to support those countries with little or no domestic oil and insufficient foreign exchange earnings from trade with the European Community to pay for imported oil.

Here are some terms used by the IMF to explain what it requires from countries that seek credit:

> *Conditionality.* The IMF requires borrowers to meet certain economic and financial obligations.
>
> *Low conditionality.* Borrowers must make reasonable efforts to solve their balance-of-payments problems. They can borrow from the first-credit tranche, CFF, and BSFF.
>
> *High conditionality.* Borrowers must receive approval of their economic program to raise taxes, cut spending, devalue the cur-

rency, and diversify trade. They can borrow from the upper-credit tranche and EFF.

Letters of intent. Borrowers sign these with the IMF before the latter issues them credit on an installment basis.

Low-conditionality drawings from the credit facilities, representing about 90 percent of total lending by the IMF, were prevalent throughout the 1970s. But by 1982, over 75 percent of total IMF lending was from high-conditionality drawings from these same credit facilities. In fact, several factors converged to make the IMF a development animal: the softening of IMF conditionality following the review of Conditionality Guidelines in 1979; the liberalization of the credit facilities; the lengthening of the assistance period; an increase in the quotas; and a policy of enlarged access for the less developed countries. The IMF became as deeply involved in the lives of the LDCs as it could. High conditionality was its latest bit of education, and it was a sobering experience, even though it started out with fundamental deteriorations in the balance of payments due to the 1979 oil price increase and ended up with long-term secular declines in export performance due to the 1981–1983 world recession. The IMF became the single most important source of funds for some less developed countries (Peru, Jamaica, Burma, and Sri Lanka)—the least creditworthy—and a catalyst for Eurodollars and private commercial funds for other less developed countries (Mexico, Brazil, Argentina, and Venezuela), the more creditworthy. High conditionality has been the main experience of the IMF for a long time.

Some say that conditionality by the IMF breeds loss of output and unemployment; ignores economic development for short-run corrections of balance-of-payments problems; stems from economic factors outside the control of the less developed countries; produces performance criteria too narrow for their successful use; and can't be accomplished because little or no funds are generated from domestic sources. So say the contentious ministers of the LDCs, who wish to cover up their own internal economic mismanagement and their own inability to adjust domestic programs to new world conditions.

Domestic mistakes. Expansionary demand policies, cost and price distortions related to multiple exchange rates, price freezes, and wage controls.

External problems. Oil. Recession. Declines in exports. Deterioration in terms of trade.

Servicing the debt. Interest and principal on what was borrowed before.

The IMF says that conditionality depends on limiting domestic credit to both government and the private sector; restricting new external debt; setting up minimum levels of foreign exchange reserves; and reducing current payments arrears and devaluation. Occasionally, the IMF says: no new multiple exchange rates, no bilateral payments agreements, no restrictions on current payments, no limitations on imports.

Let's stop for a moment and sum up. The IMF has too few resources to graduate any country. It can influence private capital flows to advanced LDCs but not to the poorest African, Caribbean, and Pacific countries. There's a lot of frustration with the International Monetary Fund. And no hope of any Article XIV country voluntarily giving up this protection and becoming an Article VIII country.

Conditionality is all right for one small country, or maybe for a few countries. High conditionality cannot be applied to all less developed countries simultaneously and be successful.[3] How can all less developed countries both reduce imports and expand exports at the same time? None of the developed countries will bear the burden of these exports from Lomé, Latin America, or Asia.

Unchecked IMF (and private) lending, with conditionality as its backbone, will not bring adjustment to balance-of-payments deficits, improvement in terms of trade for exports, or economic development leading to graduation. Conditionality locks the economic stables of the LDCs after government officials and private interests send their flight capital overseas, after consumers' imports enter countries through the black market, and after exports simply disappear statistically. Conditionality damages current growth and long-term investment. It requires the whole future of world economic development to rest on an ever-growing flow of IMF and private international bank lending. It tolerates high interest rates, slow growth, a dollar premium, and a long-term tendency to throw good money after bad.

Rescheduling. It's a way of postponing the day of default, at the cost of a bigger default when it comes. It's also called buying time.

To be rescheduled, less developed countries must accept IMF conditionality and, with that, economic austerity—hard times to pay off yesterday's debt. Given that export earnings are depressed because of protectionist policies in the developed countries and that the terms of trade are going against the less developed countries, repayment is impossible.

Rescheduling causes a vicious circle of financial fiction, human panic, and ruinous borrowing at any cost.[4] To pile more IMF credit, bank debt, and other resources on top of past lending is to opt for more inflation. And default.

Countries do default on their commercial debts.[5] In the 1930s, first Bolivia, Peru, and Brazil, then Ecuador, Costa Rica, and all of Latin America (save Argentina, Venezuela, and the Dominican Republic) defaulted. Then Hungary, Yugoslavia, Romania, Poland, and Bulgaria. Then Hitler's Germany blocked its payments for foreign debt.

Countries become more stubborn in their defaults precisely when their economies start improving. Once these countries consolidate their ravished economies and return to political stability, their determination to withstand foreign creditors grows as well. Moreover, creditor governments do not unleash retaliatory trade against the defaulters; instead, they blame the bankers for overlending, for acting like drunken sailors on shore leave.

Since the 1820s, the Latin American countries have defaulted en masse repeatedly, about every fifty years.[6] After a period of default, they reestablish their credit by settling (readjusting in the 1930s, rescheduling in the 1980s) their outstanding claims for a fraction of their face value. The stigma of default is expunged from the record, and they can then obtain new, expanded credit.

Mexico—1930s. Mexico—1980s. It holds a preeminent position as one of the world's greatest debtors. An April 1981 prospectus for a loan of $50 million on behalf of Pemex, the state oil company, said: "Full debt service has been paid when due upon all external debt issued by the Federal Government of Mexico since the adoption of the constitution of 1917." Mexico had defaulted on most of its pre-1914 obligations. It was prevented from raising new loans until 1943, when, under the pressure of World War II, the United States and Great Britain persuaded Thomas W. Lamont of J. P. Morgan and Co. and his fellow bondholders to take $50 million in full payment of the $500 million of outstanding debts.

Will Mexico be permitted to write down $90 billion to $9 billion in the 1980s? Probably.

Regional Integration

Throughout the sovereign debt crisis of Mexico, Brazil, Argentina, and other Latin American countries, Latin America's attempts at intraregional integration were foundering. Moreover, new industries were stagnating.

Domestic demand did not grow, and these industries were saddled with unused capacity, output that needed export subsidies to be sold outside Latin America in countries that viewed this as dumping and imposed countervailing duties and other "voluntary" restrictions. No amount of market widening through integration by the Latin American Free Trade Association (LAFTA) could boost domestic demand sufficiently to absorb all the industrial capacity created by duplication among each of the twenty-one countries in Latin America. No integration scheme could offer LAFTA the wherewithal to create its own machine-tool industry so that domestic industries in Latin America might become self-sustaining, free from foreign-source inputs, and unexposed to changes in the terms of trade. Never did LAFTA command enough strength to force a scale of operations in a few countries that would enable Latin American prices for exports to become competitive with world prices. Instead, nations protected their weak industries, hoarded scarce foreign exchange, and never could get out of the vicious cycle of trade restrictions, more debt, and no graduation.

One can concentrate on foreign exchange as the critical scarce resource (one can but one shouldn't) and never understand anything else. The Latin Americans, believing as they did, that their deteriorating terms of trade were causing a widening gap between export earnings and import needs, faced severe balance-of-payments difficulties and ruthlessly cut out all but the most essential imports. In the 1960s, the IMF could offer little solace because it insisted that LAFTA countries cut spending (and hence imports)—a deflationary program that was seen as a last resort—in order to receive IMF limited credit finance for reducing the severity of balance-of-payments difficulties. The Latin American countries chose, predictably, permanent import restrictions and exchange controls. True protectionists, these Latin Americans, for when the IMF greatly expanded its credit facilities and private international credit exploded—both occurrences resulting from the need to recycle petrodollars—the enormous boost in international liquidity did not change the way in which these formerly unacceptable debtors carried out their foreign trade with countries outside of LAFTA. And because the world was awash with loanable funds, LAFTA countries could borrow money to finance their balance-of-payments problems without making adjustments and corrections in their industrial, monetary, and economic policies. When the multinational banks gave away these megabucks to Brazil, Mexico, Argentina, Venezuela, and others, they did not ask for conditionality by the IMF, and none was offered. All saw the 1970s as a wonderful opportunity to finance their present and future current account deficits. And certainly everyone thought this was a new beginning through which they could open themselves up to world trade, and import restrictions, and force domestic industries to be more competitive overseas.

Worse for the Latin Americans than too much money were too few markets in the developed countries. The latter's recession became the former's depression. Even allowing for all the choices open to Latin Americans for ending restrictions or reducing them—allowing for the shift in intellectual support from import substitution to demand (and export) management—the recession's depth found the LAFTA countries deep in debt and with no new markets open to them. They seemed not to know what to do. It's often said that economics is the management of the possible; autarky, by contrast, is the management of extremes. The world community can condemn this second practice by excluding trade with governments that adhere to it (such as Burma), but this approach is not a very healthy one—especially since the world must pick up the pieces when these governments are turned out. The presidential regime of José Lopez

Portillo in Mexico, for instance, was a nationalistic drama of mirrors. Mexico during its oil boom of the late 1970s wanted to become less dependent on traditional overseas suppliers, such as the United States; however, Mexico refused to do what the other LDCs had done and join GATT. Instead, Mexico chose to come under the tutelage of imported Fabian socialists from the Cambridge School of economics, and close its borders to the world. Countries must import in order to export. This is not an aggressive American notion; it is known as foreign commerce and trade, in which all governments have engaged, with good and bad results, since antiquity, and often in the face of problems far more intractable than Mexico's. The other newly industrialized countries—Taiwan, South Korea, Ivory Coast, and Cameroons—have done this—and more. They have created industrial and agricultural systems whose products command world markets because they are price-competitive and provide quality to the customer. This is also the tried-and-true method.

When Latin Americans—perhaps because of too much money or perhaps because of too little skill in managing the possible—proclaimed in 1980 that LAFTA had become the Latin American Integration Association, the world declared itself mildly encouraged but added that it wasn't expecting anything new.[7] The developed countries believe that regional associations among less developed countries don't work, because there is little intraregional trade, a lack of common economic purposes, and, without Lomé-type ties to the advanced industrial countries, no chance for success among such associations. That sort of judgment is where the world comes down on LAFTA (or LAIA), the Caribbean Common Market, and others. In all north-south discussions, the developed countries have announced their prescription—reciprocal bilateral free trade—and the less developed countries are ready to it. If this proves to be more than patent medicine, it will be a happy day, for in the past decade, with one less developed country after another, the United States, the European Community, and Japan have haggled like tourists in a foreign bazaar who insist on obtaining their souvenirs at little or no cost. The developed countries want access to LDC markets for free. As we have seen, the friendly Lomé, Asean, (Asian Economic Association, includes Philippines, Indonesia, Singapore, Malaysia and others) and LAFTA countries tell their world customers to get lost unless the former get free access to the markets of the developed countries, too. Somewhere in all this there is a deal to be made under the banner of reciprocal bilateral free trade between the United States and Canada on the one side and the Caribbean and Latin America countries on the other. Otherwise, the less developed countries can threaten the developed countries with default on $600 billion of debt ($300 billion in Latin American debt alone). Will they go through with their threat? Probably not. Will they decide to pay out a maximum of 10 percent of their export earnings to service their debt? Probably so.

North-South

When debtor nations contemplate their debt, they generally wonder where all the money went. But there they are (Brazil, Mexico, Argentina, and Venezuela—these Latin American countries owe about one third of the total LDC debt in the world, or about $200 billion), together with the International Monetary Fund and many unhappy banks, contemplating. They are contemplating what looked like riches—oil, copper, iron, and bauxite—and how these brought no visible improvement in their life, fortunes, and ability to service the debt. They are looking hard at their debt and their negative economic growth. Per-capita national income actually fell between 1979 and 1982. All the development projects—steel mills, aluminum plants, railroads, pipelines, copper mines—of the past decade, perhaps, investment gone berserk, without technical people and management to make it work. Or the consumption of luxury goods gone mad. Or the foreign bank accounts—precious foreign exchange squandered, lost irrevocably to the nation. The debtor nations have wondered, also, what combination of high interest rates, tight money, reduced trade barriers, lowered price controls, and expanded public employment could possibly conquer inflation. Then, before their very eyes, they uncovered debt after debt from the government's state-owned corporations: the least-known group of debts that doubled what the countries owed their bankers. All of this has meant a freeze on their economies. Most of their debt is short-term. They want to postpone it, but their banks won't refinance it without high conditionality from the IMF, and IMF insists on drastic domestic austerity policies. The Latin Americans must face up to mushrooming public employment, government spending, and the massive debt of the state enterprises, along with their dependence on selling oil, minerals, and other primary products instead of manufactured goods to the industrialized countries. Even the most visionary among them knows the game is up. Where is Uncle Sam, they'd like to know, when they really need him?

Side effects—north.

American exports to Mexico dropped by one-third in 1982.[8] Mexico is the United States' third-largest trading partner, after Canada and Japan, and Mexico accounts for one half of all U.S. exports to Latin America.

American exports to Argentina fell, too. And the sharp economic contraction in Brazil and Venezuela was felt via a drop in 1983 U.S. exports, particularly in machinery and transport equipment, which make up 45 percent of total exports to Latin America.

The export of scientific and business machinery dropped by 16 percent in 1982. In 1983, the exports of computers and other high-technology items began to fall also, declining by 38 percent. So U.S. exports to Latin America dropped by 25 percent within one year, from 1981 to 1982. Lost American jobs totaled 250,000 in 1982 and 150,000 in 1983 because of lost exports to Latin America.

Side effects—south.

1981, 1982, and 1983. Per-capita national income in Latin America fell for three consecutive years. And to add to Mexico's misery, American companies reduced their foreign direct investment by $1.5 billion in 1982.

The vicious circle. High debt, autarkic economic policies, lost jobs, reduced investment, fewer exports, no imports, an empty foreign exchange till.

Visions of letting the Latin Americans solve their own problems filled some congressional heads, and the 1983 IMF appropriations bill met with resistance. But the congressmen looked hard at this illiquid debt, and while they stared at it they had second thoughts. It would be risky business. The banks certainly couldn't be counted on—not with Bank of America, Chase Manhattan, and Citicorp making loans with other banks here and abroad. And should they act on their emotion, closing down the sovereign-country debt window and casting the country out of the world's economy? Anyway, they reflected, by what right could they place a higher value on bankers' repayment schedules than on the survival of Mexicans, Brazilians, and all the other peoples who have lately begun to try to prosper? We can hardly expect them to support our other initiatives if we don't help them in their hour of crisis. If we have to help, shouldn't we do so gracefully rather than grudgingly? And if we are to be their lender of last resort, won't the Latin Americans, inevitably, wind up buying more from us than they sell us?

Summary

The argument: Bilateral free trade with Mexico and other Latin American countries means helping them solve their sovereign debt crisis. In 1984 and 1985, Mexico has been treated by the United States as if it were another Federal Reserve District. Monies have been made available to Mexico to be sure there is no financial collapse there. Mexico should be treated as if it were within the customs union of the United States and Puerto Rico. Reciprocal bilateral free trade with Mexico means loan guarantee programs for corporate American investors in Mexico and the free exportability of their Mexican-made goods back to the United States. If Mexico finds this politically unfeasible, let the Mexican states contiguous to the United States form a free trade area with the United States, and let this be a test case of how economic development occurs as markets for goods and services are broadened within a regional common market. A healthy Mexico means a further enhancement of the North American free trade area.

Results: The United States knows now that resolution of the sovereign debt crisis of the Latin American countries goes hand in hand with restarting their economies through access to U.S. and Canadian markets.

Recommendations: Reciprocal bilateral free trade means the United States guarantees market share to Mexican agricultural and manufactured goods in return for the freedom to invest and produce goods in Mexico for use there and for export to the United States. Reciprocal bilateral free trade means that the United States will put no restrictions on the number of goods Mexico sells in the United States. Some U.S. industries will suffer and some may permanently relocate to Mexico. This is structural adjustment; the United States has been doing this for the past two hundred years, most recently from the North and Midwest to the South and Southwest. Now is the time for the Mexican north and perhaps central Mexico also to benefit from the sort of structural adjustment that takes place from time to time in North America.

16
A New Order

Dare us to create a new international economic order, and, by heaven, we will.

There are ten codes of conduct for multinational firms (or transnational enterprises), and these codes form the basis of what governments expect from such firms. They are the rules of the game. The developed countries want to minimize the impact of these firms on the balance of payments, prices, and taxation; and the less developed countries want to minimize the impact of these firms on the distribution of wealth, income, and power. The LDCs insist that these firms must agree to local ownership, domestic content, and national control.

Andean Common Market (Ancom). The rules limit foreign ownership; insist on a fifteen-year fadeout to a maximum of 49 percent foreign ownership; direct the remittance of profits; and shape the manner in which technology is to be transferred. The code is the most restrictive for foreign investors in the non-Communist world.

European Community (EC). The rules insist on fair competition and the protection of workers; condemn tax avoidance; and require corporate information. Many of these rules are in the OECD (Organization for European Co-operation and Development) code.

International Labor Organization (ILO). The rules ask for more local personnel in employment and training; the use of technologies that generate employment; and the availability of more information to workers.

Nonaligned Nations (NAC). These discussions form the basis of the Group of 77 LDC argument against multinational firms and how the former will overcome the latter. These discussions form the basis of the proposed United Nations code on transnational enterprises.

Organization of American States (OAS). Like the Group of 77, eleven Latin American countries pressed for a code restricting the behavior of multinational firms, and these discussions are a part of the proposed United Nations code on transnational enterprises.

Organization for European Co-operation and Development (OECD). This organization aims at harmonizing the way in which firms are treated among member states; it disallows unfair transfer pricing and bribes. Unlike the Andean code, it has not been made official through national legislation.

Sistema Económico Latinoamericano (SELA). SELA's proposals are similar to those in the OAS proposed code. SELA also requires that multinational firms do business in a less developed country in order to give a financial benefit to the host country. These proposals are a part of the proposed United Nations code on transnational enterprise.

UN Commission on Transnational Corporations. It has put together a composite code that includes recommendations from both developed (EC and OECD) and less developed (Ancom, NAC, OAS, and SELA) countries. Each member country must pass national legislation to enforce the UN rules.

UN Conference on Trade and Development (UNCTAD). There are two statements: 1980, a Code of Conduct; and in 1981, a Code on the Transfer of Technology. A more restrictive fourteen-point code on technology transfer has been adopted by Mexico and more codes are to follow elsewhere in the Third World.

These are a few soft, presidential-press-conference-type statements about the new international economic order. Let's work on some high inside fastballs.

Statements from less developed countries all begin with: Multinational firms must

> Follow host government policies. National sovereignty is the highest form of authority, and no recourse can be made to international agreements and international law. This is the old Calvo doctrine of Latin American countries dressed up for United Nations approval.
>
> Cease corrupt practices. There must be no bribery or extortion among executives. This is the United States' Foreign Corrupt Practices Act of 1977 dressed up for world approval.
>
> Give up majority ownership. Only the Andean code retains this harsh condition in its original form, so multinationals are free to invest outside of Venezuela, Colombia, Ecuador, Peru, and Bolivia.
>
> Be subject to financial controls. The less developed countries want to end local borrowing by foreign affiliates and want to establish the principle that multinationals must make a positive contribution to the host country's net financial resources.
>
> End restrictive business practices. The less developed countries want to end intrafirm transfer pricing, particularly the "arm's length" method of pricing, and want to stop multinationals from taking over local firms in the less developed countries.
>
> Transfer technology. The less developed countries have gotten their way on this, and the developed countries are having a difficult time protecting industrial and intellectual property.
>
> Disclose information. More is wanted. More will be obtained. More will be used against the multinational firms. That's the course of the future.

Lomé's agreement with the European Community includes many of these restrictive statements on multinational firms. The

Caribbean Basin Initiative between the islands and the United States includes some of these statements, too.

The new international economic order is still strengthening itself—to make the world economy work more for the less developed countries; to make the developed countries more dependent on the less developed countries for trade and payments; to link the state firms of the LDCs to multinational enterprises; and to further the use of nonequity forms of international operations (technology agreements, components sales, coproduction agreements, management contracts, patent and trademark licensing). UNCTAD's Lima targets to reduce inequities and advance the development process were being accomplished through Lomé and, to a lesser degree, through Ancom, until the second oil shock of 1979, the subsequent recession, and the crisis of sovereign country debt.

The less developed countries want the multinational firms to do four things.[1] First, they want them to process more of their raw materials in the host countries. Many LDCs nationalized the mines in the 1970s but found they didn't control the industry any more now than they did before. They want control over the foreign-processing and distribution facilities. And this has been bitterly fought by multinational firms and their home governments by means of tariffs, countervailing duties, and other protectionist schemes, or supported by Japanese (and, in some cases, European) firms and their government to promote domestic employment and economic growth.

Second, the LDCs want more industries as substitutes for imports and expect multinational firms to continue investing in the Third World. Some LDCs with poor debt records, such as Mexico, will get less rather than more; others with great market growth potential, such as Brazil and Venezuela, will get still more no matter what the status of their debt is. Still other LDCs, such as Lomé, will be seen as good sites for light consumer durable goods, textiles and clothing, and processed food items.

Third, the LDCs want more of their goods exported to the developed countries. They insist on the multinational firms including LDC products in their marketing programs for the developed countries. This too has been bitterly fought by multinational firms and their home governments with tariffs, countervailing duties, domestic content legislation, and other protectionist schemes, or supported by Japan, Inc.

Finally, the LDCs want to have more of the services that are related to manufacturing performed in the Third World: banking, insurance, engineering, and consulting. This demand already has brought resistance from the developed countries.

The UNCTAD Lima targets are for a reallocation of industrial activity to Third World countries. To meet this target means the multinational firms must give up large amounts of management discretion and the developed countries must give up industrial power, control over services, and many things that differentiate them from the less developed countries. It's unlikely that the Lima targets will be met anytime soon by the multinational firms and their home governments.

Transfer of Technology

As we realize more clearly every day, Latin America is serious about the Lima targets, and this is the reason that its laws on the transfer of technology are among the strictest in the world. Latin America, since World War II, has established its new industries with foreign technologies that have been acquired through contracts with the United States, the European Community, and Japan. Latin America is the dominant source of royalties and feeds paid to the United States from the less developed countries. This alone is testimony to the willingness of Latin American countries to restrict the use of foreign exchange (scarce dollars) to pay for technical assistance, patents, trademarks, and other forms of help, and transfer of technology laws have proved to be extremely popular—to the surprise of many in the United States, since these laws could be subject to reciprocity legislation here: a quid pro quo reaction from Washington against laws passed in Brasília, Bogotá, Mexico City, and elsewhere in the region.

Brazil's Law 4,131, enacted in 1962, was the first such law, and it prohibited a Brazilian subsidiary from paying royalties for patent or trademark licenses to its foreign parent company. Colombia and Chile entered the ranks in 1967 with a list of restricted practices. In 1970, the Andean Common Market adopted Decision 24, which codified its members' laws of 1967 and limited foreign access to local capital and markets. Argentina, 1971; Mexico, 1972. And seven other countries set up transfer of technology programs, reformed them between 1974 and 1976 and suppressed the ability to patent innovations in pharmaceuticals, nuclear energy, and other products.

Japan's Ministry of International Trade and Industry is the inspiration for these laws to gain control over technology, both in Asia and Latin America—laws that are seen as a way to increase a country's bargaining power. Multinational firms are supposed to unpack their different products and services so that the Latin Americans can pick and choose among them rather than have to buy everything from one multinational firm.

Debundling is the theme of all transfer-of-technology laws. Local firms must have the right to buy from as many sources as possible, domestic and foreign, to combine them in any way they wish, and to refuse to accept what they don't want. Local firms are required to negotiate the price downward; alter parent-subsidiary relations (see Decision 24 of Ancom); cut down the term of the contract to fifteen years (in Argentina and Brazil), ten years (in Mexico) and two to three years (in Peru and Colombia); and impose as many restrictive practices as possible upon the foreign parent.

These laws have been a partial success for the Latin Americans, who have obtained a decrease in technology payments in absolute terms and have saved crucial foreign exchange. In this case, the Lima targets have been met. But these laws have forced multinationals to invest in other areas of the world, and in this situation, they have been a failure also.

Unfinished Agenda

It has been almost a decade and a half now since the less developed countries launched their remarkable quest for basic changes in the rules governing economic relations between themselves and the developed industrialized countries. Their arguments were made in terms of their own inequality and the growing gap between rich and poor nations, and they asserted that countries could create their own comparative advantage by restricting trade temporarily in order to make domestic producers competitive with foreign producers. So what seeped into the consciousness of governments was this: they could manipulate comparative advantage to their own best interest. Country after country raised tariffs to encourage their infant industries to compete against traditional suppliers. Prior to World War I, the United States, Germany, France, Russia, and Japan protected their infant industries from British competition. After World War II, the former colonies of Britain and France claimed that their historical status left them with a dependence on the exports of primary goods, on widely fluctuating prices for these agricultural goods and raw materials, and on foreign-controlled marketing systems. Except for a few primary products such as sugar and coffee, most goods had to be sold in the spot market without any guarantee of sales in the developed countries. For most of the 1970s, oil sales were controlled by producers, the OPEC cartel. Bauxite, copper, and tin producers could not pull off the same trick, and once the developed countries learned how to do with less oil, OPEC's control over oil prices was weakened, too. There were several believable theories about the role of the LDCs in world trade. Raul Prebisch, the chief economist for the UN Economic Commission on Latin America, hammered out the theory that the terms of trade were deteriorating for the LDCs because these countries specialized in raw materials and commodities, while the developed countries specialized in manufactured goods. Productivity gains were larger for the developed countries, and these gains, when translated into higher wages, were defended by organized labor, government, and multinational (transnational) firms. Prebisch called for import substitution; the less developed countries must create their own industries and diversify their exports, first by light manufacturing and then by heavier manufacturing; and governments could push this process along by giving tax breaks to foreign investors, forcing domestic firms (including state enterprises) to construct steel mills, bauxite-alumina facilities, and automobile assembly plants, and by doing everything possible to create a long-term, sustained economic take off. Others said the LDCs couldn't join the ranks of the developed countries because they were dependent on the latter, and until the LDCs took control of the external marketing conditions, as the oil producing nations did, they would remain dependent on the developed industrialized countries. Although OPEC did buy oil companies, make downstream investments, and invest in grandiose projects, the failures mounted: Algeria, Iran, Kuwait, Nigeria, Venezuela. Their quick fix was not a model for producer associations in other less developed countries. Arthur Lewis, a development economist from the Caribbean, pointed out that the real problem lay in the inability of the less developed countries (which are tropical countries) to mechanize their agriculture, to raise rural wages closer to the level of urban wages, and to provide basic needs (education, public health, electricity) for all their people. I agree with this last theory and add two corollaries: the explosion in population must be brought under control; and there must be an equitable access to international capital, factor, and consumer markets. The less developed countries must do some things for themselves, too.

But some things have changed. The newly industrializing countries of Asia (South Korea, Taiwan, Singapore) and Latin America (Mexico, Venezuela, Brazil) took an increasing share of global manufacturing output, while the share of the United States, Europe, and Japan declined. Now there were additional players in the game of creating a new international economic order. These players brought new uncertainty to the world's trading system. They forced the developed countries to change the rules of the game. Instead of dedicating GATT to the supervision of free trade, they pushed the Europeans and their ACP allies to insist the GATT *manage* trade. And the Community was willing to comply in order to keep the United States and Japan at bay. The Japanese saw this as an opportunity to push their version of managed trade—MITI and its household of collaborating firms—into the world economy. Only the United States seemed to hold the phrase "managed trade" at arm's length, with disdain—it offends, repels, and sickens us. After all, free trade is as American as motherhood, apple pie, and the Fourth of July. How could we believe the world had changed?

Well, of course, it has. The Tokyo Round of multilateral trade negotiations between 1972 and 1979, enacted into U.S. law by the Trade Act of 1979, committed America to managed trade, too. The Tokyo Round confirmed America's generalized system of preferences in sugar and textiles for Mexico and the Caribbean nations, and Europe's generalized system of preferences in sugar and minerals for the Mediterranean and Lomé countries. These are nonreciprocal tariff preferences for exports of developing countries, and in their wake they brought safeguards—such as escape clauses in the United States and quantitative restrictions in the European Community—to prevent undue market disruption. The less developed countries got controls over technology transfer, additional development assistance, rescheduling of debt, and more say at the United Nations, the World Bank, the International Monetary Fund, and GATT.

Latin America also obtained more control over multinational firms. For example, Brazil insisted that these foreign firms go into joint ventures with local firms to spur on its drive toward industrialization. Colombia pushed its exports of manufactured goods and supported demands for greater access to markets in the developed countries. Mexico set up the strictest law on technology transfer and insisted that all disputes between itself and multinational firms be settled in local courts rather than through international arbitration. Venezuela, through its OPEC connection, took over its oil industry and used its revenues to build up its industrial and transportation infrastructure. These Latin American countries saw multinational firms as criminals who must be brought to heel. And the new international economic order was the means to change the relationship between themselves and the firms.

Chile (copper), Ecuador (bananas and oil), El Salvador (coffee), Guatemala (coffee), Jamaica (bauxite), and Peru (copper, sugar, and fish meal) sought to protect the purchasing power of their main export commodities. Many pushed for a stabilization fund similar to Stabex and Minerex for their commodities. And, indeed, even though the commodity producers were not successful in establishing their stabilization funds, creating equality between themselves and Lomé countries, and forcing the European Community to offer its generalized system of preferences to Latin American sugar, copper, and bauxite, still there is evidence that the Latin Americans accomplished the work of the Group of 77. More minerals and agricultural goods are processed in the less developed countries. Everywhere there is evidence that these Third World countries own their own land and resources. The sovereignty issue has been resolved in favor of the less developed countries. Many favor nonmarket solutions and have insisted on barter (or countertrade) solutions for the lack both of foreign exchange and of access to markets. Between 15 and 30 percent of world trade now takes this form, and more is coming as African, Caribbean, Pacific, and Latin American countries join forces to change the world's trading system.

One clue to the gathering momentum behind the new international economic order can be found in the call by the Netherlands, Norway, Australia, and Sweden to restructure the economies of the developed industrialized countries in order to lower barriers to the exports of Third World countries. France and New Zealand also supported revenue stabilization arrangements for commodities; Germany and Japan did not. Only the Netherlands and Sweden are willing to forgive the debt of all less developed countries. These OECD countries did agree on providing debt relief and more development aid to the poorest countries. But they did not agree on restructuring their economies, giving away technology, or disciplining the multinational firms.

The fact of the matter is that the United States vacillated between accepting and opposing the proposals of the less developed countries. That spirit of indecision was reflected in our unwillingness (and inability) to come to grips with the real economic problems facing Latin America and the Caribbean. We couldn't see beyond our own rhetoric. The liberal trading system was not working as well for them as it had worked for us. Room had to be made for them as we had made room for Europe and Japan. That's the unfinished agenda of the new international economic order.

Future Decisions

World economic events have taken on a miasmic quality. Ideas, issues, policies, programs, and even regions that used to be kept separate and distinct are now coming together. Analogy is rampant. Japan teaches the world how to manage an economy successfully. Canada tries to do this, too, with less success, but becomes the pied piper to the African, Caribbean, and Pacific countries. Europe decides to capture GATT and does so this with the help of the Lomé countries. The Latin American countries want into the EC-Lomé system and also seek to gang up against the United States through

GATT and UNCTAD. The world seems to be experiencing a sort of Tower of Babel dream—a delirium in which Canadian Herb Gray (we saw his rise and fall in Part Two of this book) writes illusionary reports on control over multinational firms for Third World countries; and the world's biggest trading partner of the United States, by some magical disappearance of its nationalist phantom, comes full circle in calling for regional free trade between itself and the United States. But while the Canadian terrors may be imaginary, the restrictions by the less developed countries are real, and the world can only hope that somehow the spell won't return to Canada and that the world economy will be restored to a more beneficial and prosperous condition.

Much of the loud complaining about managed trade came on account of MITI. Japan held on to its own ways of forcing business to collaborate with government in the quest for increased domestic employment, greater economic growth, more exports, and a lot more use of Japanese technology throughout the world. Meanwhile, American firms in declining industries complained the loudest, sought protection from the U.S. International Trade Commission, and made things difficult for Japanese exporters of steel, automobiles, and motorcycles. No one in Washington was able to put an end to these petitions, and this meant that throughout the 1970s Japanese trade practices were a political football carried downfield by all executives who couldn't (and wouldn't) compete with the newest country to come in from the periphery and join the major players in the world's trading system.

Our own decision to bar Japanese products from the United States may have kept America working, but in the long run, the decision wasn't conducive to the modernization of American industry. Other notes were struck in justification of a protectionist America, including a defeatist comment from American executives, who suggested that they simply couldn't compete against the "Yankee" traders from East Asia. But unfair competition was the keynote, and the U.S. International Trade Commission was consistent in this, if nothing else. The first objective in handling the complaint, presented by the Department of Commerce, was to find economic injury; the next objective, if possible, was to find material injury and dumping and to impose nonnegotiable countervailing duties. The

International Trade Commission has succeeded. No foreign products get in if our domestic industry goes before the commission; no foreign products escape voluntary quotas, higher tariffs, or countervailing duties. The only losers, in fact, are American consumers—their standard of living, one might say, was reduced because they had to pay more for both domestic and foreign goods.

Protectionism through the International Trade Commission is a success. It works because we took the easy way out. We could have learned something from the Japanese about how to manage our work force and our resources. We brought on our own troubles with the Japanese, and we should mourn our own loss of the entrepreneurial spirit. But it's not too late to change. Dare we do it?

Many businessmen haven't been to Geneva very often lately, but when they go, they will notice European imperialists lying down with their former ACP colonies to hatch a new international economic order. Europe is the aggressor, wielding the big stick. It dominates most of the countries in the Group of 77, and those it does not dominate clamor to get in under the European Community's generalized system of preferences.

America is guilty of one charge, and that is stupidity. When we point to what's happened to GATT's most favored nations concept, we are laughed off the world's stage as a tired "old world" country out of touch with what's going on in today's up-to-date world. How sad it is that the world didn't pursue our view of an open, liberal trading system. How much better it would be for everyone had we pursued our own view. How much better it would be for everyone had both we and they given up our commitment to free trade for all.

Summary

The argument: Multilateral free trade is a thing of the past. Japan doesn't want it because it would bring access to its home market. Canada can't have it because trade with the United States is too important in terms of employment, taxes, and capital investment. The Europeans choose to perfect their common market and tie others to the European Community in bilateral trading arrangements. The Lomé countries can't have it because trade with the European

Community is too important in terms of employment and local income. The Latin Americans prefer to build up their local national economies rather than perfect their intraregional trading agreements among themselves. They are looking for a bilateral deal similar to the one the Lomé countries have with the European Community. It's time the United States offered such a bilateral trading arrangement to one or more Latin American countries. Such agreements with Mexico, Brazil, Argentina, and Venezuela will create more intraregional trade between them and the United States, expand local employment, the tax base, and domestic capital formation, and help these countries reduce their debt.

Results: We know that the time is right for ourselves and our neighbors to the south to create a new hemispheric trading system in which American, Canadian, Japanese, and European investors would build new factories and create jobs in Latin America for the purpose of selling goods locally and internationally—in the United States, in Canada, in Japan, and in Europe.

Recommendations: Reciprocal bilateral free trade means the expansion of the free market of North America to include as many Latin American countries that wish to join this new bilateral hemispheric trading system. Reciprocal bilateral free trade means that the United States will put no restrictions on the number of goods these countries can sell here. Some U.S. and Canadian industries will suffer, and some may move their factories elsewhere in the hemisphere, depending on transport costs for the commodities produced in South America. This is the type of structural adjustment that goes on in free market economies periodically. Now is the time for some of the benefits of economic development and change to filter down to the Caribbean and Latin America countries, too.

Conclusions: U.S. Policies

In the endless stream of cases before the U.S. International Trade Commission, a writer sees a million stories—the motorcycle firm trying to survive, the machine-tool firm looking for temporary relief, the steel firm refusing to modernize. The unionized workers see jobs. The consumers, if they are observant, see more expensive bikes, cars, appliances, and clothes each time protection from foreign imports is granted. And the International Trade Commission sees a job well done in enforcing U.S. trade law.

Almost two decades have passed since these protectionist decisions entered our bloodstream and made us resistant to free trade. For most of those years, economic relations between the United States and our trading partners have been characterized by churlishness—our intentionally boorish behavior and their ungracious, intractable responses—relieved only by brief intervals of temporary solutions and passing hopes of return to an earlier, more blissful period.

Each such pleasant interval, however, has been followed by an ever more brutal demand for more protection. Petty restraints are now so deeply rooted in the enforcement of international trade law that they bring out the destructive tendencies of all western societies, weakening the fabric of and threatening the demise of the international trading system.

That harshness grew out of the statist inclinations of our allies, but with the passage of time we persuaded ourselves of the malign intent inherent in their views about the role of government in international trade. It is difficult to distinguish what is real and what is fancied in our perception of them.

The conceptions of Japanese, Canadian, and European trade policy held most widely in the United States are stereotypes, and they hinder our ability to make effective policy in a number of ways. They are oversimplified caricatures of how governments deal with business. They are static and do not take into account the changes that have taken place, particularly since the Tokyo Round. They are based on assumptions that do not bear up under critical review. They misrepresent the ways in which our allies react to our ITC decisions. They do not distinguish between polemics and facts. Finally, as oversimplified images leading to oversimplified policy, they make it difficult for us to resolve the dilemma of whether we should try to become more like them as experts in managed trade or try to stay as we are, half protectionist, half free trade.

After almost three decades of studying the trade policies of nations, what continues to strike me most forcefully is the extent to which we have let our trade policy drift away from its free trade moorings toward those distant and different shores represented by Tokyo, Ottawa, Brussels, and Geneva. Even more troubling is that we are unaware of this drift and seem unable to stop it before our trade policy crosses the sea—never to return home again. What has been absent from our thinking is the maturity to lead by example and to define the boundary between acceptable and nonacceptable trade practices.

The problems presented by MITI, FIRA, CAP, Lomé, and other protectionist schemes are serious. But stereotypes do not provide us with an adequate basis for prudent response. My purpose in writing this book is to suggest what we need to know about these problems. We need to have a realistic view of our allies' concerns over trade and how they seek to accomplish their goals for a more prosperous society. We need to come up with some realistic proposals for the conduct of our trade relations with our trading partners. I believe that the time is long overdue for us to address head-on the trade policy questions that underlie our dilemma over what to do.

One: Should we make industrial policy a GATT issue?

Over the past decade, we have come to recognize that what MITI does, what FIRA requires, what Lomé demands can be listed under the rubrics of industrial policy. It has become apparent in the 1980s that these bureaucracies were dictating investment and trade decisions. In response to this fact, the ITC issued decisions for the purpose of halting the flow of goods coming into the United States. Although the number of cases had reached floodtide, and although recent 201 and 301 decisions have brought harsher remedies, the cases have been decided after the damage has been done to American producers. Open markets, which to us mean a two-way street, have been used as a long-term economic strategy by our competition in world trade to get as large a market share as possible in the United States without a quid pro quo in market share in the other countries of the world.

Unless we act forcefully by demanding that GATT make rules about the use of industrial policy in international trade, the status quo will be upheld, for the Japanese, Canadians, Europeans, and others have an interest in closing their markets while forcing us to keep ours open. A broader commitment to open markets would require a departure from the statist faith of the interventionists much greater than any of their actions now indicate is likely to occur.

Two: Should we make the U.S. International Trade Commission condemn the industrial policies of other countries?

If we asked the ITC that question, its answer would be, "That's not what the law requires." Congressional intent for 201 and 301 decisions is quite clear: once an injury occurs, the ITC is supposed to investigate the facts, make a finding, and impose an appropriate remedy. But by then it's too late.

To say that the ITC believes it needs new authority from the Congress before it does what it must do is not to say that its decisions on industrial policy actually will be challenged in the courts. When foreign government-business cartels restrict American imports or direct exports to the United States, these actions are under U.S. law unfair trade practices. The ITC can use Section 337 to declare foreign industrial policies a violation of U.S. trade law. The ITC can stop the Japanese and Europeans in their tracks. The defendants can always sue in the Court of International Trade, or on appeal to the U.S. Supreme Court.

Three: Must the United States adopt an industrial policy of its own to make its voice heard in GATT?

Some argue yes. If this is true, it follows that the United States must organize itself to forge an industrial policy, and this would change us in fundamental ways. Such a move would become the primary objective of domestic economic policy. Those who make this suggestion forget that America has no trained cadre of bureaucrats and no desire to build such a bureaucracy, either in Washington or anywhere else.

My study of trade policy, however, suggests that the United States reads the wrong books, the wrong papers, studies the wrong examples and the wrong results of how our allies handle their industrial policies. The United States provides higher tariffs, countervailing duties, trigger prices, or voluntary export restraints but demands nothing in return from the firms and industries involved. There is no evidence that these firms' increased earnings have been reinvested into modernizing factories in order to make productivity, capital-labor input ratios, and management-labor practices competitive with the best the Japanese and others have to offer. On the contrary, profits are used to buy other, nonrelated companies.

Four: Are there good reasons for disengaging the ITC from concentrating on 201 and 301 decisions?

We have to accept the fact that the decisions by the ITC are fundamentally protectionist and inhibit competitive action by the firms that seek its protection. What we must decide is when to say "no more." We know it is not sensible to continue to give steel firms and other manufacturers more protection indefinitely. If we do, we will wind up with firms that have lost their ability to compete at all, and we will have pushed ourselves toward greater inefficiencies and long-term economic stagnation.

The 1970s was a period in international trade in which American business and labor did not work hard enough to solve their trade problems. They preferred protectionism to self-reform. Now they have the ITC they want, but it is one we don't deserve and from which we won't benefit.

Five: Can America learn from its trading competitors? Certainly, the ability of Japan to create marketing evidence of its applied technical prowess and to promote a distinctive style of management-labor relations made it possible for the Japanese to outdistance us in the competition for world markets. And despite the impressive record of MITI, it is wrong to speak evil of Japan,

Inc. The Japanese have created a government-business relationship based on the precepts of their society, and this link has been effective in creating jobs at home that are dependent on exports abroad. None of these are reasons for throwing up further barriers to trade with them. If the Japanese really want more market share in the United States, let them pay for access to it through an auction system based on the highest bidder's price. Clearly, some market share must be allocated to America's neighbors north and south rather than to the Europeans and the Japanese.

The lack of restraint shown by Canada under the Trudeau administration cannot be justified, but its interventions must be viewed in light of its nearness to us. The FIRA program, for example, was a response to nationalism run wild, and its economic failure is a well-deserved end to such a misguided policy. Of course, the European Community sought advantage over us (and against Japan, too, it should be noted) by forcing its ex-colonies to join in a conquest of GATT.

We can open the Lomé System to the Latin American countries, set up a hemisphere counterpart to the European Community, or force a change in how GATT votes. Or we can do all three. In fact, we can do no less. It lies within our power to stake out markets for the United States and go after them as Japan does. Certainly, the creation of a U.S. Department of International Trade and Industry could be helpful to the United States in this undertaking. Yes, we can learn. But in order to do so, we must be open to change.

Six: Is the world ready to engage seriously in the next round of trade negotiations, the Reagan Round?

Trade negotiations over tariff reductions and the application of most favored nations by GATT members seemed like radical ideas when Canada and the United States decided to go ahead with them in the 1930s. In the early post–World War II years, beginning in 1948, Europe was obviously willing to do everything it could to keep up our support. And so were Japan and the Third World, as well. Most of the trade discussions (Dillon and Kennedy Rounds, particularly) were advanced by the United States, and the issues were resolved in America's favor. Although our allies outwardly accepted the results, they didn't give their inward consent.

But the situation changed in the Tokyo Round. We changed

from leader to follower. Despite our formal acceptance of economic injury, material injury, the subsidies code, and other protectionist items as guiding principles, we really didn't like what we had agreed to. Our instincts are against protectionism and state intervention. In this respect, our actual policies moved closer to those of our allies.

Our allies changed, too: they returned to their past practices, such as cartels. In the Tokyo Round, we codified their view of the world's trading system, rather than our own. They will be reluctant to go back to a more open system.

Seven: What does this say about the ability of the United States to get some of the things it wants from the next multilateral round of trade negotiations?

The task will be a formidable one. It appears our allies are dealing from a position of strength; they will not match our concessions with equivalent ones. Now that they have us on the run, they will want more. But there is a positive side to this. Our firms, our workers, and, perhaps, our government will find the strength to turn themselves around and do a better job. Our concessions will benefit us with cheaper goods. The absence of new agreements is not necessarily bad. In fact, it may be good for the consumers.

Eight: Are our views of the trade practices of Japan, Canada, the European Community, and the Third World out of date?

Yes, our stereotypes are out of date. The prevailing U.S. image of these trading partners tends to make them caricatures of their true selves, leading some observers to conclude that they will press on in their quest for dominance and will win. This view neglects the U.S. willingness to retaliate and to redesign its economy in order to make it competitive once again with the best that foreigners have to offer. Because the changes we favor means we are going to be less concerned with the welfare of our competitors, in the short run our activities will be seen as bad for their best interests. Whether in the long run such changes will bring a new responsiveness to our need for an open trading system may depend in part on how well we are able to sell its merits in the late 1980s.

How the United States responds to these changes is the most important question of all, and the answer, when it becomes clear, will affect the thinking of the Japanese, Canadians and Europeans about what they should do to support or oppose an open, liberal trading system for the world.

Reciprocal Bilateral Free Trade

We know now how we should respond to the problems facing us in international trade. I call the new American policy reciprocal bilateral free trade. The United States must negotiate a North American free trade agreement first with Canada, and then together with the Canadians, we should negotiate additional bilateral agreements with Mexico, the Caribbean countries, and other Latin American nations. Such agreements will widen the market for goods produced in the hemisphere, will raise levels of employment and income, and will improve the chances for paying off the debt. Reciprocity in trade and investment is what we are about today.

The Story

It's a curious phenomenon of journalistic life today that the most important current business story—how the United States adjusts to new economic conditions in the world and what it does to restructure the world's trading system—is a story that by its very nature never appears on the business pages. "U.S. Convinces Allies—Free Trade Again" is a headline we'll never see. Nor, of course, will any columnist comment on this story, or any in-depth background pieces analyze for us how it happened and what it all means. Nor for that matter will any writer tell us how we got into the fix we are in or how we can get out of it. No assignments will be made from the financial editor's desk; no Sigma Delta Chi awards will be conferred for the story of the century.

In the beginning pages of the book, America's views on international trade were declared obsolete. We let steel, auto, and textile executives manage our trade policy, and they didn't create comparative advantage for us. The principal new finding was that in a quest for jobs and markets, all developed countries were engaging in protectionist activities, and the United States is about to jump in with both feet as well. This book describes how the less developed countries were following in the footsteps of their former colonial powers. In the judgment of this writer, all these interventionist activities could result in the end of free trade among the countries of the world. To be sure, there is uncertainty about when it will end—an uncertainty that can never be altogether eliminated. Clearly, the end can be postponed, but not indefinitely. The United States will fight back and may win some small battles or even the big and final battle. This—the matter of free (or fair) trade versus managed trade—is "the story," and would make sense for the news media to assign young reporters, who are seeking to gain their reputations, to follow this story.

Needless to say, these assignments are not being made, nor is the story being reported. As far as I know, only the Chicago *Sun-Times* covered the story week after week, but the writer was just a contributing columnist—me. When the paper was sold and a new financial editor took over, this six-year-old column on international business was terminated. A few of my stories are reported in these pages.

But the world still hasn't noticed.

Paraphernalia

Parts of this book were presented earlier in the weekly international business column for the Chicago *Sun-Times* and as lectures to MBA students at Northwestern University and at the University of Illinois at Chicago. I thank readers of the *Sun-Times* and students and faculty at both universities. Thanks go to my colleague Lawrence G. Lavengood, a professor at the J.L. Kellogg Graduate School of Management at Northwestern University, for reading the manuscript and giving me his critical and useful comments. Finally, I thank family and friends for their patience with me while I wrote this book.

Endnotes

PROLOGUE

1. Chicago *Sun-Times,* 20 February 1984, 52.

CHAPTER 1
Free Trade

1. Andrzej Olechowski and Gary Sampson, "Current Trade Restrictions in the EEC, the United States and Japan," *Journal of World Trade Law* 14, no. 3 (May–June 1980): 230–31. See also Kiyoshi Kojima, "Hidden Trade Barriers in Japan," *Journal of World Trade Law* 7, no. 2 (March–April 1973): 137–68.
2. Olechowski and Sampson, 230–31.
3. Ibid., 227–28.
4. Ibid., 228–30.
5. Michael Borrus, James Millstein, and John Zysman, *U.S.-Japanese Competition in the Semiconductor Industry* (Berkeley: Institute of International Studies, University of California at Berkeley, n.d.), no. 17, 5.
6. Ibid.
7. Ibid.
8. Ibid.
9. Ibid., 49.
10. Ibid., 50–51.
11. Ibid., 68–69.
12. Michael C. Munger, "The Costs of Protectionism: Estimates of the Hidden Tax of Trade Restraint." St. Louis: Center for the Study of American Business, Washington University, Working Paper #80, July 1983, 3–4.
13. Ibid.
14. Colin Clark, "The Balance of Payments or Are Import Restrictions Necessary?" London: Economic Research Council, October 1977, 1.

CHAPTER 2
Fear: Parent of Protectionism

1. Chicago *Sun-Times,* 15 May 1980, 35. Only excerpts of the letter were published in the paper.
2. Ibid., 5 May 1980, 63.
3. Ibid., 15 May 1980, 35.
4. Victor A. Canto, Richard V. Eastin, and Arthur B. Laffer, "Failure of Protectionism: A Study of the Steel Industry," *Columbia Journal of World Business* 17, no. 44 (Winter 1982): 43–57.
5. Peter Drucker, "Where Union Flexibility's Now A Must," *Wall Street Journal* 23 September 1983, 32.
6. Elizabeth E. Bailey, "Quantum Leap in Productivity," *New York Times,* 2 September 1983, 30.
7. Canto et al., 56.
8. Ibid.
9. Thomas F. O'Boyle, "Steel Management Has Itself to Blame," *Wall Street Journal,* 17 May 1983, 32.
10. *New York Times,* 18 December 1983, 18E.
11. Ibid., 22.
12. *New York Times,* 7 December 1983, 24.
13. Donald F. Barnett and Louis Schorsch, *Steel: Upheaval in a Basic Industry* (1983).

CHAPTER 3
The Fix Is In

1. *New York Times,* 22 January 1980, A21.
2. Ibid.
3. David A. Heenan, *The Re-United States of America: An Action Agenda for Improving Business, Government and Labor Relations* (Reading, Mass.: Addison-Wesley Publishing Co., 1983).
4. Douglas Lamont, *Foreign State Enterprises: A Threat to American Business* (New York: Basic Books, 1979).

CHAPTER 4
MITI

1. Murray Sayle, "The Yellow Peril and the Red-Haired Devils," *Harper's* (November 1982): 23–35.
2. Chalmers Johnson, *MITI and the Japanese Miracle: The Growth of Industrial Policy, 1925–1975* (Stanford, Calif.: Stanford University Press, 1982).
3. U.S. Federal Trade Commission, *Effects of Restrictions on US Imports.* Special

report prepared by Morris E. Morkre and David G. Tarr. Washington, D.C.: U.S. Government Printing Office, June 1980.

4. Murray Sayle, "Bureaucracy and the Barriers That Do Not Exist," *Far Eastern Economic Review* (April 16, 1982): 64–65.

CHAPTER 5
Comparative Advantage

1. *Structurally Depressed Industry Law,* Statutes of Japan, 1978 and 1983.
2. Michael Borrus, with James Millstein and John Zysman, "Responses to the Japanese Challenge in High Technology: Innovation, Maturity, and U.S.-Japanese Competition in Microelectronics," (Berkeley: Institute of International Studies, University of California at Berkeley, advance copy, 1983), 112–13.
3. Japan Economic Institute Report, No. 12A (April 1, 1983), 6–7.
4. Allan M. Rugman, "Canada: FIRA Updated," *Journal of World Trade Law* 17, no. 4 (July–August 1983): 352.
5. FIRA *Foreign Investment Review* (Spring 1982): 35.
6. Maurice Yeates, *Main Street: Windsor to Quebec City* (Toronto: Gage Publishing, 1978).
7. Robert Lewis, "Alberta for Albertans," *Maclean's* 93, no. 45 (November 10, 1980): 29.
8. Douglas Lamont, *passim.* "Elf Aquitaine: Breaking Its Bounds to Gain a Foothold in U.S. oil," *Business Week* (8 March 1982): 108–10.
9. Foreign Investment Review Agency, "Barriers to Foreign Investment in the United States." Toronto: Policy, Research and Communications Branch, n.d., I–VI.
10. Douglas Lamont, *op. cit.*
11. Thomas J. Moore, "Passage of Trade Legislation Urged," Chicago *Sun-Times,* 11 September 1980, 96.
12. John D. Murray, "The Tax Sensitivity of U.S. Direct Investment in Canadian Manufacturing," *Journal of International Money and Finance* 1, no. 2 (August 1982): 117.
13. Ibid., 119.
14. Section 303 of the Tariff Act of 1930. 19 U.S.C. 1303.
15. U.S. Senate Report No. 782 (1965) 39, Report of Senate Finance Committee on H.R. 9042, 89th Cong., 1st Sess. The quotation is from the "minority views" of Senators Ribicoff, Hartke, and Gore in opposition to the auto pact. Cited by Stanley D. Metzger, "The United States-Canada Automotive Products Agreement of 1965," *Journal of World Trade Law* 1, no. 1 (January–February 1967): 106–7.
16. Ibid.
17. Charles Stedman, "Canada-U.S. Automotive Agreement: The Sectoral Approach," *Journal of World Trade Law* 8, no. 2 (March–April 1974): 178.
18. Economic Council of Canada, *Looking Outward: A New Trade Strategy for Canada* (Ottawa: Information Canada, 1975).

CHAPTER 6
Foreign Investments

1. M. Watkins et al., *Foreign Ownership and the Structure of Canadian Industry,* Report of the Task Force on the Structure of Canadian Industry (Ottawa: The Queen's Printer, 1968). Wahn Report. Eleventh Report of the Standing Committee on Defense and External Affairs Respecting Canada-U.S. Relations (Ottawa: The Queen's Printer, 1970). Government of Canada, or the Gray Report, *Foreign Direct Investment in Canada* (Information Canada, Ottawa, 1972).
2. Lamont, *op cit.*
3. Ibid.
4. Alex Murray, University of Windsor. Cited by Alan M. Rugman in "The Foreign Ownership Debate in Canada," *Journal of World Trade Law* 10, no. 2 (March–April 1976): 174.

CHAPTER 7
National Energy Policy

1. "Canadian Oil Shares Drop Sharply on Fears of Government Takeover," *Wall Street Journal,* 30 October 1980, 29.
2. Robert Metz, "Behind the Drop in Canada Oils," *New York Times,* 31 October 1980, 34.
3. Frederick Rose, "Canada Alters Energy Policy," *Wall Street Journal,* 1 June 1982, 5.

CHAPTER 8
Sectoral Free Trade

1. *A Review of Canadian Trade Policy,* (Ottawa: Canadian Government Publishing Center, 1983), 67.
2. Ibid., 69.
3. Ibid., 72.
4. Ibid., 76.
5. Ibid., 94.
6. Ibid., 97.
7. Ibid., 98.

CHAPTER 9
Managed Trade

1. S.A.B. Page, "The Revival of Protectionism and Its Consequences for Europe," *Journal of Common Market Studies* 20, no. 1 (September 1981): 27.

2. Ibid., 29. See also Linda M. Gard and James Riedel, "Safeguard Protection of Industry in Developed Countries," *Weltwirtshaftliches Archiv*, 1980, vol. 116, no. 3, 471–92.

CHAPTER 10
GATT

1. See R.W. Middleton, "The GATT Standards Code," *Journal of World Trade Law* 14, no. 3 (May–June 1980): 201–19.
2. See Endre Ustor, "The MFN Customs Union Exception," *Journal of World Trade Law* 15, no. 5 (September–October 1981): 377–87.

CHAPTER 11
The European Community

1. Civ. Bruxelles, 5 June 1966, *Corn & Food Trading Co.* v. *Belgian State*, IV CDE (1968): 550–60. Cited by J.H.H. Bourgeois in "The Tokyo Round Agreements on Technical Carriers and on Government Procurement in International and EEC Perspective," *Common Market Law Review* 19, no. 1 (1982): 7. Also *Florida Lime & Avocado Growers Inc.* v. *Paul* US 132, 1963. Cited by Middleton, "The GATT Standards Code."
2. "Hohe Hürden für Importantos," *Die Zeit*, 29 May 1981.
3. *Le Monde*, 20 January 1981, 23.
4. London *Financial Times*, 5 December 1983, 18.
5. Jacques Steenbergen, "The Common Commercial Policy," *Common Market Law Review* 17 (1980): 229–49.
6. Roland Vaubel, "How the EC Became a Protectionist Trash Bin," *Wall Street Journal*, 7 September 1983, 27.
7. Ian Smith, "EEC Sugar Policy in an International Context," *Journal of World Trade Law* 15, no. 2 (March–April 1981): 95–110.
8. Ian Smith, "GATT: EEC Sugar Export Refunds Dispute," *Journal of World Trade Law* 15, no. 6 (November–December 1981): 534–42.

CHAPTER 12
Preferential Trade Agreements

1. "GATT: Third Multifibre Agreement," *Journal of World Trade Law* 16, no. 2 (March–April 1982): 178–80.
2. David B. Gaines, William C. Sawyer, and Richard Sprinkle, "EEC Mediterranean Policy and U.S. Trade in Citrus," *Journal of World Trade Law* 15, no. 6 (November–December 1981): 431–39.

CHAPTER 13
Lomé

1. K.R. Simmonds, "The Lomé Convention and the New International Economic Order," *Common Market Law Review* 13 (1976): 324.
2. Ibid., 334.
3. G.K. Helleiner, "Lomé: Market Access and Industrial Co-operation," *Journal of World Trade Law* 13, no. 2 (February–March 1979): 182.
4. K.R. Simmonds, "The Lomé Convention: Implementation and Renegotiation," *Common Market Law Review* 16 (1979): 431.
5. K.R. Simmonds, "The Second Lomé Convention: The Innovative Features," *Common Market Law Review* 17 (1980): 415–36.

CHAPTER 14
Graduation

1. Matthew McQueen, "Lomé and the Protective Effect of Rules of Origin," *Journal of World Trade Law* 16, no. 1 (January–February 1982): 122–24.
2. Ibid.
3. René Barents, "New Developments in Measures Having Equivalent Effect," *Common Market Law Review* 18, no. 2 (1981): 289–91.
4. Peter Oliver, "Measures of Equivalent Effect: A Reappraisal," *Common Market Law Review* 19, no. 2 (1982): 234–37.

CHAPTER 15
Debt

1. Isaiah Frank, "The Graduation Issue for LDCs," *Journal of World Trade Law* 13, no. 4 (July–August 1979): 289.
2. Graham Bird, "The International Monetary Fund and Developing Countries: Retrospect and Prospect," *De Economist*, 131, no. 2 (1983): 165.
3. Lindley H. Clark, Jr., "The IMF Helps to Make the Debt Problems Worse," *Wall Street Journal*, 27 September 1983, 33.
4. Anthony Harris, "The Micawber Approach to Debt," *Financial Times*, 21 December 1983, 12.
5. Anatole Kaletsky, "When the Debtors Said No," *Financial Times*, 28 December 1983, 13.
6. Ibid.
7. Diana Tussie, "Latin American Integration: From LAFTA to LAIA," *Journal of World Trade Law* 16, no. 5 (September–October 1982): 399.
8. Sanjay Dhar, "U.S. Trade with Latin America: Consequences of Financing Constraints," *Quarterly Review of the Federal Reserve Bank of New York* 8, no. 3 (Autumn 1983): 14–18.

CHAPTER 16
A New Order

1. Constantine Vaitsos, "Transnational Enterprises and the Lima Target," *Journal of World Trade Law* 13, no. 3 (May–June 1979): 223.

Index

Absenteeism, 5
ACPs, 108, 111; and European Community, 120, 163–175, 177–179; and private capital, 191; and standards code, 129; and sugar, 143–144, 169–170; *see also* Africa; Caribbean; Less-developed countries; Lomé Convention
Africa, 163–164, 165; and European Community, xvii, 120, 163, 164–171; minerals, 173, 177–178; trade agreements, 4; *see also* ACPs; Less-developed countries; Lomé Convention
African-Caribbean-Pacific countries, *See* ACPs
Agency for International Development, 138
Agricultural machinery, 98
Agriculture: and Australia, 99; and Canada, 98–99; and European Community, xix, 99, 109–110, 115–116, 140, 142–149, 158, 165–166, 169, 173; and GATT, 109, 114, 115, 116; and Japan, 99, 116; and less-developed countries, 132–133, 164, 168–175, 177–178; and Lomé countries, 165; and United States, 109, 141, 143
Aikawa, Gensuke, 46–47
Aircraft, 101, 115, 136–137
Alaskan oil, 5
Alberta, Canada, 59, 77, 82–84, 87, 90, 94, 100, 102
Alcohol content regulation, 183–184
Algeria, 157, 212
Alsands project, 87
American Iron and Steel Institute (AIST), 19, 20, 21
American Motors, 30, 65
Andean Common Market (Ancom), 205, 206, 209–210
Andre, Harvie, 83
Antidumping laws, 13, 71, 172, 173–174; and GATT, 125–126, 132
Aquitaine Co., 85
Arab Common Market, 130
Argentina, 26, 114, 188, 210, 217; debt, 192, 193, 197, 198, 200; and International Monetary Fund, 194; U.S. exports to, 201
Argus Corporation, 86
Asian Economic Association (ASEAN), 199–200
Australia, 214; agriculture, 99; sugar, 145, 146–147
Austria, 113
Autarky, 198–199
Automation, xxi; and European Community, xix, 107, 141
Automobile industry, 10; and Canada, 4, 65–67, 69–70, 77–78, 90, 93, 94, 96, 97, 101; and European Community, 34, 117; and Japan, xiii, 33–35, 38, 45, 53,

Automobile industry (*continued*) 66, 117, 215; and labor costs, xiii–xiv; and United States, xv–xvi, xxi, 5, 9, 30–34, 35–36, 40, 74; voluntary marketing agreements, xiii, 5, 125

Bailey, Elizabeth E., 24
Balance of payments, 193–198
Bananas, 169, 171, 213
Bank of America, 201
Bank of Canada, 86
Bank of Japan, 49
Banking services, 209
Barents, René, 183
Barnett, Donald F., 27
"Barriers to Foreign Investment in the United States," 61
Barter, 214
Basic oxygen furnace, 25
Basket extractor mechanism, 153
Bauxite, 169, 173, 200, 211, 213
Beaufort Sea oil, 85
Beef exports, 172
Belgium, 22, 135, 148; and equivalent effect, 181–182; textiles and clothing, 154, 155–156
Bell, Joel, 81
Bengis, Ingrid, 32
Bethlehem Steel, 26
Bieber, Owen, 33
Bilateral trade agreements, 15, 41, 53, 199, 202, 225; with Canada, 60, 62, 76–77, 96, 101, 102–103, 175, 189, 215, 225; and Caribbean, xxiv, 175; and European Community, 11, 113, 139, 151–152, 154, 163–175, 189, 216; and Latin America, xxiv, 175, 217, 225; and less-developed countries, 163–175, 217; and Lomé countries, 15; and Mexico, xxiv, 62, 120, 175, 189, 202–203, 217; and steel, 28
Black Madonna, 29
Bolivia, 196, 207
Bombardier, 101
Border checks, 182–183
Border taxes, 121–123, 125–126, 127
Borrus, Michael, 5–6
Botswana, 172
Bounties, 65, 71–72, 125, 126, 158; and Canada, 99
Branch plants, xvii–xviii
Brazil, 145, 146, 154, 184–185, 217; citrus, 158, 185, 187; debt, xviii, 13, 118, 188, 191, 192, 194, 196, 197, 198, 200, 201; industries, 208; and multinationals, 213; shoe exports, xviii; steel industry, xxi, 23, 25, 26, 188; and subsidies, 188, 187; sugar, 109; technology transfer laws, 209–210; and United States, 201
Bribery, 207
British Columbia, 59, 102
British Leyland, 34
Brock, William, 97
Brussels Tariff Nomenclature, 4, 178–179
Buffer Stock Financing Facility, 193
Burke-Hartke bill, 111
Burma, 194, 198
Buy American legislation, 8, 12; and Canada, 77, 100, 101

Cafeteria approach to benefits, 24
California, 59, 135
Calvo doctrine, 207
Cambridge, Economic Policy Group (U.K.), 118
Cambridge school of economists, 9, 11, 199
Cameroons, 199
Canada, xxii, 10, 214, 216, 223; agriculture, 98–99; Automobile Pact, 4, 65–67, 69–70, 77–78, 94, 96, 111; bilateral trading agreements, xxiv, 60, 62, 76–77, 91, 96, 101, 102–103, 175, 189, 215, 225; bureaucratic costs, 12; clothing industry, 96, 97, 100, 102; currency depreciation, 59, 86–87; electronics, 101–102;

employment, 59, 87, 94, 95; energy policy, xvii, 62, 66, 70–71, 81–91, 94, 95, 97; and exchange rates, 86, 87; footwear industry, 97, 98; foreign investment in, xvii–xix, 58–59, 61–67, 73–79, 89, 90, 94, 95, 99; forest products, 99; and GATT, 96; history of trade policy, 95–98; interventionism, 58–67, 69–71; mass transit equipment, 96, 98; minerals, 99–100; and multinationals, 75–76, 78, 82–83, 89, 215; research and development, 72, 74; steel industry, 96, 97, 98, 99–100; subsidies, 70, 99; taxes, 63–65, 66, 82–83, 88; and Tokyo Round, 96, 113, 223–224; trade deficits, 70; trade practices, 98–102; and United States, xvii–xviii, 4, 41, 59, 60–67, 70–79, 91, 93–103, 119, 120, 141, 220, 223–224
Canada Development Corporation, 60, 66, 74, 99
Canadian Oilwell Drilling Association, 86
Canagrex, 99
Capital, mobility of, xxi
Caribbean, 62; bilateral trading agreements with, xxiv, 175; and European Community, xviii, 108, 111, 120; and sugar, 189; and United States, 41, 52, 120, 188, 189
Caribbean Basin Initiative, xxiv, 152, 188, 189; and multinationals, 208; and Tokyo Round, 212
Caribbean Common Market, 130, 199
Cartels, 37, 57, 107, 119, 224
Carter administration, 17, 21–22, 31
Cassis de Dijon formula, 183
CCCN, 178–179
Center for the Study of American Business, 37
Central America, 62
Central American Common Market, 130
Ceramics, 5, 8, 37, 49
Chaffee, John H., 27
Chase Manhattan, 201
Chicago *Sun-Times,* 19
Chieftain Development, 85
Chile, 193, 209, 213
China, 32
Chrysler, 65, 94; bailout, xiii–xiv, xvii, 9, 30–34, 35–36, 40
Citicorp, 201
Citrus: and Brazil, 158, 185, 187; and European Community, 109, 151, 158; and Israel, 109, 158
Clark, Colin, 9
Clark, Ed, 81
Clark, Joe, 81, 84
Clayton Act, 72–73
Clean Air Act, 20
Clothing: and Canada, 96, 97, 100, 102; and European Community, xix, 107, 140, 155–159; and less-developed countries, 172
Coal, 100
Cocoa, 169, 177–178
Coffee, 177, 211, 213
Cohen, Marshall "Mickey," 81
Colombia, 207, 209, 213
Color TV, xix, 107
Committee on Foreign Investment in the United States, 61, 74–75
Common Agricultural Policy (CAP), 109–110, 142–143
Commonwealth countries, 96
Comparative advantage, 57–68, 69–70
Compensatory Financing Facility, 193
Computers, export of, 201
Conditionality, 193–197
Conference of Eastern State Governors, 64
Conference of Western State Governors, 64
Conservative party (Canada), 81
Consumer costs of trade policies, 8–9, 36–40, 216

Consumer protection controls, 183
Continental Oil, 85
Copper, 169, 173, 175, 178, 200, 211, 213
Coproduction agreements, 208
Co-Prosperity Zone, 111, 164
Corn gluten feed, 142
Costa Rica, 196
Cotton, 168, 177
Countertrade, 214
Countervailing duties, 71–72, 99, 101, 126; against less-developed countries, 208–209; and Tokyo Round, 113; and United States, 185, 187, 208, 215, 222
Court of International Trade, 221
Coutts, Jim, 81
Craftsmanship, xiv
Crown corporations, 59–60, 99
Customs unions, 158
Cyprus, 152–153, 157

Dairy products, 114, 141, 142
Dassonville formula, 181–812
Datsun, 46
Defense Production Sharing Agreement (U.S.—Canada), 96
De Gaulle, Charles, 76, 151
Denmark, 148, 154
Depreciation rates, 20, 26
Devaluation of currency, 9, 11–14, 59, 86–87; *see also* Exchange rates
Die Zeit, 135
Dillon Round, 112, 223
Dodge, Joseph M., 47
Dollar, xxii–xxiii; and exchange rate, xiv, 39, 123; and import prices, 140
Dome Petroleum, 85
Domestic content requirements, xix, 51, 138, 208–209
Domestic International Sales Corporation (DISC), 121–122, 126–127
Downs v. *United States*, 125
Drucker, Peter, 22
Dumping, xiv, 13; and GATT, 123–124; and Japan, 215; and steel, 26, 27; *see also* Antidumping laws
Dunkel, Arthur, 139
Duty drawbacks, 122

East Germany, 137
Ecuador, 196, 207, 213
Egypt, 114, 143, 152–153; textiles, 152–153, 154, 155, 157
El Salvador, 213
Electrical machinery, 100
Electronics, 125, 153, 180; and Canada, 101–102
Elf Aquitaine, 60, 61, 85
Embargoes, 3
Employment: and Canada, 59, 87, 94, 95; and dollar, xxii–xxii; and exports, xv, xxii; and imports, xix
Energy, 12; and Canada, xvii, 62, 66, 70–71, 81–91, 94, 95; and European Community, 173
Environmental controls, 183
Episcopal Church, 29
Equatorial Guinea, 163
Equivalent effect, 181–184, 187
Escape clause mechanism, 73, 124, 135, 213
Ethiopia, 163
European Coal and Steel Community, 131–132, 138
European Community, 10, 73, 107, 135–149, 151; and ACPs, 120, 163–175, 177–179; and Africa, xviii, 120, 163, 164–171; agriculture, xix, 99, 109, 115–116, 140, 142–149, 158, 165–166, 169, 173; automobiles, 34, 117; bilateral agreements, 11, 113, 139, 151–152, 154, 163–165, 189, 216; and Canada, 96; and Caribbean, xviii, 108, 111, 120; and citrus, 109, 151, 158; clothing industry, xix, 107, 140, 155–159; and energy, 173; and equivalent effect, 181–184; and GATT, xii,

xviii, 11, 108–116, 118–120, 131–132, 140, 142–143, 145–149, 154, 158, 180, 184, 214; import shares, 139–140; and India, 168; and lobbying, 27–28; and local content, 178–180; and Lomé Convention countries, 4, 11, 108, 120, 131, 132, 139, 141, 143, 145, 153, 156–157, 163–175, 177–181, 213, 216–217; manufactured goods, xix; and Mediterranean, xviii, 151–153, 156–159, 178, 180, 184, 213; minerals, 173, 212–213; motorcycles, xix, 107, 140; and multinationals, 180, 205; and nontariff barriers, 4, 183; preferential trade agreements, 179–180; and standards code, 129; steel industry, xxi, 18, 22, 23, 26, 107, 116–117, 131–132, 140, 141–142, 188, 225; subsidies, 145, 146–147, 148; and sugar, 109, 143–149, 165–166, 168, 169–170, 174; and textiles, xix, 4, 107, 108, 140, 151–159, 168, 172, 178, 180; and Tokyo Round, xviii, 108–116, 118–120, 138–139, 169, 212–213; and United States, 115–116, 149, 158, 220; and Yugoslavia, 137

European Court of Justice, 181–184

European Development Fund, 178

European Free Trade Association, 130, 178, 180

European Investment Banks, 178

European Monetary System, 140

European Parliament, 148

Exchange rates, xiv, xxii–xxiii; and Canada, 86, 87; and export subsidies, 123; and Japan, xxiii, 39, 47–48; and less-developed countries, 184, 191, 195, 197–198; and West Germany, 135

Export-Import Bank, 101

Export subsidies. *See* Subsidies

Export trading companies, xxiii–xxiv

Extended Fund Facility (EFF), 193, 194

Exxon, 82, 85

Federal government, xv–xvi; and Chrysler, xiii–xiv, xvii, 30–34; and steel industry, 20, 15–28

Federal Reserve, xviii

Federal Trade Commission Act, 72–73

Fertilizer, 135

Fiat, 34

Fiber optics, 49

Fietje case, 183–184

Finland, 113

Fish and fish products, 99, 213

Flyer buses, 101

Food processing, 98–99

Footwear, 4, 117, 154; and Canada, 97, 98; and European Community, 180

Ford, xiv, 65

Foreign Corrupt Practices Act, 207

Foreign flag ships, 9

Foreign investment: in Canada, xvii–xviii, 58–59, 61–67, 73–79, 89, 90, 94, 95, 99; in Mexico, 201; and reciprocity, 60–63, 96; in United States, 61, 74–75

Foreign Investment Review Agency (Canada), xvii–xviii, 58–59, 61, 62–63, 64, 66–68, 74–75, 77, 78–79, 89, 90, 94, 95, 99, 220, 223

Foreign sales corporations, xxiv, 101, 111, 126–127; and taxes, 121–123

Foreign State Enterprises, 61–62

Forest products, 99

Forklift trucks, xix, 107, 141

Forward exchange credit, 168

France, xxii, 22, 141, 151, 214; government procurement, 137; industrial planning, 75; local financing, 76; subsidies, 75; textiles, 154, 156

French Overseas Departments, 144

Fruit juices, 5, 8, 27

Galbraith, John Kenneth, 81
Gallagher, "Smiling Jack," 85
GATT, 107, 121–134; and agriculture, 109, 114, 115, 116; Article I, 135 –136; Article III, 135, 137, 138; Article IV, 125–126; Article VI, 131–132, 145, 185; Article XI, 138; Article XII, 115; Article XIII, 138; Article XIV, 138; Article XVI, 110, 122–123, 127, 145, 146–147; Article XVIII, 115, 185–186; Article XIX, 22, 111, 124–125; Article XX, 135; Article XXIV, 129, 130, 132; Article XXXVI, 109, 145, 146, 185; Article XXXVII, 186; Article XXXVIII, 145, 146, 185; and Canada, 96; and DISC, 127; and dumping, 123–124, 125–126, 132; and European Community, xi, xviii, 11, 108–116, 118–120, 131–132, 140, 142–143, 145–149, 154, 158, 180, 184, 214; and government procurement, 100, 137–138, 187; and graduation, 185–186; and industrial policy, 220–222; and Japan, 7; and Latin America, 214–215; and less-developed countries, 4, 114, 115, 116, 118, 122, 123, 130–131, 132–133, 138, 184–188; and Lomé Convention countries, 108, 142, 145–146, 163, 165, 214; and Mexico, 199; and most favored nation status, 3–4, 14, 69, 115, 129–133, 158, 185, 186–187, 216; and new economic order, 212, 213; reciprocity rules, 185; and regional trade agreements, 4, 130–131; and safeguards, 115, 124–125, 187; and standards codes, 127–129, 135–136, 187; and steel, 116–117; and subsidies, 121–124, 127; and trade negotiations, 108, 112–116, 119–120, 223; and United States, xxiv, 14, 121, 122–129, 133–134, 139, 220, 222, 223
General Electric, 46
General Motors, xiv, 65
Government procurement, 113; and GATT, 100, 137–138, 187; and multinationals, 136–137
Graduation, 177–189, 191, 192–193, 195
Grains, 98, 142, 143
Grand Coulee Dam, 100
Gray, Herb, 59, 74–75, 76, 77, 215
Greece, 187–188
Green currency system, 109, 116
Group of 77, 167–170, 171, 173–174, 206, 213, 216
Guadeloupe, 144
Guatemala, 213
Guinea-Bissau, 163
Gulf Canada, 85
Gustaitis, Andy, 88

Hamilton, Ontario, 89
Harmonization process, 182–183
Havana Charter, 148
Hawaii, 91
Heenan, David A., 32–33
Helleiner, G.K., 168
Heritage Fund (Alberta), 87
Hi-fi equipment, xix, 107, 140
Hitachi, 7
Honda, 34, 48
Honduras, 114
Hong Kong, 113, 154, 155
Hopper, Bill, 81
Houdaille case, xv, 51
Howe, C.D., 78
Hudson's Bay Oil & Gas, 85

Iacocca, Lee, 30, 32
IBM, 7
Ibuka, Masaru, 47
Imperial Oil, 82, 85
Import licenses, 114
Import shares, 139–140
Import substitution, 73, 122, 208, 211–212
Income Tax Conventions Interpretation Act, 97
India, 113, 114, 185; and European

Community, 168; and International Monetary Fund, 193; textiles, 154, 155
Indonesia, 188, 199–200
Infant formula milk, 136
Infant industries, 115, 184, 211
Injury test, 111, 115–116, 187
Interim agreements, 157, 158
Internal Revenue Service, 75–76, 90, 126–127
International Dairy Products Council, 114
International debt. *See* Sovereign country debt
International Labor Organization (ILO), 205–206
International Meat Council, 114
International Monetary Fund, 167, 191, 192, 193, 198, 213; and Argentina, 194; conditionality of loans, 193–197, 201; and Latin America, 200
International Sugar Agreement, 143, 145, 146
International Trade Administration, xv
International Trade Organization, 148
Inventory control, xvi, 5, 10
Investment Canada, 63, 68, 95, 102
Iran, 212
Ireland, 154, 187–188
Iron, 200
Israel, 91, 152, 157; and citrus, 109, 158; and graduation, 187–188
Italy, 22, 139, 141; sugar surplus, 144; textiles, 154, 155, 156
Ivory Coast, 177–178, 185, 199

J curve and devaluation, 11–13
Jamaica, 113, 194, 213
Japan, 5–7, 222–223; agriculture, 99, 116; automobiles, xiii, 33–35, 38, 45, 53, 66, 117, 215; Co-Prosperity Zone, 111, 164; domestic markets, access to, xv, 6–7, 14, 39–40, 43, 45, 216; dumping, 215; emission control standards, 135; and exchange rate, xxiii, 39, 47–48; and GATT, 7; and graduation, 187–188; import share, 139; industrial targeting, 73; labor costs, xv, xxi, 5, 23; and less-developed countries, 166, 208, 209; lobbying, 27–28, 43, 51–52; and managed trade, 117–118, 119, 212, 214, 215; Ministry of Communication, 47; motorcycles, 45, 124, 215; nontariff barriers, 4, 48–49, 50–51, 135; productivity, 5, 44; and protectionism, 10, 14, 116; research, 49; semiconductors, 5–6, 45; shipbuilding, 49; and standards codes, 127–129; steel industry, xxi, 18, 19, 21, 23, 25–26, 39, 49, 53, 116–117, 188, 215; subsidies, 75; textiles, 49, 108, 157; and Tokyo Round, 113; voluntary market agreements, 26, 33–34, 45, 125; *see also* Ministry of International Trade and Industry (MITI)
Japan-American Society, 47
Japan External Trade Organization (JETRO), 51–52
Japan Fair Trade Commission (JFTC), 58
Japan, Inc., myth of, 6, 52
Johnson, Chalmers, 48
Jordan, 157
J.P. Morgan and Co., 197

Kaletsky, Anatole, 139
Kennedy Round, 108, 112, 223
Kenya, 172
Kingston, Jamaica, 164
Kishi, Nobusuke, 46–47
Kuwait, 212

Labeling requirements, 183–184
Labor costs, 14; and Japan, xv, xxi, 5, 23; and steel industry, 22–25, 141; and United States, xiii, and West Germany, xxi
Labor givebacks, 12
Laffer, Arthur, 22, 24–25
Lalonde, Marc, 82, 83–84

Lamont, Thomas W., 197
Lanzier, Bruce, 85
Laser, 49
Latin America, 10–11; bilateral trade agreements, xxiv, 175, 217, 225; commodities, 213; debt, 196–197, 200–201; and GATT, 214–215; and multinationals, 206, 207–208, 213; per capita income, 201; regional integration, 197–200; steel industry, 26, 28; and technology transfer, 209–210: and United States, 41, 164, 189, 201–202, 214–215, 217, 225
Latin American Free Trade Association (LAFTA), 130, 141, 197–198, 200
Latin American Integration Association, 199
Leather products, 180
Lebanon, 157
Less-developed countries: and agriculture, 132–133, 164, 168–175, 177–178; and balance of payments, 193–198; bilateral trade, 163–175, 217; and clothing, 172; common markets, 130–131; corruption, 207; debts, xiv, 13, 37, 118; differential treatment, 184–188; and European Community, 209; and exchange rate, 184, 191, 195, 197–198; and export subsidies, 122, 123, 133; and GATT, 4, 114, 115, 116, 118, 122, 123, 130–131, 132–133, 138, 184–188; graduation, 177–189, 191; and government procurement, 138; investment in, 171; and Japan, 166, 208, 209; loans to, 173; managed trade, 118; market access, 184–185, 198–199, 208–209; and most favored nation status, 115, 165, 172, 186–187; and multinationals, 205–209, 210, 213; and standards code, 128, 138; and sugar, 143–144, 169–170, 171, 173, 189, 213; technical assistance to, 138, 167, 178; and textiles, 100, 154–155, 156–157, 168–169, 172, 212; and Tokyo Round, 166–167, 171, 174, 187, 212–213; and United States, 13, 15, 159, 166–167, 186, 214–215
Letters of intent, 194
Levesque, René, 83
Lewis, Arthur, 212
Liberal Democratic party (Japan), 49–50
Liberal party (Canada), 81, 82, 97
Liberia, 163
Licensing agreements, 6–7
Livestock, 98, 99, 114
Lobbying, 27–28, 29, 43, 51–52
Local content, 178–179, 205–206
Local debt financing, 76
Lockheed, 36
Lomé Convention, 163–175; and agriculture, 165; and bilateral trade agreements, 15; and European Community, 4, 11, 108, 120, 131, 132, 139, 141, 145, 153, 156–157, 163–175, 177–181, 213, 216–217; and GATT, 108, 142, 145–146, 163, 165, 214; and market access, 188, 199–200; and multinationals, 208; preferential trade agreements, 163, 171–172, 173, 177, 179–180; and sugar, 143–145, 147, 165–166; and textiles, 156–157; *see also* Less-developed countries
Long Term Agreement, 108, 125, 154
Lopez Portillo, José, 11, 198–199
Lougheed, Peter, 59, 60–61
Lumley, Ed, 59
Lumpiness, 13
Luxembourg, 22

MacEachen, Allan, 81, 86
Machinery and equipment, xv, xxi, 100–101
McQueen, Matthew, 178, 180
Madagascar, 172, 177
Malaysia, 199–200

Malta, 152–153, 157
Managed trade, 107–120, 212–214, 215
Management, xiv, xx–xxi, 44–45; and steel industry, 17, 19–21, 23, 25
Manchukuo, 46
Manila UNCTAD conference, 171
Manufactured goods, xix, xxii, 178
Marathon Oil, 19–20
Maritime Provinces, 63–64, 87, 97
Market access: and Japan, xv, 6–7, 14, 39–40, 43, 45, 216; and less-developed countries, 184–185, 198–199, 208–209; and Lomé Convention, 188, 199–200
Market share, xxiii, 139–140; and Japan, 6; and less-developed countries, 188; mandatory, 111
Martinique, 144
Mass transit equipment, 96, 98, 101
Materials costs, 5
Mauritius, 153, 177
Meat Import Laws (U.S.—Canada), 99
Mediterranean countries: and European Community, xviii, 151–153, 156–159, 178, 180, 184, 213
Mercantilism, 5, 8, 14, 76
Metz, Robert, 85
Metzger, Stanley D., 65
Mexico, 114, 133, 185; bilateral trading agreements, xxiv, 62, 120, 175, 189, 202–203, 217; and codes of conduct, 206; debt, xviii, 11, 13, 118, 192, 196–197, 198–199, 200, 208; foreign investment in, 201; and GATT, 199; imports, 201; industries, 208; and International Monetary Fund, 194; and multinationals, 213; steel industry, xxi, 25, 26, 188, 218; and technology transfer, 210, 213; textiles, 212; and United States, 41, 124, 141, 168, 197, 199, 201, 202–203, 217
Michelin Tire Case (Canada), 72
Millstein, James, 5–6
Mineral Leasing Act, xv, 61–62
Mineral water, 50
Minerals: and Africa, 173, 177–178; and Canada, 99–100; and European Community, 173, 212–213; processing, 208; and subsidies, 114
Minerex, 213
Minex, 173
Ministry of International Trade and Industry (MITI), xvii, 3, 14, 33, 39–40, 43–53, 75, 212, 215; and auto industry, 35; and cartels, 57; and industrial policy, 220; nontariff barriers, 4, 6, 35, 39–40; and petroleum refining, 57–58; and steel industry, 26; and technology transfer, 210; *see also* Japan
Minority Business requirements, 101
MITI and the Japanese Miracle (Johnson), 48
Mitsubishi, 7, 48
Mitsui, 48
Modine Corporation, 65
Montreal, Quebec, 100
Morita, Akio, 47
Morocco, 152–153, 157–158
Most favored nation status: and Canada, 96; and GATT, 3–4, 14, 115, 129–133, 158, 185, 186–187, 216; and less-developed countries, 115, 165, 172, 186–187
Motorcycles, xiv, xvii, 37; and European Community, xix, 107, 140; and Japan, 45, 124, 215
Mulroney, Brian, 63, 79, 91, 95, 100
Multifibre Agreement (MFA), xix, 108, 125, 151, 152–157
Multinational corporations, 207–208; and Brazil, 213; and Canada, 75–76, 78, 82–83; 89, 215; and Caribbean, 208; and codes of conduct, 205–206; and European Community, 180, 205; and less-developed countries, 205–209,

Multinational corporations (*continued*)
210, 213; and Lomé Convention countries, 207–208; and origin rules, 180–181; and standards codes, 136–137; and technology transfer, 207

Nakasone, Yasuhiro, 51
National Energy Policy (NEP), xv, 62, 66, 70–71, 81–91, 94, 95, 100, 102
National industrial policy, xxiii, xxiv, 41, 32–33, 36; and steel industry, 18, 21
National Machine Tool Builders Association, ix
NEC, 7
Negative interest-equalization tax, xxiii, xxiv
Netherlands, 22, 148, 156, 214; and alcohol content, 183–184; textiles, 156, 157
New Brunswick, 63–64
New international economic order, xviii, 163, 184–188, 205–217; and GATT, 212, 213; and Lomé Convention, 165
New York Central Railroad, xxi
New York Times, 24, 26–27
New Zealand, 214
New Zealand/Australia Free Trade Agreement, 130
Newfoundland, 84, 85, 97, 103
Nicaragua, 129–130
Nicholas and Co. v. *United States,* 125
Nickle, Carl, 83
Nigeria, 178, 185, 212
Nissan, 34, 46, 48
Nixon, Richard M., 76
Nomenclature of the Customs Cooperation Council (CCCN), 178–179
Nonaligned Nations, 206
Nontariff barriers, xiv, xix, 3, 14; and European Community, 4, 183; and Japan, 4, 48–49, 50–51, 135; and U.S. trade laws, 73
Norcen Energy Resources, 86
Northwest Territories, 84, 85, 94
Norway, 113, 214
Nova Scotia, 63–64
Nuclear energy, 210
Numerical control machines, 45

Oakville, Canada, 78
O'Boyle, Thomas F., 25
Obsolescence, 14
Ocelot Industries, 85
OECD. *See* Organization for Economic Cooperation and Development
Oil, 5, 211, 213; and Canada, xvii, 59, 60, 77, 81–91, 97; and Mexico, 13–14, 198–199
Oil seeds, 98
Olechowski, Andrej, 3–4, 8
Olive oil, 143
Ontario, Canada, 89–90, 97, 100
OPEC, 13, 20, 84, 211, 212; and automobiles, 34–35
Open hearth steelmaking, 25
Oranges, 27, 132–33, 158; *see also* Citrus
Oregon, 59
Organization for Economic Cooperation and Development (OECD), 205, 206, 214
Organization of African Unity, 163–164
Organization of American States, 206
Origin, rules of, 178–181
Orthodox Christians, 29–30
Overthrust Belt, 88

PAIT case (Canada), 72
Pakistan, 154, 155, 193
Parti Quebecois, 103
Pasta, 139
Patent licensing, 208, 209
Payment-in-kind (PIK), 143
Peabody, Robert B., 19
Pearson, Lester, 78
Peckford, Brian, 84
Pemex, 196–197

Pennsylvania Railroad, xxi
Peru: debt, 194, 196, 213; and multinationals, 207, 210
Petro-Canada, 81–88
Petrochemicals, 57–58, 100–102
Petrodollars, 191–192
Pharmaceuticals, 50, 74, 136, 210
Philippines, 193, 199–200
Pitfield, Michael, 81
Poland, 192
Polish National Catholic Church, 29
Portugal, 158, 187–188
Prebisch, Raul, 211
Preferential trade agreements, 151–159, 193; and European Community, 179–180; and GATT, 163; and Lomé Convention, 163, 171–172, 173, 177, 179–180
Pricing, 75–76, 207
Prince Edward Island, 63–64
Procureur du Roi v. *Dassonville,* 181–182
Produce, 99
Productivity, xxiii, 5, 8, 24, 44
Protectionism, xix–xxi; 36–40; and automobile industry, 30–36, 40–41; costs of, 7–9; and fear, 17–28; and steel industry, xvii, xix–xxi, 17–28, 29–30, 34, 49, 111, 112, 116–117
Proxmire, William, 31
Public health controls, 183
Puerto Rico, 91

Quality control, xvi
Quantitative restrictions, 181–184
Quartz watches, xix, 107, 140
Quebec, 59, 87, 89, 97, 103
Quebec Hydro, 77
Quotas, xiv, xvii, xix; automobiles, 5; consumer costs, xxiii, 8; and Japan, 45; and steel industry, xx, 20, 24, 26, 117; and sugar, 132; voluntary, 3, 24, 216

Random access memories, xvii
Ranger Oil Canada, 85
Reagan, Ronald, 97; dollar policies, xxii; and foreign sales corporation, 127; and Japan, xv, 28, 51; and steel industry, 22
Reagan Round, 116, 223
Reciprocity in International Investment Act, 61–62
Regina, Saskatchewan, 61
Regional Integration, 197–200
Regional trade agreements, 4, 133, 151–153, 157–159; and GATT, 4, 130–131; and less-developed countries, 178
Renault, 34
Research, xvii; and Canada, 72, 74; and Japan, 49; and subsidies, 72, 74; and United States, 49
Resource diversion, 13
Reunion, 144
Re-United States of America, The (Heenan), 32–33
Revenue Act, 51
Reverse preferences, 164, 165
Robinson-Patman Act, 37, 72–73
Robots, xx, 49
Rum, 169, 171, 172
Rumania, 61

Safeguards: and GATT, 115, 124–125, 187; and Lomé, 168, 171, 172; and United States, 213
Safety regulations, 3
Saint Thérèse, Canada, 78
Sampson, Gary, 3–4, 8
Sarnia, Ontario, 100
Sayle, Murray, 48, 50
Scale economies, 94
Schorsch, Louis, 27
Scientific machinery exports, 201
Scotch whiskey, 181–182
Sectoral trade, 62, 93–103, 152
Securities and Exchange Act, 61
Seed oil, 143
SELA, 206
Self-sufficiency, 7–8
Semiconductors, xvii, 5–6, 45, 49
Service industries, 12
Sherman Act, 37, 72–73
Shipbuilding, 49, 101, 153

Shipping, 5, 9
Siderbras, 188
Simmonds, K.R., 164–165
Singapore, 155, 185, 199–200
Sistema Economíco Latinoamerico (SELA), 206
Sistema Moda (Italy), 156
Somalia, 109
Sony, 7, 46, 47, 48
South Africa, 111, 188
South Korea, 154, 157, 185, 191; steel, 188; world market, 199
South-South arrangements, 130
Sovereign nation debt, xiv, 13, 37, 118, 191–203; and Argentina, 192, 193, 197, 198, 200; bilateral treaties, 202–203; and Brazil, xviii, 13, 118, 188, 191, 192, 194, 196, 197, 198, 200, 208; defaulting, 196–197, 200; forgiveness of, 214; and Mexico, xviii, 11, 13, 118, 192, 196–197, 198–99, 200, 208; and regional integration, 197–200; rescheduling, 196, 213; and Venezuela, 192, 194, 198, 200
Soviet pipeline, 142
Soya, 143
Spain, 158: citrus, 109; graduation, 187–188; steel exports, 117
Special Trade Representative, xv, 97
Sri Lanka, 194
Stabex, 164, 165, 167, 168, 169, 173, 213
Standards code, 113, 127–129, 133, 135–136; and European Community, 129; and Japan, 127–129; and less-developed countries, 128, 138
Steel industry, xiv, 10; and Brazil, xix, 23, 25, 26, 188; and Canada, 96, 97, 98, 99–100; dumping, 26, 27; and European Community, xx, 18, 22, 23, 26, 107, 116–117, 131–132, 140, 141–142, 181, 225; and federal government, 20, 25–28; and GATT, 116–117; and Japan, xx, 18, 19, 21, 23, 25–26, 39, 49, 53, 116–117, 188, 215; labor costs, 22–25, 25–28; and Latin America, 26, 28; and less-developed countries, 188; and Mexico, xxi, 25, 26, 188, 218; protectionism, xvii, xix, 17–28, 29–30, 34, 49, 111, 112, 116–117; quotas, xx, 20, 24, 26, 117; trigger prices, xx, 9, 17, 21–22, 24, 26, 100, 117
Structurally Depressed Industry Law (Japan), 58
Subsidies, 111, 121–124, 158–159; and Brazil, 185, 187; and Canada, 70, 99; costs, 12, 144; and European Community, 145, 146–147, 148; and France, 154, 156; and GATT, 185; and Japan, 75; and less-developed countries, 184, 187; and Tokyo Round, 114; and United States response, 71–72, 74–75
Sudan, 163
Sudbury, Ontario, 90
Sugar, 91, 211, 213; and ACPs, 143–144, 169–170; and Australia, 145, 146–147; and Brazil, 109; and Caribbean, 189; and European Community, 109, 143–149, 165–166, 168, 169–170, 174; excise taxes, 125; and Italy, 144; and Lomé Convention, 143–145, 147, 165–166; and less-developed countries, 143–144, 169–170, 171, 173, 189, 213; and United States, 103
Supplementary Financing Facility (SFF), 193
Surface Transportation Assistance Act, 101
Surge provisions, 38–39
Swaziland, 172
Sweden, 113, 115, 148, 214
Sweetgrass, Montana, 88
Switzerland, xxiii, 113
Synthetic oil, 88

Synthetic textiles, 155
Syria, 157

T-shirts, 153
Taiwan, 52, 154, 157, 185, 191; markets, 199; steel, 188
Tariff Commission, 37
Tariffs, xix, 222; consumer costs, xxiii, 8; and less-developed countries, 185–186; and origin, 178–179
Taxes: and Canada, 63–65, 66, 82–83, 88; and DISC, 126–127; and export subsidies, 121–122; and foreign investment, xxiii; and foreign sales corporations, 121–123; and GATT, 121–123; rebates, 125–126; and transfer pricing, 75–76
Taxes occultes, 122, 126
Technology transfer, xiv, 10, 138, 167, 178, 209–210; and codes of conduct, 205–206
Texaco, 84
Texaco Canada, 85
Texas Instruments, 7
Texasgulf Sulphur, 60, 61
Textiles, xiv, xvii; and Belgium, 154, 155–156; and Canada, 96, 97, 98, 100, 102; and European Community, xix, 4, 107, 108, 140, 151–159, 168, 172, 178, 180; and France, 154, 156; and India, 154, 155; and Italy, 154, 155, 156; and Japan, 49, 108, 157; and less-developed countries, 100, 154–155, 156–157, 168–169, 177, 212; protectionism, xxi, 4, 5; and Lomé Convention, 156–157; and Mexico, 212; and United Kingdom, 154, 156; and United States, 4, 5, 8, 49; voluntary restraints, 125
Third World. *See* Less-developed countries
Timber, 5
Tin, 211
Tojo, Hideki, 46–47
Tokyo Round, xviii, 4, 112–116, 127; and Canada, 96, 113, 223–224; and Caribbean, 212; and countervailing duties, 113; and European Community, xviii, 108–116, 118–120, 138–139, 169, 212–213; and Japan, 113; and less-developed countries, 166–167, 171, 174, 187, 212–213; and managed trade, 118–119, 212–213; and United States, 113, 212, 220, 223–224
Toronto, 90
Toronto Stock Exchange, 85
Toshiba, 7
Toyota, xiv, 34
Trade Act, 38, 71; Section 201, 22, 24, 27, 37, 73, 168, 221, 222; Section 301, 24, 27, 73, 77, 221, 222; Section 303, 71–72; and steel, 22, 24, 27
Trade Agreements Act, 71, 72
Trade Agreements Extension Act, 124
Trade and Tariff Act, 20–21, 28
Trade associations, 38, 111
Trade Reform Act, 126
Trademark licensing, 208, 209
Transfer pricing, 75–76, 207
Transistors, 46
Transportation industry, 74
Treaty of Rome, 107–108, 138–139, 154, 155, 156, 180, 182–184
Trigger prices, xvii, 222; and steel industry, xx, 9, 17, 21–22, 24, 26, 100, 117
Trudeau, Pierre Elliot, 59, 60, 63, 99, 223; energy policy, 81–85; industrial plan, 70, 76–77; and sectoral trade, 95, 97
Truman, Harry S., 124
Trust Fund (TF), 193
Tuna fishing, 51
Tunisia, 152–153, 157
Turkey, 152–153, 158, 191
Turko Resources Ltd., 86
Turnover, 5

UNCTAD. *See* United Nations Conference on Trade and Development
Underwriters Laboratory, 127–128, 136
Unfair trade practice law, 72–73
Uniate Christians, 30
United Auto Workers, xiv, 31, 33
United Kingdom, 9, 22; bureaucratic costs, 12; and Canada, 96; egg exports, 148; and Mexico, 197; research, xvii; steel imports, 117; subsidies, 75; sugar imports, 145; textiles, 154, 156
United Nations, 213; code on transnationals, 206
United Nations Conference on Trade and Development (UNCTAD), 169; code of conduct, 206–207; and GATT, 165; and Lomé Convention, 165, 166–167, 169, 170, 171, 173–174, 180; and new international economic order, 208, 209, 215
United Nations Economic Commission on Latin America, 211
United States: agriculture, 109, 141, 143; automobile industry, xiii–xiv, xx, 5, 30–34, 35–36, 40, 74; and bilateral trade agreements, 15, 41, 53, 60, 62, 120, 175, 189, 202–203, 217; and Brazil, 201; and Canada, xvii–xviii, 4, 41, 59, 60–67, 70–79, 91, 93–103, 119, 120, 141, 220, 223–224; and Caribbean, 41, 120, 152, 188, 189; and ceramics, 5, 8, 37; and countervailing duties, 185, 187, 208, 215, 222; devaluation, 12–13; and European Community, 115–116, 149, 158, 220; and foreign investment, 61, 74–75; and GATT, xxiv, 14, 121, 122–129, 133–134, 139, 220, 222, 223; import shares, 139; industrial policy, 220–222; labor costs, xiii; and Latin America, 41, 164, 189, 201–202, 214–215, 217, 225; and less-developed countries, 13, 15, 159, 166–167, 186, 214–215; and Mexico, 41, 124, 141, 168, 197, 199, 201, 202–203, 217; shipping, 5, 9; steel industry, xiv, 10, 17–28, 29–30, 34, 49, 111, 112; and subsidies, response to, 71–72, 74–75; and Tokyo Round, 113, 212, 220, 223–224; trade deficit, 12
U.S. Department of Commerce, 21, 38, 215
U.S. Department of Defense, 136–137
U.S. Department of International Trade and Industry, 97, 223
U.S. International Trade Commission, xii, xv, 36–40, 77, 215–216, 219; and bounties, 158; and Canada, 99; and industrial policy, 221, 222; and injury test, 72; and steel industry, 24, 26
United States Steel, 17, 22, 26, 38, 141; and Marathon Oil, 19–20
U.S. Supreme Court, 125
United Steelworkers Union, 23
University of California, 5–6
Updike, John, 35

Valuation for customs, 114
Value-added taxes, 111, 121, 123, 126, 168
Vans, xix, 107, 141
Venezuela, 212, 217; debt, 192, 194, 198, 200; and multinationals, 207, 213; U.S. exports to, 201
Volkswagen, 30, 34, 135
Voluntary marketing agreements, xiii, xxiii, 5, 45, 124–125; and automobiles, 33–34, 117; costs, 8; and steel, 26
Volvo, 34

Wages, xv, xx–xxi
Wages Integration Fund (Italy), 156
Washington state, 59
West Germany, xx–xxii, 22, 45, 148; and alcohol content, 183; automobiles, 135; and East Germany, 137; and exchange rate,

xxiii; and Japan, 135; subsidies, 75; testiles, 154
Wheat stockpiles, 141
Williamsburg economic summit, 22, 51
Windsor, Ontario, 70, 78, 89–90, 93
Wood Gundy Ltd., 88
World Bank, 213
World Health Organization, 136

Yeates, Maurice, 58
Yen, xxiii, 39, 47
Youngstown, Ohio, 20
Yugoslavia, 50, 130, 137, 152–153
Yukon oil, 84

Zaire, 178
Zambia, 178
Zysman, John, 5–6

About the Author

Douglas Lamont is the author of *Foreign State Enterprises: A Threat to American Business, Managing Foreign Investments in Southern Italy* and articles in *The New York Times,* the *Harvard Business Review* and other magazines. Mr. Lamont is a visiting professor of management at the Kellogg Graduate School of Management, Northwestern University, and an international business consultant to firms on several continents. He earned a B.S. (Econ.) from the Wharton School of Finance and Commerce, the University of Pennsylvania, an M.B.A. from Tulane University, and a Ph.D. (Business Administration) from the University of Alabama. He has taught international business on the faculties of Notre Dame University, the University of Alabama and the University of Wisconsin-Madison. For many years, he was the dean of the Walter E. Heller College of Business Administration of Roosevelt University in Chicago; he also was the international business columnist for the Chicago *Sun-Times* and the financial personality for radio stations WIND and WBEZ-FM in Chicago. Mr. Lamont has appeared on *The Phil Donahue Show* and *Wall Street Week* to discuss the foreign trade and financial problems of the United States. Mr. Lamont serves on the International Policy Committee of the Chamber of Commerce of the U.S., the Taxation Committee of the National Association of Manufacturers and the Illinois District Export Council (to which he was appointed by the Secretary of Commerce). He chairs the Policy and Legislative Action Committee of the International Business Council MidAmerica, and serves as its vice president and a member of its Board of Directors. He is a member of the executive committee of the Chicago World Trade Conference. Mr. Lamont has testified before committees of the Congress on international trade and financial problems facing the United States.